Thinking About
Beowulf

Thinking About
Beowulf

JAMES W. EARL

Stanford University Press
Stanford, California
1994

Stanford University Press,
Stanford, California

© 1994 by the Board of Trustees of the
Leland Stanford Junior University

Printed in the United States of America

CIP data appear at the end of the book

Stanford University Press publications are distributed
exclusively by Stanford University Press within the United
States, Canada, and Mexico; they are distributed exclusively by
Cambridge University Press throughout the rest of the world.

For my father, my best teacher

Preface

I have written a number of introductions to this book over the years, and two of them, linked only by their common function, form the following Introduction. Two others form Chapter 1. They introduce the themes—literary, philosophical, anthropological, psychoanalytic—developed in the chapters that follow. Those chapters, arranged roughly in order of their composition over fifteen years, trace the growth of my interests and the changes in my thinking about *Beowulf* during that time. Inevitably, since the chapters were written independently over many years, I return repeatedly to familiar texts and themes—each time, I hope, in a new light and at higher magnification.

I began with a quite traditional sense of the poem's traditionality, its origins in oral poetry, its early date, and the dominance of fate and necessity among its themes. But these easy opinions gradually faded. Perhaps because I was first trained in patristics and early Christian tradition, over the years I was drawn ineluctably to the most literate poems in Old English, like "Christ I," "The Rhyming Poem," and King Alfred's verse prefaces. The oral tradition has occupied me less, because I am unconvinced of the largest claims for its relevance to the analysis of most of the Old English poetry we have. It was in light of the literate tradition that I eventually came to appreciate even *Beowulf*'s remarkable originality and literateness, qualities that have been much underestimated.

In the first half of this book I explore the literary treatment of concepts like space and time, history and transcendence, and orality and literacy, in *Beowulf* and other Old English poems. My method in this part of the book, if one can be deduced from such various exercises over such a long time, is mostly phenomenological—the form of intellectual and religious history perfected by Paul Ricoeur (may his influence prosper in literary studies). The second half is dominated by psychoanalysis. This interest began with psychoanalytic anthropology, under the influence of Victor Turner and René Girard; but Freud inevitably drew me on to issues of individual consciousness, creativity, and reader response. I end by probing the creative autonomy of the *Beowulf* poet, as well as the reader, and our mutual interest in the hero's freedom beyond his fate.

The poet's concern with fate already implies this freedom: a concern with fate is a concern with freedom, after all. But in traditional readings of the poem fate totally overwhelms freedom as a theme. The reasons for this emphasis are to be sought as much in ourselves and in our culture, however, as in the poem, the poet, or Anglo-Saxon culture. Unfortunately, more recent critical theories also prohibit discussion of authorship, originality, and freedom. These topics are as charged and vexed today as they were in the Middle Ages. Determinism and materialism haunt most of our new critical discourses—Augustine's attack on them in the *Confessions* has surprising relevance for us today. For many critics, free will is not a meaningful concept in any context, much less in *Beowulf*, where it seems to be so forcefully denied. To a large extent, of course, we see in the poem what we want to see. The question is, why do we want to see what we see? Why, for example, are creativity, authorship, and human freedom such nontopics for critics today?

What holds these chapters together is not a single developing argument—far from it—but the intellectual pleasure I have found in thinking about such issues in *Beowulf*, an enigma leading me on from thought to thought, theory to theory, eluding me now as much as ever. These are not researches into *Beowulf* in the usual sense, *Beowulf-studien*, philological and historical studies of the text and its context. Rather, they are exercises in thinking about the poem. Each chapter introduces elementary issues in Anglo-Saxon history and culture, then explores their relations to the text and to the reader. In introductory discussions throughout the book I try to bring the poem to the wider intellectual audience that it deserves, beyond the small number of scholars who can read it in Old English. Anglo-Saxonists will have to bear with me at times for the sake of an imagined audience of anthropologists, intellectual historians, psychoanalysts, students, and other humanists.

Caveat Lector

Readers more interested in *Beowulf* than in recent debates about the nature of literary criticism might want to turn directly to the second introduction, on p. 15. The first introduction is intended to answer the new demand that critics situate themselves in relation to all the various theoretical discourses clamoring for attention right now. Readers of the future, when these debates have receded, might also wish to skip ahead.

> And therefore, whoso list it nat y-here,
> Turne over the leef, and chese another tale. . . .
> Blameth nat me if that ye chese amis.

Acknowledgments

With this book I pay a small part of my debt to William Kerrigan for 25 years of friendship and conversation about literature and ideas. Also for my wife, Louise Bishop, perfect partner in life and work, I take this occasion to celebrate our mutual love and support; her faith more than my industry brought the book to completion.

I am indebted to the Oregon Humanities Center for a term's leave to work on this book; also to Clare A. Lees of the University of Oregon for a thoughtful reading of the manuscript.

Portions of this book have appeared in earlier form. The section in Chapter 1 "The End of the World" was published as "Apocalypticism and Mourning in *Beowulf*" in *Thought* 57, no. 226 (Sept. 1982): 362–70; reprinted by permission of the publisher, copyright © Fordham University Press. Chapter 2 appeared as "Transformations of Chaos: Immanence and Transcendence in *Beowulf* and Other Old English Poetry" in *Ultimate Reality and Meaning: Interdisciplinary Studies in the Philosophy of Understanding* 10 (1987): 164–85. The section in Chapter 3 "King Alfred's Talking Poems" appeared in *Pacific Coast Philology* 24 (1989): 49–61. Chapter 4 was published as "The Role of the Men's Hall in the Origin of the Anglo-Saxon Superego" in *Psychiatry* 46 (1983): 139–60. The section of Chapter 5 "Identification with the Hero" is included as "Identification and Catharsis" in Joseph H. Smith and William Kerrigan, eds., *Pragmatism's Freud: The Moral Disposition of Psychoanalysis*, © 1986 Forum on Psychiatry and the Humanities of the Washington School of Psychiatry; reprinted by permission of The Johns Hopkins University Press, Baltimore/London. The section of Chapter 5 "Freud and Augustine" was published as "Augustine, Freud, Lacan" in *Thought* 61, no. 240 (Mar. 1986): 7–15; reprinted by permission of the publisher, copyright © Fordham University Press. Chapter 6 appeared in Allen J. Frantzen, ed., *Speaking Two Languages: Traditional Disciplines and Contemporary Theory in Medieval Studies* (1986), pp. 65–89; reprinted by permission of the State University of New York Press. I am grateful for permissions to reuse the material.

J.W.E.

Contents

Two Introductions 1
Fractal Poetry, Fractal Criticism, 1
The Further Originality of *Beowulf*, 15

1. The Birth and Death of Civilization 29
The Heroic Age in Greece and England, 30
The End of the World, 40

2. Transformations of Chaos 49

3. Oral-Literate: Two Case Histories 79
Transcribing Caedmon, 81
King Alfred's Talking Poems, 87

4. *Beowulf* and the Men's Hall 100

5. Two Psychoanalytic Excursions 137
Identification with the Hero, 138
Freud and Augustine, 152

6. *Beowulf* and the Origins of Civilization 161

References, 191

Index, 201

Thinking About
Beowulf

Two Introductions

Fractal Poetry, Fractal Criticism

In literary criticism everything depends upon the assumptions we bring to the text. Some of these are imprinted deeply in our characters and in our culture, and some are the result of intellectual struggle and insight. These latter are the easiest to articulate, since they are conscious, so I begin with them. Later chapters will deal with more elusive unconscious factors. To begin, then: What intellectual attitudes do I bring to my reading of *Beowulf* and other Old English poetry? What are the most conscious principles of my criticism, and why do I hold them so dear?

The Nominalist Critic

I tell my students, *Everything is more complicated than you think.* Privileging the world over thought like that (every *thing* is more complicated than you *think*) would have made me a "nominalist" in Chaucer's world; in ours I am only a borderline postmodernist, a prehumanist perhaps, out of my time.

As a philosophy, nominalism arose well after the Anglo-Saxon period, so it must seem an odd lens through which to read *Beowulf*; but for me it serves as a useful corrective for many of the distortions of contemporary critical theory. Nominalism struggles against

the generalizing tendency of all language and against the human tendency (especially in the West) to reify ideas. It struggles instead to
perceive the reality of individual things, which is the only reality there
is. Medieval nominalism radicalizes the individual thing. Therefore
nominalism is the natural enemy of allegory, typology, and, more
important today, theory—though these do remain possible, with diminished claims, in a nominalist world. Nominalism's most famous
avatars are Peter Abelard and William of Ockham, whose razor is my
favorite critical tool.

To the nominalist, "universals" (ideas, types, abstractions—the
stuff of theories) are only names (hence "nominalism"), words only,
without substance or essence. The world is not diminished for all
that, however, because the world—*mirabile*—is not composed of
ideas or of language. My title "The Nominalist Critic" is a bit of a
joke, then, since no nominalist would grant that "the nominalist" or
even "nominalism" exists. Language plays jokes like this on us all the
time, which is one reason we should not rely too exclusively on language in our thinking. The world is more than a text, and we are
more than subject-positions in it. That is one of my quarrels with
postmodernism—including semiotics and deconstruction, which are
in some respects quite nominalistic.

If nominalism is not wholeheartedly postmodern, it is distinctly
and distinctively modern. Hans Blumenberg thinks it was a necessary condition for the birth of the modern, in humanism: "Only
after nominalism had executed a sufficiently radical destruction of
the humanly relevant and dependable cosmos could the mechanistic
philosophy of nature be adopted as the tool of self-assertion" (p. 151).
A recent study of Renaissance poetry begins, "The use of nominalist theological distinctions allows for readings of literary texts that
focus on what we tend to find 'modern' in this literature" (Langer,
p. 3). Umberto Eco's *Name of the Rose* effectively dramatizes nominalism's modernity: according to Eco, inductive reasoning—that is,
science—as well as semiotics, is possible only in a nominalist world;
you can follow a trail of clues through the labyrinth of the empirical world only if you keep reminding yourself that the objects and
people you are tracing are individuals, not just ephemeral manifestations of Platonic ideas or general principles. Practical reasoning
always begins with the unique object at hand.

metaphors

In the world of ideas, on the other hand, we should wield Ockham's razor freely to keep our artificial intellectual structures as simple as possible. We can do this because, as Ockham would have put it, ideas are *post rem*, not *ante rem*: they do not precede things but proceed from them.

There is another side to medieval nominalism: it also affirms the absolute contingency of the world, asserting that it is only one of the infinite number of worlds God could have created if he wished. If we grant God's absolute freedom, it follows that nothing is necessary. Extending this claim by irresistible analogy to human creativity—a characteristic gesture of the Renaissance—has the effect of affirming the imaginative freedom of both the author and the reader. Nominalism therefore highlights the originality of the poet and the creativity of interpretation. To claim that Chaucer was a nominalist, for example, as Rodney Delasanta does, is to claim his radical originality, his freedom to create not only conventional types but individualized characters who do not conform to readily interpretable medieval patterns. Thus our reading is complicated by ambiguity, and the conflict of interpretations rises sharply.

Philosophy aside, my humanistic concerns for the individual, free will, and the world seem to have grown characterological roots and cannot be uprooted. These are matters of belief, after all—of political persuasion and kinesthetic conviction as much as philosophy—and are not open to proof or disproof. My own kinesthetic conviction I carry around in an epigram I call "The Nominalist in Love":

> The world is every map's perfection;
> So you perfect imagination.

Or as linguists used to say, "The map is not the territory."

Ideas about the world are idealizations—tautologically. For some, this discovery reveals language and literature as only so much illusion and deception. Language lies, betraying even its own most earnest intentions. For many others, filled with big ideas and high ideals but impotent to transform the world with them, the world itself seems to declare itself untrue, an illusion promoted by the language of a pernicious dominant ideology. For the disillusioned critic the question then arises, of what use are idealizations like "world," "culture," and "literature" at all, if they are so easily deconstructed? At first

such questions might appear to be a nominalistic attack on universals; but those who live in a world of ideas, and habitually confuse
words and things, have been concluding instead that we are trapped
inside Nietzsche's prison-house of language. The world itself is a
text; we live, Quixote-like, in a novel, or a film—not a surprising
thought, perhaps, given the present state of American culture, and
the crisis of higher education. This depressing discovery, however,
seems to elate literary critics, who can now claim privileged access
to the world's meaning, as theologians and philosophers used to do.
The insufficiency of language to reveal the world seems to explain
the insufficiency of the world itself.

The critic has simply lost faith in the world, of course, and with
it faith in the power of language and literature to reveal and redeem
it. Now language seems emptied of both intention and reference; it
reveals nothing but itself; since everything is a text, literature is nothing very special; and what world could there be outside the text, if
we as well as the world are constructed entirely by language?

Without a little faith, of course, poems are indeed only so many
cynical, threatening gestures—especially religious and love poems,
which account for most of medieval literature; but all literature is
affected by this loss. Old English Christian poetry is now revealed
as anti-Semitic and complicit with social violence (Hermann); as
for love, it is now possible to interpret Chaucer—even *Troilus and
Creseyde*—without reference to the concept (Patterson). This is literary criticism in the age of AIDS: do not trust anyone; do not believe
their honeyed words; protect yourself.

So, donning a rubbery, impenetrable prophylaxis of jargon, the
critic earnestly repudiates both the "transcendental signified" and the
"transcendental signifier" (oddly interchangeable bits of jargon for
the world and the self), proclaiming the social good from within a
sealed world of ideas. Symptoms of narcissism abound in the new
critical discourses. Critics routinely romanticize the primordial soup
of prelinguistic subjectivity (Lacan's Imaginary, Kristeva's Chora),
rationalizing that since the self is constructed by language, the infantile self is not really a self—so even what Freud called primary narcissism is not really narcissism. It is now axiomatic that the unconscious
is structured like a language—we would not want it to be too inac-
cessible to the critic! More likely, of course, language is structured

like the unconscious: that would put the horse before the cart, even if language and the unconscious were a lot less "readable" that way.

Critics caught performing these gestures—especially Marxists and feminists—find themselves dogged by "essentialism," alternately embracing and repudiating it. Essentialism is the opposite of nominalism; it is what the Middle Ages called "realism," the belief that ideas constitute a higher reality, of which individual things are only examples or manifestations. When I say "the critic," for example, I am essentializing for comic effect. When such essences are pursued in earnest, however, interpretation starts to feel more like a force than an abstraction, as if it were motivating history rather than being deduced from it. Our ideas, our critical categories and terms, come to feel *ante rem*; they seem to push things into being and push them along. Theorists of class, race, and gender cannot be nominalists, notwithstanding their concern for the body and material culture, because class, race, and gender are always treated as such essences.

Semiotics and deconstruction, however, as I noted before, are nominalistic in certain ways. Fredric Jameson actually analyzes "Deconstruction as Nominalism" (pp. 217–59). What he calls Paul de Man's "nominalism" may have as little to do with Abelard and Ockham as the "political unconscious" has to do with Freud; but still, his treatment of deconstruction echoes Blumenberg's treatment of nominalism. Deconstruction's disorienting attacks on logocentrism and essentialism are already instinctive in a nominalist. As Blumenberg says, "Nominalism is a system meant to make man uneasy about the world" (p. 151). So is deconstruction.

DeMan says there came a time in his own historical researches when "I found myself unable to progress beyond local difficulties of interpretation. In trying to cope with this, I had to shift from historical definition to the problematics of reading" (quoted in Jameson, p. 220). This shift, he says, "is typical of my generation." Typical, that is, of the very years I have spent reading *Beowulf*. So even I, in the slow-moving backwater of *Beowulf* studies, have been distinctly affected by this global warming in the critical climate, this postmodern greenhouse effect—benign enough for now, though eventually, I am sure, it will have to be reversed. In the meantime, the chapters of this book trace that same shift from historical definition to the problematics of reading.

But language is language, and the world the world. If only we could reduce the world to a text, it would be our oyster! Who really wants to grant the world existence on its own terms? Who wants to grant subjectivity to the Other, or objectivity to oneself? Nowadays these are considered political issues, but to me they are first of all psychological. Political and psychological descriptions of our decentered, dislocated, scattered, and marginalized existences share no linguistic boundaries. They are epiphenomena, separate languages pendant to the same world; all they share, that is, is the world that gives them being. Politics, psychology, and philosophy are three such languages. The world is their Rosetta stone.

Take away the stone, and nothing remains; nothing but a politics of illusion, a psychology of narcissism, and a philosophy of nihilism —our three cultural plagues. We are a generation of guilt-ridden, materialistic American intellectuals, grasping the world in practice and fleeing it in thought. But this is no more than Augustine, Abelard, and Freud said, each about his own time and in his own language.

It was once claimed that aerodynamically the bumblebee should not be able to fly, but it does. It has also been deduced from Saussurian linguistics that language should not be able to deliver us the world, but it does. Helen Keller is a greater authority than Heidegger on this point. We say "water," but until it flows from the pump onto our hands at the same time, we are indeed trapped in the prison-house of language: we cannot speak the Other; we cannot step outside the discourse; there is nothing outside the text; history is ideology, and culture a facile totalization; love is sexuality, and sexuality textuality; the university, the universe itself, is as superficial as a shopping mall. Any theory that wishes to disinherit the world these days has good reason—but no reason can ever be good enough.

Anyone who is not an English professor must wonder what any of this has to do with *Beowulf*. "A long preamble of a tale!" I told you you should have skipped ahead.

The Unlimited Semiotician

A corollary to my first axiom, that everything is more complicated than you think, is that *the closer you look, the more you see.* That is the connection between *Beowulf* and the Mandelbrot set that adorns the cover and title page of this book. The metaphor is visual, not linguistic. Poems, by my experience, have what Mandelbrot calls fractal coastlines. They sit on their pages like so many discrete little islands, but the closer we look, the more indefinable and complex their edges become; ambiguity and intertextual connections become apparent, and soon all attempts at measurement veer toward infinity. As with the Mandelbrot set, it isn't just that the closer you look, the more you see; it's that what you see is always so unexpected, in spite of all the symmetries and repeating structures. Subtleties revealed at higher magnification routinely nullify earlier impressions. What first appeared simple, on closer inspection branches endlessly downward into increasing complexity. Language is fractal in this way; and literature, particularly poetry, specializes in this vertiginous effect, as it plunges asymptotically toward the immanent and the transcendent.

This phenomenon was well understood in the Middle Ages, even before the invention of nominalism in the twelfth century. Of special interest to me are the insistent materialism of Anglo-Saxon culture and the concreteness of the Old English language—both precociously nominalistic. In law, these tendencies were expressed in the rule of precedent, an endlessly complicating engagement with historical reality. In preaching (notably Aelfric), they were expressed in a fixation with the literal level of interpretation. In poetry, they encouraged ambiguity and enigma, and individualized effects more often associated with Dante, Chaucer, and the Renaissance than with the early Middle Ages. The striking physical and psychological realism of the Old English elegies, for example, is, paradoxically, part and parcel of their mystery. The Anglo-Saxon reluctance to essentialize is expressed as a complexity that refuses to be simplified, a riddling quality in the world, and a thick metaphoricity in language about the world.

Anglo-Saxonists commonly evoke the complex interlace patterns of Celtic and Germanic art as a visual analogue to these qualities in the poetry. It is as though the illuminators of manuscripts like the Lindisfarne Gospels and the Book of Kells were struggling to create a Mandelbrot set without computers. Many Old English poems, not just the riddles and elegies, seem to shout at the reader, "Untie this knot!" To casual readers, the riddling interlace structures of *Beo-*

wulf are most evident at the level of its architectonics, in the use of
digression, apposition, and repetition; but students of Old English
know the more immediate frustration of trying to translate a poem
in which sentences can seldom be diagrammed, if they can be defined
as sentences at all. It has been 25 years since I first read the opening
page of *Beowulf*, and I still have to untie the knots and tie them again
every time I read it:

> WE OF THE SPEARDANES IN DAYS PAST
> of peoples kings power have heard,
> how then princes fame performed!
> Oft Scyld Scefing from scathing hosts
> many peoples mead-seats parted,
> the earl frightened after he first
> was found bereft, for that rewarded,
> waxed under clouds, worthy of praise,
> till each of all those sitting around him
> over the whale-road had to obey,
> to give him gold. That was a good king.
> To whom a child was afterwards born,
> young in the yards, whom God sent
> for nations comfort, saw crimes need,
> that they before had suffered lordless
> a long while. Him Life's Lord,
> Heaven's Ruler gave world's honor,
> Beowulf was known, fame sprang far,
> the son of Scyld in the Scedelands.
> So should a young man do good deeds
> with brave fee-gifts on a father's breast.

These are not the graceful and precise dislocations of Virgil's Latin
or the simple paratactic accumulations of Old English prose. Much
of *Beowulf* is even more complex than this and odder to the modern
ear, but these lines are odd and complex enough to startle any reader
out of linguistic complacency—though translators are always trying
to ease their difficulty for us.

  As puzzling as the narrative and the syntax are here, bold metaphors like "took away mead-seats" only manage to render the definition of good kingship more concrete: Scyld Scefing's fame here is not
glory in its Roman-Christian sense of celestial radiance, but simply
wealth, success, and power over others. Of the three Old English

words in these lines that might be translated glory, one (*þrym*) also means multitude, force, or power; another (*ar*) also means property or possessions; the third (*blæd*) also means success, and puns on an identical word meaning fruit or flower, in the phrase *blæd wide sprang*. At the end of this passage, a young man's good deeds are specified bluntly as "fee-gifts" to his followers. The enigmatic reference to "crimes need" (*fyrenðearf*) probably refers to the crimes of the previous king, Heremod, which are explained later in the poem. Even the enigmatic metaphor "on a father's breast," whatever else it might connote (it is sometimes compared to the biblical metaphor "in Abraham's bosom"), is literalized in the following scene, when treasures are actually heaped on Scyld's breast at his funeral. There is much puzzlement in these lines, but little abstraction, here or in the rest of the poem.

There were elements in early Christianity bound to reinforce these proto-nominalistic tendencies toward enigma and concreteness in Anglo-Saxon England, though patristic Christianity was nothing if not abstract and theoretical. The gospel narratives themselves are highly realistic, after all, no matter how enigmatic the parables or the underlying theology. But even more relevant to our task as interpreters is the fact that biblical interpretation was understood in the Middle Ages to be endless, contradictory, and unsystematic— though nonetheless revelatory of the world as well as the Word. In a psychological register we might say that for Augustine Scripture was strongly overdetermined. Philosophically, he understood (much like Saussure) that words are only signs referring to other signs. Augustine concluded from this proposition, however, that there are any number of true interpretations of a text (see *The Teacher, Confessions* XIII, and Vance). Holding the theory did not require him to devalue the world—emphatically not; knowledge of the truth does not make the world go away.

For Augustine, not only words but things are signs, and all signs point to the transcendent, which not only names the world, but gives it being. Augustine questions the world not only with his words but with his eyes, and it answers him with its beauty (*Confessions* X.6). That all things are signs does not reduce the world to a text, though, even if the world can be described in language, even if it can be figured meaningfully as a book (*Confessions* XIII.15). Augustine is not a nominalist, of course, eight centuries before Abelard; rather, he is a neo-Platonist of a new sort: even though his head is in the clouds, his feet are firmly on the ground. For him the allegorical is always rooted in the literal. Not only the Bible but the historical world itself overflows with meaning. Augustinian interpretation may look like chaos to us as we read through his meandering sermons on the Psalms, for example, but like the reality it maps, it is infinite, stable, and beautiful. The more you read, the more coherent it becomes. Augustine's interpretation seeks the transcendent. It seeks (if I may return to my visual metaphor) what Mandelbrot calls the Strange Attractor, that underlying presence, or nonpresence, that gives its shape to chaos.

Augustine's hermeneutic and later medieval nominalistic revisions of it have been reformulated for us today, with different emphases, in Wittgenstein's linguistics, in Heidegger's and Ricoeur's phenomenologies, and in the pragmatic semiotics of Peirce and Eco—among others. Ricoeur calls it "the rule of metaphor." Eco calls it "unlimited semiosis." Eco interprets Peirce as saying that *there is no end to interpretation*; but the infinitude of interpretation does not mean there is nothing outside it. There may be no transcendental ground from which interpretation springs, as Augustine thought, but nevertheless "there is a true *conclusion* of semiosis and it is Reality." Peirce himself says, "The real, then, is what, sooner or later, information and reasoning would finally result in, and which is therefore independent of the vagaries of me and you. . . . The very origin of the conception of reality shows that this conception essentially involves the notion of a community." Eco again: "The transcendental meaning is not at the origins of the process but it must be postulated as a possible and transitory end of every process" (*Limits*, p. 15). I think I can accept this description of the stone, happy to think of myself as an unlimited semiotician—of life, language, and literature in general, and *Beowulf* in particular.

Though the world is not a text, *Beowulf* certainly is. It is only a map and not the world itself. The most fundamental error in literary criticism is to mistake the map for the territory—in this case, *Beowulf* for the world of Germania, Scandinavia, or Anglo-Saxon England. But *Beowulf*, like any text, is only a map—and an imaginary map at that. (Interestingly, the Mandelbrot set is constructed of imaginary numbers.) What transcendent reality might *Beowulf* be mapping? As

fractal poetry, it is an infinitely magnifiable imaginary map, truly surprising at each new magnification. If scholarship tells us anything,
it is that this poem's semiosis is unlimited. Commentary could be
extended indefinitely. For me, reading *Beowulf*, even after all these
years, is not like talking to an old friend; it remains always a distant
stranger, an enigmatic voice in a foreign tongue, speaking from beyond the grave. And it is hard enough to understand those closest
to us.

I no longer trust those who say they know what *Beowulf* means, or
even what it is about. The poem is hedged about with so many uncer-
tainties—historical, textual, linguistic, hermeneutic—that even the
simplest and most straightforward statements can provoke a battle
royal among scholars. (*Beowulf* an epic? Beowulf a *hero*?) Freud more
than anyone has helped me understand how deeply the reader is implicated in the reading of a text like *Beowulf*. "Unlimited semiosis"
could describe Freud's interpretation of dreams as well as Augustine's interpretation of Scripture. Both are endless, subjective, and
overdetermined. Our mental associations run along numberless roots
under the vast fields of memory. "The power of the memory is prodi-
gious, my God. It is a vast, immeasurable sanctuary. Who can plumb
its depths? And yet it is a faculty of my soul. Although it is part
of my nature, I cannot understand all that I am" (*Confessions*, X.8).
Here Augustine is describing himself; but he could just as well be
describing the unlimited semiosis of Scripture, the Mandelbrot set,
or *Beowulf*.

Thus the analysis of a poem is endless, subjective, and overdetermined. I will suggest by the end of this book that we might approach
the poem as if it were a dream—even as if we had dreamed it ourselves. This approach is certainly at the far end of the shift from historical definition to the problematics of reading, at least as I conceive
the problematics of reading. Why approach a poem in such a way?
Not to find its "true meaning," obviously, but rather to expose our
unconscious responses, which are the invisible roots of our conscious
ones. Dreams are strong misreadings. I am not the poem's author—
but am I not, psychologically at least, in imagining him, in identifying with him consciously and unconsciously?

The ego meets the text along a fractal coastline, part of the larger
fractal coastline between the individual and culture, a coastline with

symmetries and complementarities of far-reaching—in fact unlimited
—complexity. These symmetries are reiterated in the larger structures of consciousness and knowledge, which we internalize in what
I would rather call a cultural than a political unconscious. The cultural unconscious cannot be essentialized as an ideology, because it
is not composed of ideas. It is grafted inextricably to our subjectivity, bound by endless branching associations to the imagery of our
personal experience. It may be communal to some extent, but not
collective in a Jungian sense. Everyone remains always an individual,
and every poem remains an individual production. How surprising
and pleasing, then, that poems—like fractals—seem to reproduce so
uncannily the larger structures of the world.

In unlimited semiosis, as in the interpretation of dreams, interpretations grow, copulate, and multiply, and the result is something
like the infinitesimal regressions of the Mandelbrot set. Freud says
in *The Interpretation of Dreams*, "There is at least one spot in every
dream at which it is unplumbable—a navel, as it were, that is its
point of contact with the unknown" (p. III, n. 1). The closer we
look at a poem like *Beowulf*, the more it recedes into local difficulties
of interpretation, unsuspected levels of complexity, new dimensions
of meaning, which in turn vanish into more complexities the closer
we look. Familiarity does not breed contempt or boredom, because
the poem always remains unfamiliar, always in contact with the unknown—and not in just one spot, but many.

Beowulf is hardly unique in providing this vertiginous, unfulfillable
desire to pause after each word and feel new patterns forming along
the tangled branching roots of our associations. There are many factors in canon formation, but one of the most important has been the
high premium traditionally set on texts with this sort of radical indeterminacy—what used to be called richness or ambiguity. Still, *Beowulf* and the other canonized Old English poems are extreme cases.
Their high uncertainty forbids easy rationalization; their raw power
provokes contradictory responses.

At life size (IX) *Beowulf* is an epic, perhaps a primary epic, a fictional world, a projected ideal of the Anglo-Saxon imagination, a
folktale, a sermon, an elegy, a mirror for princes, and so on. Issues of
unity and genre predominate, with historical considerations of origin and transmission.

Mandelbrot set, detail: branching complexities along the borderline.
(Courtesy Art Matrix, Ithaca, N.Y.)

At 2x, digressions appear, and J. R. R. Tolkien discovers a two-part structure, like the two hemistichs in each of its lines, the youth and age of the hero; Robert Kaske discovers the twin themes of *sapientia* and *fortitudo*; and Fred Robinson discovers apposition; structuralists discover light/dark, male/female, and other binary structures. At this magnification there is much talk of oral/literate, pagan/Christian, early/late, exemplary/cautionary, and so on.

At 3x, the three episodes crystallize as a structure: there are three monsters, three tribes, three parts of the soul, three stages of sin, three stages of history, three aspects of time, the Trinity, the triple dynamics of author/text/reader—triads of all sorts. Celtic influence now mingles with Germanic and Christian. And 3x, it turns out, is the domain of feminism, because at 3x Grendel's Mother is recovered from masculine dualistic analysis (Chance, p. 248).

At 50x, or 3182x, we have no way of knowing what local difficulties of interpretation will appear. What looked like a dualistic time consciousness at 2x, time/eternity or present/nonpresent, and looked like a tripartite time consciousness at 3x, past/present/future, and then opened to a fourfold historical typology at 4x, comes to assume the fibrous but elusive texture of lived time, as Heraclitus, Augustine, or Bergson might have described it. Relatively simple concepts, structures, and distinctions dissolve into the spider-webbing complexities of the Geatish-Swedish Wars, of line-by-line textual, intertextual, linguistic, and hermeneutic problems, footnotes to footnotes to footnotes. Certainty evaporates. Questions and clues lead everywhere.

It is a critic's nightmare, except that the set of all possible meanings is, after all, *Beowulf*—stable, mappable, and as beautiful to those who study it as the Mandelbrot set. How far into this forest do you want to chase the meaning of this text? This meaning of this detail of this text? General statements are only approximations that do not apply at higher magnification. Suddenly the poem, which seemed at first a secure repository of so many traditions, resolving so many tensions, bristles with novelty and announces its originality as the work of a strong poet, a text that will not be tamed.

Anglo-Saxonists, like biblical scholars, have long felt free, in the name of philology or folklore, to disregard the authorship of *Beowulf*. Recently they have also been enjoying the endorsement of other critical theories for this traditional neglect (orality, New Historicism, and Marxism, among others, as in the work of John Miles Foley, Martin Irvine, and John P. Hermann). The invention, originality, and creativity of this poem, however, both in its largest conception and its smallest details, invite and encourage us to imagine the author from whom they sprang. Harold Bloom says in *The Book of J*,

As we read any literary work, we necessarily create a fiction or meta-phor of its author. That author is perhaps our myth, but the experience of literature depends upon that myth. . . . The proper use of a fiction of authorship is not to aid in an interpretation but to clarify an inter-pretation once it has developed out of a sympathetic and imaginative reading of a difficult text. (pp. 19, 34)

Bloom isolates the J text of the Pentateuch, the oldest of its documents, and discovers it to be the work of a strong poet, a work of a highly original literary genius, whom he claims moreover was a woman. For obvious reasons her work has been subjected to three thousand years of misreadings—some strong, most weak. Her origi-nal genius has been neglected until now. Bloom's reading is another strong misreading, of course.

My unconscious responses to *Beowulf* prompt my conscious ones in quite different directions than Bloom's. I do not think the *Beo-wulf* poet was a woman, and I do not know when or where he lived. But I do know that the reader is necessary to the analysis of the text, and that every reader is different. Fractal symmetries revealed in a two-edged analysis launch an infinite process of interpretation, as we approach both the transcendental signified and the transcendental signifier asymptotically, vertiginously, overwhelmed by the richness and beauty of the problem, and the freedom, the arbitrariness be-stowed on us by our knowing that the analysis will be interminable, the semiosis unlimited.

The Further Originality of *Beowulf*

A Few Axioms

Each year when the time comes to revise my "Introduction to *Beo-wulf*" lecture, I rediscover the importance of the poem's many tradi-tions. *Nearly every feature of the poem*, I find myself repeating in ever more subtle formulations, *is a traditional function of its traditional functions*. (That's a late, epigrammatic variation of this axiom.) The digressions, the elliptical and fragmented narratives, the repetitions, the diction, the numerous fundamental themes, the ever-expanding bibliography of sources and analogues in several languages—the poem now seems deeply embedded in history, in literary history, in anthropology, comparative linguistics, and mythology, in theology, and in many other fields of knowledge and research.

Another axiom—or a theorem, actually, derived from the first—is that *the poem imitates oral style*. It's only an imitation, mind you—but still, you have to know what is being imitated in order to understand it. This theorem is based on Larry Benson's demonstration that even the most literate Old English poems, such as "The Phoenix" and the *Meters of Boethius*, have the same oral-formulaic density as *Beowulf*. I have never been convinced by attempts to explain away the importance of this simple observation. Mine is a liberal position, then a canny agnosticism that allows me to incorporate oral-formulaic criticism into the lecture as easily as patristic-exigetical criticism. No need to choose among competing theories!

Revising the lecture after each year's new critical reading, however, I have refined it like a well-tested scientific model until it has now become burdened with its own epicycles, equants, and eccentric deferents to account for a complex of retrograde notions—some in the text, clearly, but some in myself. So perhaps it is time to apply Ockham's razor and discard the traditional paradigm for a new one, as Roberta Frank has recently done with Germanic legend. Criticism is hardly a science, but it cannot be a wrong instinct to seek a few relative certainties on which to build—even if as moderns we know these are historically contingent, and as postmoderns we know they are illusory—as long as we keep them simple. Semiosis may be unlimited, but only within the limits set by the text. We are free, but not free enough to rewrite the text.

Three things have brought me to my little revolution—three new axioms for which I have been unable or unwilling to devise clever epicycles.

The first of these was the unexpected and unwished-for gift of Kevin Kiernan. The jury is still out on his theory of the poem's composition, and it may remain out indefinitely; but in the meantime, and probably forever, the issue of the poem's date is wide open. In the last decade, strong arguments have been put forward for locating the poem in every century from the seventh to the eleventh and in every part of England. After reading Kiernan's book and Colin Chase's, and articles by David Dumville (*"Beowulf"*) and Michael Lapidge, I now consider it axiomatic that *the problem of the poem's date is insoluble*

—which means in practical terms that *we should not build theories and interpretations of the poem that depend too heavily on an eighth-century or any other date*. And because the poem's style is archaic, imitating an early style, the text itself cannot rescue the great tradition running from W. P. Ker and R. W. Chambers to Tolkien, Dorothy Whitelock, C. L. Wrenn, and John Niles, elaborating the implications of an early provenance; nor can it validate new theories of a late one. Is *Beowulf* early, middle, late, or diffused throughout the period in a living oral tradition? It is like asking if an electron is here, there, or everywhere at once: answers are only probabilities, and in our case not even calculable ones. Therefore, all theories that depend on dating we will now bracket and put in a file labeled "contingency *x*."

Without a date, conventional literary history is impossible. Does *Beowulf* reflect the conversion, express the Golden Age of Bede, pay tribute to Offa or Wiglaf of Mercia, legitimize the West Saxon royal line, conciliate the Danish settlement, respond heroically to the Vikings, or praise the Anglo-Danish dynasty of Cnut? Is its resemblance to other poems, such as "Exodus" and "Andreas," cause, effect, or just accident? Not only should all such theories about the poem be bracketed, but inversely, *we cannot safely use the poem to help us interpret Anglo-Saxon history; we cannot assume the poem is representative of any period, or even, finally, representative of anything at all*. Like the Homeric poems, *Beowulf* portrays an imaginary society with an imaginary culture; its relations to Anglo-Saxon and Scandinavian historical reality are oblique and problematical to the highest degree, as much a matter for cultural and literary criticism as historical investigation.

Here we might take the lead from Homeric scholarship. M. I. Finley, in his classic *The World of Odysseus*, showed that the ethnology of the culture of the Homeric poems differs dramatically from that of Homer's own world, as well as from that of the Dark Age that Homer was ostensibly describing. Recent scholars like Jean-Pierre Vernant use the Homeric poems in the reconstruction of Dark Age culture only by taking such differences into account. They do not use Homer as a historian, in spite of the many inviting but misleading similarities between Homer's world and Greek history as it is revealed in archaeology and epigraphy.

Regarding *Beowulf*, my own early work is a case in point. Canny

agnosticism notwithstanding, until Kiernan's book I never seriously
entertained the possibility of a very late date, and I came to assume
that the poem indeed represents the conversion period—not that it
illustrates it, necessarily, but at least that it expresses its problems and
attitudes, it thematizes it. In the essay that became the fourth chapter of this book, "*Beowulf* and the Men's Hall," written before Kiernan's book appeared, I originally concluded that like the Homeric
poems in Greece, *Beowulf* must have been born along with literacy
and civilization in England, no later than the Age of Bede. Given this
proposition, I could deduce much about the meaning of the poem,
and much about the conversion too. It was a comforting theory—
but probable only to factor *x*. Though the elegance and coherence
of the theory might be argued to weigh in favor of the propositions
underlying it, that is only a wish and a circular argument. *Beowulf*
scholars have to revise their work regularly.

My second new axiom was neither unexpected nor unwished for.
It had been taking form for several years in my reading in both Greek
epic and Norse edda, but in the end it was Jeff Opland's discussion of the Bantus that finally brought it home to me that *the epic, a
long narrative poem of the heroic age, is not necessarily a traditional oral
genre.* When I first studied *Beowulf*, Albert B. Lord's *Singer of Tales*
was still novel; it convinced us that if you ask a Yugoslavian *guslar*
for an epic, he might oblige with a ten-hour performance. It was
easy to believe the same of an Anglo-Saxon *scop*; and so it was also
easy to believe that *Beowulf* is the sole surviving Old English epic
among the many that perished or were never recorded at all. This
train of thought simply assumes that *Beowulf* is the work of a *scop*, an
oral poet.

But if we weigh the positive evidence of other oral cultures (not
just the Yugoslavian Muslims that Milman Parry and Lord studied)
and avoid negative evidence entirely, a far different picture emerges.
The primary epic is primary precisely because it is *not* traditional.
Opland notes of the Xhosas, "There exists in the oral tradition no
epic as such, although epics are now being written" (pp. 21–22). Epic
may serve a specific historical function in the transition from the oral-
traditional stage of a culture to the literate-civilized stage, gathering
together a comprehensive vision of a way of life that has already been
lost but which, preserved in poetry, can still be evoked as a cultural

ideal. The relation of a culture to such an ideal is one of my persistent interests. Epic is produced on the borderline and looks back to a heroic world that no longer exists and probably never did; it is a summary statement of oral tradition, in a form that the oral culture itself never developed, because it did not need it.

This theorem results from examining H. M. Chadwick's classic notion of the Heroic Age in light of recent research in oral culture and orality. Parry suggested that perhaps "the way of life of a people gives rise to a poetry of a given kind and a given degree of excellence" (p. 469). Opland suggests further that "a corollary of such a thesis, if it can be proven, would be that human societies similar in structure tend to produce similar literatures" (p. 11). Proven or not, this has become an unspoken axiom of comparative literature, and though it can be applied only very generally and tentatively, it does provide a paradigm, a frame for research. Within this framework, the research I would most like to see right now would ask why the South Slavic Muslim *guslari* sing long narrative songs, while their Christian neighbors sing only short nonnarrative lays. Is this difference determined by other cultural factors? The Muslim epics are odd enough that I wonder what special needs they might be fulfilling in their culture. (And I wish oralists now working so fruitfully in this area would stop calling both kinds of oral poetry epic.)

Meanwhile, the relation of *Beowulf* to Homer remains an interesting and legitimate issue, not because they are both oral and traditional, but precisely because they are literate, original and transitional —similar monuments erected on similar borderlands. Thus *Beowulf*'s originality—the fact that it does not belong to a preexisting Germanic oral genre—might account for its being the only poem of its type in Old English. (It should be obvious from what I have already said that I find no grounds for concluding that "Waldere" and "Finnsburh" are fragments of epics rather than lays, whatever their resemblances to *Beowulf*; and I would rather not imagine other lost epics.)

Identifying *Beowulf* as a primary epic might seem to weigh for an early date, but not necessarily: Anglo-Saxon history was a centuries-long series of convulsions, from the migration and conversion, to the Danes and unification, to the Vikings and the Normans; and the epic could as well suit the age of Wulfstan as the age of Gildas. Robert Hanning showed us, and recently Nicholas Howe has shown us

again, that the same cultural myth was revised and recycled throughout the Anglo-Saxon period, just as the Greek tragedians were still
wrestling with the Homeric world centuries after Homer.

More important, the identification of *Beowulf* as primary epic
would release some of the poem's most important features from the
grip of oral-traditional analysis. If there were no oral genre of Germanic epic, then the poet and his audience would have no generic
expectations. Thus the architectonics of the poem—its use of digressions, for example—should not be regarded as traditional or typical,
but rather as the invention of the poet. These digressions may be allu-
sive in the manner of "Widsið" and "Deor" and may give us some
of the same scholarly headaches; but in its use of digression, *Beowulf*
is totally unlike these shorter poems. An earlier generation of scholars understood this novelty and tried to dissolve *Beowulf* back into its
component heroic lays, short songs that the poet supposedly wove
into his own larger fabric, rather than imagine an oral-traditional epic
exemplar. E. V. K. Dobbie preserves the best thought of this school:
"Neither the Caedmonian poetry nor the heroic lays brought from
the Continent could have afforded a sufficient model" for *Beowulf*
(*Beowulf and Judith*, p. lv).

In light of these two new axioms (that the problem of dating is
insoluble, and that the epic is not necessarily an oral genre), it is difficult enough to maintain that the poem is highly traditional; the third
makes it impossible. Karl Kroeber remarks that *Beowulf* is a "marvelous medieval epic for which no one has yet found a single identifi-
able medieval reader" (p. 328). A footnote refers us to the concluding
sentence of Dobbie's introduction: "That *Beowulf* was the great epic
of the Anglo-Saxons, from which later periods of Anglo-Saxon culture drew inspiration, is a proposition which cannot be refuted but
which is repugnant to common sense" (*Beowulf and Judith*, p. lviii).
The basis for these assertions is of course the complete absence of
any reference to our poem or its hero in any other medieval document. The silence is deafening. All the other characters in the poem
(except Unferth) are more or less richly attested elsewhere. I will let
Dobbie, who suddenly seems a well of common sense, draw the conclusion that is my third new axiom: *"There is no reason for believing
that [Beowulf] was anything more than a fictitious hero invented by the
poet"* (*Beowulf and Judith*, p. xxxiv; my emphasis). It is hardly a new

idea; it is obvious; it is widely recognized; but its implications have never been thought through. It means that the poem is at least as original as it is traditional.

Pursuing this line of thought, I was quickly led to Benson's 1970 ✓ article, "The Originality of *Beowulf*." This article, like Tolkien's, is a landmark reassessment of Chambers's fundamental criticism of the poem. But Benson puts the case for originality a good deal less radically than Dobbie's single sentence. "By 'original,'" he concludes, "I do not, of course, mean that he [the poet] invented everything that he used. Obviously he did not invent the story of Finn or Sigmund or Hrothgar or even the character Beowulf himself. All the events he relates, including, of course, the basic story of Grendel and his dam, are based on traditional materials" (p. 37). A strangely generous conclusion to a withering reassessment of the evidence! Benson detects an oral tradition of the character Beowulf in Unferth's speech, "Are you the Beowulf . . . ?" It is an interesting possibility, but pretty speculative. If you are going to apply Ockham's razor, let it be said afterward, *swenges ne wyrnde*—"he did not withhold the stroke."

Benson also believes that the main plot of the poem and the analogous episode in *Grettissaga* are related by a common folktale (the Bear's Son's Tale), though the common elements are very sparse and both developments of the folktale therefore highly original. Because he unhesitatingly relies on an eighth-century date for *Beowulf*, he has to imagine the original folktale persisting though six centuries until the saga was written in the fourteenth. But what if the poem is of the eleventh century, the same as the saga's setting, a period of heavy Anglo-Saxon–Norse relations? There would certainly be easier ways of accounting for the appearance of the two variants than their assumed folkloric roots.

But we don't want to rely on an eleventh-century date either; and if we're going to bracket the conjectural, we had better bracket the folktale too, which is as conjectural as Lady Macbeth's childhood. What convinced Benson that the two accounts are related in the first place? "The only relatively uncommon characteristic that Beowulf and Grettir share is skill in swimming," he says (p. 30). But Karl Wentersdorf, Robinson, Frank, and I have all argued independently that Beowulf's legendary skill in swimming might actually be a scholarly illusion, based on misreadings of the poem that have become ratified by repetition over the last century. I suspect, in fact, that it was Grettir's swimming skill in the first place that influenced early scholars to read Beowulf as a great swimmer.

In any case, without a traditional lay of Beowulf and Breca, without a date, and without a folktale source, Benson's meditation on the originality of the poem could have taken a more radical turn. The deafening silence surrounding Beowulf could be explained in part by Kiernan's thesis that the poem was composed at the very end of the Anglo-Saxon period and thus had no time to be influential; but even so, we would still have to assume that the main plot and the hero were invented by the poet, as Dobbie said, and woven tightly into the fabric of traditional history in the manner of Woody Allen's *Zelig*, with the result that no trace of the hero can be found outside the poem. Thus I share Joseph Harris's view more than Benson's: "As a whole, then, *Beowulf* presents a unique poet's unique reception of the oral genres of the Germanic early middle ages; like the *Canterbury Tales* it was retrospective and comprehensive, *summa*-rizing a literary period in a literary form so new and so masterful that it apparently inspired no imitators" (p. 16). The poem is even more unique than this, however; for the audience wants to know, first of all, *Who is this hero named Beowulf*?

The Name of the Hero

To think through the implications of the poet's originality—indeed, his idiosyncrasy—would be to reassess every long-held interpretation of the poem based on its traditionality, much in the spirit of Kiernan's book. Kiernan advised us not to assume that the poem's textual history is deep; I am adding that we should not assume that the poem's oral history is deep either. All the evidence tells us *this is a new story*, with only the vaguest relation to the Bear's Son's Tale or any other forebear. A reader or auditor of the poem (if it ever had any) would not have known the hero or the plot ahead of time; may not have had even a vague sense of how such a story might unfold; would not have known, for example, that the Sigemund digression foreshadows a final dragon-fight. The dragon-fight, after all, is not even suggested by the Bear's Son's Tale, but is an elegant, unexpected, and ambiguous fulfillment of it. The audience would not even have known the name of the hero until it was finally revealed at line 343. An Anglo-Saxon reader would perhaps have found the structure of the poem as startling and confusing as modern readers first found (and still find) "The Waste Land." Indeed, they might have found *Beowulf* as startling and confusing as modern readers do.

Rather than generalize about the implications of a late, literary, original, idiosyncratic *Beowulf*, let me illustrate them with the example at hand, the name of the hero. As in the case of the so-called swimming-match, we will see that commentators, editors, and translators have gone so far as to change the text in order to bring the poem into line with a supposedly homogeneous oral tradition. But there is nothing self-evidently traditional about Beowulf's name, his character, or his story.

From the scholar's point of view, the most astonishing feature of Beowulf's name is its oddity. Not attested elsewhere, it does not even alliterate properly with his father's, Ecgtheow. But for the reader, what is most astonishing is that it is so conspicuously withheld for so long. If the story is traditional, this withholding is only a clever artificial effect; but if the story is new, the reader is being held in serious suspense for a long time. Who *is* this guy? One hundred and fifty lines go by after he enters the poem, before he finally announces "*Beowulf is min nama.*" But that hardly answers the question: *So*? Who *is* this guy?

The effect on the audience is complicated by the fact that the name is new, unexpected, and unfamiliar, but at the same time very familiar indeed; for as odd as the name is, another Beowulf has already appeared in the poem. "Beowulf Scyldinga," Hrothgar's grandfather, is named twice in the first 53 lines. Thus the hero's untraditional name is given its own traditionality right within the poem. The increasingly common emendation of this name to "Beow," the corresponding name in the West Saxon genealogies (first suggested in 1906), is a little scandal of recent scholarship. "Most scholars now agree" that "Beowulf Scyldinga" is a scribal error, claims E. Talbot Donaldson (p. 31, n. 3); but an informal poll of Anglo-Saxonists hardly supports that claim.

Let us consider the case logically; let us sharpen our razors. Either the manuscript reading "Beowulf" in lines 18 and 53 is a scribal error, or it is not. If it is a scribal error, it is not the usual sort of mechanical slip of the eye or hand, but a case of mistaken identity, and a reiterated one at that. How could it have happened? I invite alternative scenarios to the following, which is the only one I can imagine.

For the manuscript reading to be wrong, we have to imagine that the scribe, having been instructed to copy a poem about a hero named Beowulf (note that Kiernan's theory of the poem's composition is already excluded), decided that the "Beow" introduced as *breme* (famous) right on the first page of his exemplar must have been an error by the previous scribe ("Hey, dropped a few letters there!"). So he corrected it (or thought he did) to the name of the hero he was told the poem was about—Beowulf. In order to make this error (assuming still that it is an error), the scribe obviously must have known the name of the poem's hero, Beowulf, but just as obviously could not have known who that hero was—a king of the Geats, not the Danes. He also could not have known, from tradition or the genealogies, that "Beow" was indeed the correct name of Scyld's son, since he "corrected" it to "Beowulf."

Further, we have to imagine that after the proem, in the very first line of the first fitt, our scribe found the same "error" again; and though he must have thought it a pretty odd coincidence ("Hey, dropped the same letters *again*?"), he probably felt confident correcting it again, because if you haven't read the poem before, that line really does seem to be launching the story of the hero: "*ða wæs on burgum Beowulf Scyldinga. . . .*"

Then, by the time the *real* hero Beowulf was finally named, sixteen whole manuscript pages later, our imaginary scribe must have forgotten, or have lost track of the story, or just neglected to go back and recorrect himself once he realized what he had done ("Oops!"). Or maybe he didn't consider it a very big mistake—though that hardly seems likely.

Thus, if "Beowulf Scyldinga" is a scribal error, we must imagine a scribe alternately alert and inattentive, unfamiliar with both characters, Beow and Beowulf, but still confident enough to tamper unhesitatingly with their names in his text, and lazy enough not to correct his errors when he discovered them. Perhaps the lasting value of Kiernan's book will be to have finally put all such notions about the scribe to sleep. Even if we accept no more of his argument than his observation that the manuscript was carefully proofread by the scribes, we have no basis for emending "Beowulf Scyldinga" out of the poem.

What, on the other hand, if the first Beowulf is *not* a scribal error? We have every reason to believe that the author, if not the scribe, did know the traditional name Beow but that he invented the hero's name, Beowulf. So if the first Beowulf is not a scribal error, it too must be an invention. We ought to be asking, then, what effect might be gained by having the hero's name prefigured in the poem's opening lines, offered as a variant form of the name of a traditional patriarch of the Danes (and the West Saxons), even though the hero is a Geat.

If both names have been invented, it is hard to avoid the inference that our hero is the earlier Beowulf's namesake and that his name signals his father's close tie to the Danish royal house. That is, Beowulf would appear to be named for Hrothgar's grandfather, perhaps as an expression of Ecgtheow's debt of gratitude to Hrothgar. How natural and reasonable, then, appears Beowulf's mission to Denmark: we feel it immediately, as Beowulf's name is announced to the reader and Hrothgar in quick succession, and Hrothgar immediately explains his relationship to Beowulf—"I knew him as a boy." And how natural and reasonable too, appears Hrothgar's attempt to solve the problem of his succession by declaring Beowulf his son, for he is by name a Danish aetheling already. Perhaps he is even the king's foster son—though here we are straying beyond the axiomatic, rejuvenating Lady Macbeth again—though we are following the poet's clues and accepting the text's own invitations to speculate.

It is enough to conclude that the originality of *Beowulf* (the *further* originality of *Beowulf*) is in this case not only the simplest and most logical explanation of the facts but also the most elegant, deepening the thematic and structural interest of the poem dramatically. It is only a theory, of course, but at least it is the simplest theory possible.

I first made this case for preserving the manuscript reading "Beowulf" on Ansaxnet, the Anglo-Saxonists' computer network, in the form of a scholarly referendum. I was hoping to pressure Howell Chickering into restoring the manuscript reading in his popular and influential edition of the poem. The majority of respondents did indeed vote to unemend the text (this is the informal poll referred to above), but my argument met with a storm of protest anyway. Peter Baker, who voted with the majority, nevertheless objected:

> My real quarrel with the emendation and the case against it is that both assume the one-time existence of an "original" *Beowulf* analogous to the first edition of a novel—better, really, because free of inadvertence. Such texts may have existed in the Middle Ages, but I'll bet that patchwork texts were at least as common—ones that incorporated great swaths of received material, written or oral, translated or un-, revised or not, with all the inaccuracies of the source text carefully preserved and maybe some added for good measure. The lines between compiler, author, and scribe seem very blurry. So what moment does the notion of the "correct" reading point to? I sure can't tell. I think it a pretty good bet that Beowulf 1 was at one time Beow, Beaw, or Beowa, but that time could be just about any time, including the pre-written history of *Beowulf*, and I see no particular reason to privilege that moment over the one that produced the text we now have.

This is an invincible argument, as long as we assume that the poem has a deep oral and textual history. But if the poem is as original as I am suggesting, the manuscript should not be treated as just one of many possible versions. We would not approach a text by Chaucer or Langland this way, even though we have numerous manuscripts of each. In any case, the vote did not change history: Chickering issued a closely reasoned rationale for the emendation, building on Baker's analysis and citing virtually every previous editor's suspicion that the text is corrupt; he did not bow to the public will.

I may seem to have painted myself into a corner here. Earlier, when arguing that the poem cannot be dated, I suggested that theories of its composition are only probabilities, like the location of an electron. The conception of the text as dispersed through any number of possible texts might seem congenial to this sort of quantum criticism. But I do not want to treat the text itself, which history has somehow delivered to us as raw if mysterious data, as only a probability. As nominalist critics and unlimited semioticians, our ideas about the text are indeed indeterminate, and certainly the text we have is only one of an infinite number of texts the poet could have written in his freedom; but the actual text is no less actual for all that—especially since we have only one manuscript.

If our new heightened skepticism regarding the poem's origins and traditionality seems to threaten our always-perilous critical footing, so be it. In the absence of facts, scholarly speculation tends to follow the course of least resistance, or most desire, as Allen Frantzen eloquently argues. Now that we have a clearer sense of what we don't know, and most previous interpretations of the poem have been bracketed as "contingency *x*," what remains is the text itself, in the latest senses of that word, still open to a phenomenological description and to almost any critical method except those we have been using up to now. If we cannot anchor our thinking about *Beowulf* in history any longer, we may have to entertain at long last the freedoms of modern and postmodern critical thinking—at least within the parameters set by the fractal text, and its Strange Attractor, the poet.

Chapter 1

The Birth and Death
of Civilization

Beowulf is a poem about the origin and the end of civilization. It opens with the mythical origin of Denmark and the building of the great hall Heorot, where a *scop* recounts the creation of the world. The hall is a cosmic symbol; but no sooner is it built than its destruction is announced:

> The hall towered
> high and horn-gapped, war-whelm awaited
> of fierce flames, nor was it long before
> the edge-hate of oath-swearers
> after warfare must waken at last.
>
> (ll. 81–85)

The poem will end with the death of the hero and the imminent destruction of his nation. Thus *Beowulf* explores the Heroic Age out of which history is born and the apocalyptic end toward which history inevitably moves. The death of the Heroic Age at the end of the poem, then, is a past destruction symbolizing a future one; but the end of the Heroic Age is also the beginning of our own. In this context, distinctions between past and future, origins and ends, are surprisingly hard to maintain. Here I would like to think about this looking back and looking forward—which may be universal themes in human thought—in their particular Anglo-Saxon forms, where past and future seem to collide.

29

The Heroic Age in Greece and England

Students of *Beowulf* since the generation of Chadwick, Ker, C. M. Bowra, and C. S. Lewis have instinctively turned to Homer for comparisons. Lewis's discussion of primary epic in his *Preface to Paradise Lost* is a good example of this traditional comparative method. Parry and Lord's theory of oral composition gave this old comparison new urgency and a keener edge, and a new generation of oral-formulaic theorists appeared, preeminently Foley, equally at home in Greek, Old English, and Serbo-Croatian. More recently, Opland has reminded us in his study of the Anglo-Saxons and the Bantus that oral poetry involves an anthropology as well as a critical method. The Bantu analogy is especially instructive, since the Bantus are still a traditional society and have not yet perished; but in the long run, classical anthropology will probably be more helpful in elaborating an anthropological approach to Anglo-Saxon England and *Beowulf*, because early Greece provides such a complete case history of the transition from tribe to state and of the role that poetry—especially epic—plays in the origins of civilization.

Classicists were quicker than Anglo-Saxonists to learn from the new science of anthropology. What is now often dismissed as "armchair" anthropology has come a long way since J. G. Frazer and Jane Harrison and has more to teach us about northern Europe than Jessie Weston's *From Ritual to Romance* can. Today the anthropologist's focus is less exclusively on myth and ritual and more on social organization; less on the origins of religion than on the origins of civilization.

It is less well known among Anglo-Saxonists that classical scholars often turn to Anglo-Saxon England for comparisons—not to *Beowulf* primarily, since our poem can only be a rude country cousin to Homer, too rustic to shed light or confer prestige on the great one; but classicists explaining the origins of Greek culture to an English audience commonly invoke the familiar history of Anglo-Saxon origins. H. T. F. Kitto observes that "Greek-speaking peoples from further north migrated into this region—no doubt very gradually—and imposed their language . . . much as the Saxons did on England. . . . Some of these have, to generations of Englishmen, been more familiar than our own Egberts and Egwiths and Aelfrics, for Atreus' sons Agamemnon and Menelaus were Achaeans, and Achilles and the other heroes of whom Homer was to write" (pp. 15–16). This rough and romantic analogy of Greek and Anglo-Saxon origins has grown more precise and more interesting as archaeology, anthropology, Indo-European studies, and historical linguistics—especially the decipherment of Linear B—have influenced the analysis of Greek origins. In general, classical scholars have been more aggressive in their analysis of origins than their Anglo-Saxon counterparts. Anglo-Saxonists could learn something from classical anthropology.

The historian of Greek origins faces a problem much like the Anglo-Saxonist's. The Minoan and Mycenaean cultures of the Bronze Age left clear and dramatic traces in the ground, as well as in writing, making it possible to trace the development of culture up to the year 1200 B.C. But around that time there was an abrupt breakdown of Bronze Age civilization, involving the Dorian invasion of Greece, the appearance of "Sea Peoples" around the Mediterranean, the fall of the Hittite Empire, and a general disruption from the Baltic to Mesopotamia. Finley attributes these events to "a combined tribal migration and invasion reminiscent of the later Germanic movements into the Roman Empire." He itemizes the known features of this migration and concludes, "All that is analogous with the later Germanic movements, as is the fact that trading and cultural interchanges and influence, at least with Greece, had been going on for centuries before the raids began" (*Early Greece*, pp. 59–60). Around 1200 B.C. a Dark Age commences, which persists until about 800 B.C. (The term "Dark Age" bothers classicists less than it does medievalists.) When the curtain rises again, the literate, powerful, centralized palace cultures of the Mycenaean warrior kingdoms are gone, and in their place are the fledgling city-states of the Archaic Age, soon to give way to the better-known glories of the Classical Age.

What happened during this Dark Age? We know that the Dorian invasions ended the Mycenaean Age; and we know that four centuries later the Archaic Age was ushered in by the rediscovery of writing. Other than Homer's immediate backward look into the dark, evidence for what happened in these centuries is scant. But despite the fact that Dark Age history is nearly a blank, it is one of the glamour areas of classical scholarship today. For classicists, the subsequent history of Greece is justification enough for seeking out its roots by whatever means.

Not so for Anglo-Saxonists. We too have our Dark Age, the two centuries from the fall of Roman Britain at the beginning of the fifth century to the arrival of Augustine's mission at the end of the sixth. Here too, the invasion of illiterate tribal peoples, the Anglo-Saxons, extinguished the relatively bright light of an antecedent urban culture. When writing is reintroduced by Christianity, the curtain rises on a society of farming villages ruled by a warrior aristocracy, organized into small competing kingdoms. And like Homer's work, the *Beowulf* poet's backward glance is one of the brightest lights we possess for illuminating the Dark Age.

As in Greece, records of the settlement period, as we call the Anglo-Saxon Dark Age, are nearly nonexistent. There is Gildas's lamentation from the British camp; there are a few evanescent settlement villages, all made of wood, like West Stow (see West); there are cemeteries, brooches, some pottery (see Myres) and other grave goods; and until quite recently there has been general agreement among historians that without more evidence than this, what we cannot speak of we must pass over in silence. Whitelock typically avoids speculating about the culture's evolution during this time: "It might have been possible to fill up some of the gaps by imaginative surmise, but I have preferred to restrict myself to what the surviving evidence states or implies" (*Beginnings*, p. 9). Precious little evidence survives from the "heathen" period, as she calls it. Anglo-Saxonists learned too well, perhaps, to avoid the excesses of Arthurian and fantasy enthusiasts (beginning with the Normans), who have taken advantage of this period's darkness to romanticize it. For decades the master scholar of the settlement period was J. N. L. Myres, whose meticulous, unromantic study of fifth- and sixth-century pottery is still the surest empirical basis we have for tracing the history of the migration; but unlike the painted pottery of Greece (see Hurwit), Anglo-Saxon poetry says little about social and cultural evolution. Nicholas Brooks laments, "Historians of Anglo-Saxon England have been strangely reluctant to produce any general model of state formation. . . . One would be more confident of justifying our empirical concentration upon the extant evidence and our rejection of models, were it not a reflection of the insularity of much English scholarship" (p. 56).

Only recently historians and archaeologists have begun filling in the gaps (Hodges, Bassett, Stafford, Arnold, Carver), and their re-

sults are now beginning to be absorbed by those studying literature (Dumville, Sims-Williams). For the most part, however, literary
scholars remain content to begin Anglo-Saxon history with the conversion rather than the settlement (note even Sims-Williams's title,
Religion and Literature in Western England, 600–800) and to deduce
earlier "pagan" ideas and institutions from their more or less incongruous blending with later Christian evidence. The Christian orien-
tation of most historians tends to foster this approach. That is why
we find words like "heathen" and "pagan" in the scholarship. I prefer
words like "tribal," "traditional," or even "primitive." The usual approach is unavoidable to an extent, but it is subject to its own sorts
of distortion and devalues the impact of the migration and settlement on subsequent Anglo-Saxon development.

Everything we know tells us that the Anglo-Saxon kingdoms of
597 were remarkably different from the Continental tribes of 400.
The settlement was a period of rapid social change, during which
the Anglo-Saxons, without the aid of Christianity, made—or almost
made—the critical transition from tribe to state, from primitive to
civilized, from a society organized primarily by kinship and governed
by blood feud to one organized by centralized authority and sworn
oaths among men, and governed by law. When the Church arrived,
the culture was already ripe for conversion. It gave relatively little resistance and quickly entered the mainstream of Christian European
civilization as a major new force. England's subsequent history jus-
tifies a closer look at the transformations of the Dark Age that set it
on its particular trajectory—by whatever means.

The most obvious approach to this problem is to note what distinctions we can between the tribes before they came to Britain and
the kingdoms the missionaries found when they arrived there. Our
best impressions of the former are still drawn from Tacitus (whom
we have learned to read with caution) as well as Gregory of Tours
and other chronicles. Other sources are archaeology, especially village excavations like West Stow, or Thorsberg in southern Denmark
(Jankuhn), which was abandoned in the fifth century probably by
migrants to Britain; and also studies of Germanic institutions, like
J. M. Wallace-Hadrill on kingship and Georges Dumézil on cult and
class structure.

It is a commonplace of Germanic studies that the early Continental tribes had two sorts of rulers, *reges et duces*, one chosen by blood, the other by strength. The king was ruler in time of peace; as *cyning* he ruled the *cyn*, the tribe defined in terms of blood and organized by kinship. The lord, on the other hand, was ruler in time of war; but even in peace he ruled a warrior class, the *comitatus* or "companions," whose oath to him superseded, or at least conflicted with, the omnipresent obligations of kinship. These two forms of social organization seem to have been distinct in the early period. The king and the lord were separate powers. We can speak of a warrior aristocracy, perhaps, but not a warrior king. Edward James has recently resifted all the evidence regarding these features of early Continental kingship and confirms this general picture.

I would not insist that this stage of dual powers actually existed, however—though it does seems likely. It is totally hypothetical, an "imaginative surmise" suggested by earlier and later evidence, much of it of dubious reliability.

Could this reconstructed past be the Heroic Age? No, for heroic literature describes an age of warrior kings and only hints at this earlier stage. In oral culture—as in literate culture too—the Heroic Age is a slippery form of history, ever advancing to absorb all but the most recent past. Anything that occurred more than two generations ago can be represented as happening in a single time frame, often a single lifetime. Compressed as it is, however, the heroic past does have a dynamic structure, a thematic history: times were better, and then got worse. Simply put, the idealized past implies a fall into the present.

What function does such an artificial idealization serve? When we detect it in later Anglo-Saxon artifacts, we should remember that it is not exactly a reconstruction of earlier history, but a narrative representation of contemporary social concerns, energies, and ideals, projected onto the past. Narratives of the Heroic Age represent idealized relations of blood and oath, war and agriculture, upper and lower class, male and female, kin and king, hall and hut, and all the other conflicts and complementarities of the society telling the story—in addition to preserving past narratives which had the same function for previous generations. Heroic narratives are vastly overdetermined, and their hermeneutic problems are largely unsolvable.

As Jeffrey Hurwit says of the Greek epics, "Homeric society . . . is a composite, a fiction of overlapping details and circumstances drawn from those periods through which the oral tradition passed. The stratigraphy of Homer is not easy to make out; but the stratum of Mycenaean memories and relics, while it is there, is thin, while the Dark Age stratum appears to be deeper" (p. 51).

Later Germanic myth preserved, in the stories of the Aesir and the Vanir, the history of an agricultural people conquered by a warrior people. Such a conquest may have happened, but it need not have happened in order for these stories to carry symbolic weight, to perform serious cultural work. Whatever happened, the myth defines the dynamic relations between the agricultural and warrior classes. A hint of this narrative appears in the opening lines of *Beowulf*, in the name *Scyld Scefing*, Shield, son of Sheaf. War follows upon agriculture, but agriculture is prior in time and importance. These two "functions," as Dumézil calls them, are in perpetual if changing balance; though one has clear authority over the other, it somehow remains secondary. Food always comes first. Another hint appears, perhaps, in the characterization of Hrothgar, who is repeatedly asserted to be a good king, in spite of the fact that he is militarily impotent. The young Beowulf plays *dux* to his *rex*, adds *fortitudo* to his *sapientia*. When the two functions are combined in the same person, like the older Beowulf, we sense fulfillment of the concept of kingship, but the functions are still theoretically separable.

Such a balance of functions may have characterized Dark Age culture, or it may have been achieved gradually during that time. In any case, whatever stability this dual system might have had on the Continent, it was largely destroyed by the migration to Britain in the fifth century, which produced a profound reshaping of the traditional social structure. Social scientists have developed a demographic model of "frontier migration," which typically involves a preponderance of men; Clover has brought this concept to her study of the Icelandic settlement (pp. 120–28). The gender imbalance in the Anglo-Saxon case was probably even more exaggerated, since the settlement followed a long military campaign. Such a conquest would have resulted in a transformation of power structures, leaving the kindred at an extreme disadvantage in relation to the enlarged

powers of the warrior class. Perhaps this transformation is paradigmatic of the origins of civilization generally; it certainly resembles
the situation in Dark Age Greece, as Vernant sees it.

I agree with Freud's great thesis that civilization originates in the
repression of the two human instincts, violence and sexuality. It must
be remembered, though, that the term sexuality here includes everything I have been calling kinship. One does not have to be a Freudian
to agree with this thesis: Finley, in his discussion of justice in the
Greek Dark Age and in the Homeric poems, points out that "Historically there is an inverse relationship between the extension of the
notion of crime as an act of public malfeasance and the authority of
the kinship group. . . . The growth of the idea of crime, and of criminal law, could almost be written as the history of the chipping away
of that early state of family omnipotence" (*World of Odysseus*, p. 77).
Girard, in his study of vengeance in Greek religion and tragedy, develops the same idea in the more precise vocabulary of psychoanalytic
anthropology (pp. 14–27). The primary allegiance of the individual
to the nation rather than the family is achieved by creating a central legal authority to guarantee vengeance in the name of the state
rather than the kindred. This development provides the theme for
legal history in both early Greece and Anglo-Saxon England. It is no
accident that legal historians discover in both cases, and these cases
especially, the germs of constitutional law and democracy. Without romanticizing these concepts, I think Greece and England do
share something in the early evolution of their governments, which
fostered the development of individual rights and limitations upon
kingly power.

A provocative analysis of this problem is Vernant's *Origins of Greek
Thought* (pp. 38–48). The redistribution of power after the fall of the
Mycenaean kings, he concludes, resulted in the emergence of a more
limited sort of kingship, requiring the political wisdom of the aristocracy for its support. One is reminded of the Anglo-Saxon *witan*.
This wisdom, *sophia*, became more interesting in itself to subsequent
ages than the institutions it was invented to serve, but it is still best
understood in its original context.

The Anglo-Saxon case is very complex. There is enough conflicting evidence to suggest that no general model of the settlement is
possible, but different areas underwent distinctive transformations

from Roman to British to Anglo-Saxon rule. Martin Carver compares the situation to that of colonial Africa, where power took so many very different forms. Handbook clichés about the extermination of the Britons, or about the settlement of Anglo-Saxons in unpopulated geographical niches, or about the gradual expansion and evolution of kingship may apply locally; but at the level of village and farm, continuity seems to have been as much the rule as disruption. Steven Bassett and Pauline Stafford both see a pattern of the Anglo-Saxons filling the Britons' shoes, and even heavy assimilation; Stafford notes in recent studies a "new emphasis on aristocratic organizations and re-organizations" (p. 79).

We can reconcile these seemingly opposed models by imagining the Anglo-Saxon conquerors installing military lordship over large tracts of land—like those listed in the Tribal Hidage—and thus planting the seeds of a new form of military kingship. Such kingship would only have imitated preexisting British kingship as described by Gildas. Carver sees a development in East Anglia from small units of lordship in the fifth century, to an emerging aristocracy in the sixth, to kingship in the seventh; but Anglo-Saxon protofeudalism in land ownership and taxation might have existed right from the conquest instead of emerging gradually. Doubtless the situation was complex and variable; but even in East Anglia, Stafford says, "The earliest and most continual demands of a lord were for material provision for himself and his followers, forced hospitality, provision for his hunting and the maintenance of the structures of his hall and court. From the beginning, these huge estates were organized to meet these requirements. They were originally in the hands of kings and great lords, two groups which were once not so clearly distinguishable" (p. 31).

Add to this picture the demographic distortions typical of frontier migration, especially gender imbalance, and a general model emerges that would allow for a variety of local differences. During the period of conquest and settlement dominated by men and their military organization—during those several generations when equal numbers of men and women were being reestablished—we have the makings of a heroic age not unlike that on the American frontier during the westward expansion, characterized by military organization, war with the native inhabitants, large land claims, power struggles, masculine violence, exploitation, and lawlessness. This state of affairs would have been modified gradually by traditional forms of law and order, the slow reemergence of women, stable kinship structures, and settled agricultural communities. This period, and not the more stable Continental past, is what we find reflected in narratives of the Heroic Age like *Beowulf*. *Beowulf* depicts a struggle to impose order on real social chaos.

Literary historians find the Dark Age interesting primarily because the Anglo-Saxons, like the Greeks, imagined it as the setting for an idealized cultural history. *Beowulf* seems to throw such a bright light into the darkness that when we finally come to realize how unreliable it is as history, we are tempted to abandon our search, since the stolidly reliable brooches and pottery of the Dark Age seem so mundane and uninformative by comparison. But Homeric scholars like Finley and Vernant know that the epics, with their peculiar blend of present, past, and imagined elements, cast their own sort of indirect light. Epic is a response to the social and cultural transformations of the Dark Age, a new civilization's analysis of its own origins. It recalls a past whose loss is still poignantly felt and establishes its memory as a permanent fixture in the culture. Epic themes can be seen best against the background of the cultural evolution that provoked and preserved them.

Beowulf, for example, is a typical hero of civilization. Just as Odysseus is forced to leave his new family and go to war when his son is placed before the plow, just as Hector has to leave his wife and son to face Achilles, and just as Aeneas has to abandon Dido, so Beowulf rises above the claims of kindred and sexuality to embrace the more abstract claims of civilization. He is the man without a kindred, or whose kindred is as big as all Scandinavia (see Farrell). Geat, Swede, and Dane, he himself, astonishingly, never marries. The poem's attitude toward women and kinship is severe even by epic standards. Think of another hero whose mother is so conspicuously anonymous even when she is being praised:

> Indeed she can say,
> whichever woman bore that son
> in the manner of men, if she still live,
> that the God of Old was good to her
> In childbearing. (ll. 942–46)

Beowulf is distinctly a masculine poem, reflecting the masculine *sophia* of the *Exeter Book* poem "Maxims I":

> As the sea is calm
> when the wind does not waken it,
> the people are peaceful when men have deliberated.
> They sit in council together, and among companions bold men
> hold power naturally.   (ll. 55–58)

It is a man's world, run by the king, the law, and the wisdom of men. There are no kind words here for women, kinship, or the primitive law of blood revenge; rather, "The lady should be at her table" (l. 63).

The repression of sexuality—that is, kinship—is among the many reasons the Church was and is such an effective bearer of civilization: "Anyone who prefers father or mother to me is not worthy of me. Anyone who prefers son or daughter to me is not worthy of me" (Matt. 10: 37). "If any man comes to me without hating his father, mother, wife, children, brothers, sisters, and yes his own life too, he cannot be my disciple" (Luke 14: 26). The Anglo-Saxons found in this teaching the fulfillment of their social development during the Dark Age. The obligations imposed by Christ do not conflict with those of kinship, because they supersede them. In this regard, Christianity breaks definitively with tribal thinking.

Reading *Beowulf* as a representation of the masculinist interests of an emerging civilization might seem to favor an early date of composition. The traditional eighth-century date would be analogous to that of Homer in the eighth century B.C. and suits my feeling that the poem thematizes the concerns of the settlement and conversion periods—that is, the origins of civilization. But we must not be dogmatic. The Greek tragedians revived the Homeric Dark Age narratives again in the fourth century B.C., though their concerns were different from Homer's. As Vernant sees it, tragedy is a particular moment in cultural history, poised between myth and philosophy ("Greek Tragedy," p. 288). The Anglo-Saxons had no such moment, because Christianity arrived to complete the transition to civilization so quickly—that is, unless those puzzlingly anachronistic heroic poems like *Beowulf* and "The Battle of Maldon" themselves represent the tragic moment. The extent to which *Beowulf* strikes us as tragic rather than epic perhaps argues for a later date, then, making it analogous to the Greek tragedies' dark reinterpretation of the Heroic Age.

Of the thousands of tribal cultures that have entered civilization, most were dragged kicking and screaming out of their age-old traditions and quickly died, or simply succumbed to the culture of the conqueror. Greece and England are rare exceptions. England entered the mainstream of European civilization without losing the coherence and vitality of its native culture and its history because the development of military kingship during the Dark Age had already undermined the Anglo-Saxon kinship system, provoking precisely those forms of renunciation that prepared the way for Christianity and civilization.

The End of the World

When we think about the Heroic Age, it seems natural to idealize the past. Then we ask, in what particular ways and for what particular purposes did the Anglo-Saxons and the *Beowulf* poet idealize the past? England and *Beowulf* emerge from this questioning not as typical examples of Germanic state and epic poem, but marked by their differences from any imagined universal model. Now I would like to ask similar questions in the opposite direction: how do we think about the *end* of civilization, and how did the Anglo-Saxons and the *Beowulf* poet in particular think about it? *Beowulf* tells us that the past Heroic Age and the future end of history are surprisingly closely related.

It is a common joke among Anglo-Saxonists that there is no future in Old English—a reference to the lack of a simple future tense in early Germanic languages. Paul Bauschatz has written eloquently on the implications of this peculiarity of Germanic languages for time consciousness in narratives like *Beowulf*. Concepts like fate (*wyrd*), which we associate with the future, the Anglo-Saxons associated with the past instead. Fate is not what will happen to us in the future but a pressure that the past exerts upon us in the present.

The difference between Germanic, Christian, and modern conceptions of the future are neatly illustrated in the word "doom." In the Anglo-Saxons' heroic poetry *dom* meant fame, reputation, judgment, or fate—how one is judged by others. Christianity appropriated the word for its own future-oriented meanings—destiny and final judgment. In our post-Christian age, the word has been emptied of all

Joan

positive connotations, yoked into the formula "gloom and doom," and now signifies only a meaningless future destruction—nuclear war as doomsday. Whether or not the early Germanic languages had a future tense, however, variations on the myth of the end of history do characterize Germanic as well as Christian culture, though in different ways. These variations, which I will call the apocalyptic and the eschatological, converge in Anglo-Saxon England and in *Beowulf*.

An apocalypse, according to its Greek derivation, is an uncovering, a revelation, a revealing of something hidden. The idea of an apocalypse, then, depends upon a prior sense that something is hidden—something we know, insofar as we know it is hidden; but something we do not know, insofar as it is hidden from us. This sense of a partially apprehended reality seems to be universal, though the symbols used to express it are manifold, and their deployment in mythical narratives such as the Christian apocalypse takes innumerable forms. Here we are primarily interested in Christian and Germanic symbols, but we might ask first what experiences and impulses gave rise to them.

Where do human beings derive the sense that there is a reality hidden, or partially hidden, from them? Our earliest records reveal that humankind already felt estranged, diminished, and desirous in relation to some invisible reality expressible only in symbols. We may *Logos* imagine, if we like, in early man, or primitive man, a naïveté that could not distinguish symbols and their objects (could not distinguish between the earth and a woman, for example, or a man and a bull, or the sun and a chariot), but it is more likely that people saw from the beginning that mythical symbols refer us elsewhere.

Even the infant recognizes, in the earliest stages of its psychogenesis, that the imagining of a desired object is not the object itself, and cries for it. The symbols of our desires point to what is absent. Myth, a language of such symbols, refers to its own world (the mythical world) and its own history (mythical time). Ernst Cassirer's phenomenology of these concepts is still very useful (pp. 71–151). Mythical realities only occasionally manifest themselves in the material world, and even then only in the meanings of symbolic objects, actions, and statements. Religious life everywhere is devoted to the absent world, from which humans naturally feel estranged. This feeling of absence provides some of the universal themes we find in mythology and religion.

Myth is the narrative treatment of these symbols, the exploration of their meanings in narrative form. Myths of the absent world have to account for both its nature as a world and its absence. Narrative naturally treats these themes temporally, and we are familiar with the resultant myths of loss, decay, fall, exile, genealogical descent, and so on, which portray the absent world as temporally prior—that is, as an idealized past from which we are alienated by some act of separation. Statements about this past state and about the events that separated us from it are, of course, statements about human experience and values, about human existence and its meanings, in a language freed from reference to the physical world—in a language of imagination. In this language, our alienation from the transcendental is identified with our analogous alienation from the past, and in the process the past is made transcendental, an object of desire.

In sum, our symbols are symbols of something, of an ideal world, a world created by the imagination in the absence of and desire for what we have to imagine. The meanings of symbols constitute an absent world, and myth accounts for our alienation from it, symbolized as some form of loss. In this framework we can see that the myth of the apocalypse symbolizes a desire to have that world revealed to us directly, to erase the distinction between the real and the ideal, to lift the veil that separates us from the world we can know only in symbols, to possess at last (again) the clear understanding of their meanings—to possess physically the very objects of our desire; to have, rather than imagine; to see, and not as through a glass darkly.

The apocalypse is not really a myth of the end of the world, then, as we sometimes say, attached to a complementary myth of the world's creation; rather, it is a myth of the end of our alienation from an ideal superhistorical reality, attached instead to the myth of the fall. It is a revelation of the world that is hidden from us because of our fallen nature. The apocalyptic myth has both a prospective aspect and a historical one; it places us between a past moment of loss and the promise of a restoration.

The apocalypse, we should note, is by no means a universal myth. It is in fact distinctively Judeo-Christian. Biblical religion is distinctive for its insistent historicization of myth: "sacred history" is the biblical form of myth. The ideal structures of experience are revealed not in a mythical world but in the immanent recurring structures of history; the transcendent world is revealed in history itself. God is revealed in the very fabric of our worldly experience. The fall and exile are not ideas, as they are for the Platonic and Neoplatonic myth, and they do not occur in a mythical world. In Scripture they are insistently historical events. Augustine struggled to understand the historical nature of the fall. He explored how it was embodied in the structure of his own life as well as in sacred history.

As for the apocalypse, then, because it is the future revelation of what is now hidden from us, it is, like the fall, necessarily conceived as a historical event. To see why this is unique to Christianity, we can look at analogous myths that are not historicized, the relatively common eschatological myths.

The eschaton (Greek "last thing") *is* the end of the world, and the notion of a universal destruction is naturally attached to myths of creation. One of the clearest examples of an eschatological myth we possess is in Norse eddic poetry, the final expression of the mythology of the early Germanic and Scandinavian peoples. There is one fact about this particular myth which is of special interest to us: the last battle, Ragnarök, is the conclusion of a mythic history in which human history figures hardly at all. The *Voluspá* recounts only the creation and the destruction of the world; although the creation of human beings is described briefly in the poem—they are made from driftwood the gods find as they stroll by the sea—human history is not really touched upon. In fact, this story is so tangential to the whole mythical history that it cannot be taken seriously as an account of humanity's place in the cosmos.

This fact should not be surprising; the mythical world is not the physical world, after all, and mythical history is not human history. Hesiod's *Theogony* never bothers to account for humanity either. It is as if the mythical history of the world is not terribly concerned with people, or at least not with historical people. But of course this history is entirely human, since mythical statements are actually statements about the mental or spiritual world, and thus imply man; but mythical man is not historical man, and mythical statements are not historical but ideal. The *Rig Veda*'s "Hymn to Man" (*Purusha*) begins

> Man, shining light in the City,
> Has a thousand heads, eyes, and feet,

> He covers the earth on all sides,
> Rules supreme over inner space.
>   (LeMée, p. 36)

It is as if the mythical cosmos were understood to be internal, ideal, and imaginary, a world of the mind that need not account for man because he is already and everywhere present in it:

> Man indeed is this Universe,
> What has been and what is to come,
> Master of immortality.   (p. 38)

Man, conceived quite apart from history, is both the context and the content of myth, even in the absence of explicit statements about his worldly history, as in the *Vǫluspá*, the *Theogony*, and the *Rig Veda*.

The myth of the end of the world, then, is a symbolic statement about the world of myth, not a prophecy about the future of the historical world. It has more to do with the problem of death than with future history. The meanings of the myth are to be sought in its psychological and social motivations, which in the case of the northern peoples reflect their extreme view of the transience of life and existence; and this belief is culturally determined by social, environmental, and other factors. So, because Ragnarök is not conceived as a historical event, it is not an apocalypse of the Christian sort. Though the myth itself is a revelation in the sense that it reveals what it symbolizes, it is not a myth of revelation. Ragnarök takes place in the mythical world and does not dissolve the distinction between the ideal mythical and real historical worlds, between desire and reality.

The difference between this northern eschatology and true Christian apocalypticism is especially interesting because they encounter each other in our poem. The spread of the Church across Europe was not simply the replacement of native religions and mythologies with Christian belief. We would not think to minimize the impact of Greek or Roman thought on early Christianity, and we should likewise expect the conversion of any strong culture to be a dynamic affair. Christianity's encounters with cultures already organized by native belief necessarily resulted in the modification of both parties. When Christianity came to England, it encountered a culture already organized by a fully eschatological mythology. Both cultures could recognize affinities between their beliefs and institutions. The hopeless eschatology of the primitive Anglo-Saxons helped them accept the Church with minimal resistance and maximal results. I would not want to argue that this native eschatology seriously affected Christian doctrine, but it did influence Anglo-Saxon Christianity by emphasizing apocalyptic themes more than in southern cultures and by emphasizing especially the negative aspects of the apocalypse. The result was the dark Christian vision familiar to students of Anglo-Saxon culture.

Although the roots of Anglo-Saxon apocalypticism can be traced deep into the Continental Christian tradition, we have the impression that England—especially the vernacular culture—was peculiarly saturated with these themes, not only in homilies but also in poetry, much of which is explicitly apocalyptic, and much of which is infused with apocalyptic images and ideas. It would not be too much to say that this culture was fairly obsessed with the apocalypse, especially the themes of judgment and punishment. It seems almost a part of the national character, or at least the character of the national Church; and the reasons are ultimately to be sought in the mythical, religious, and social structures of the native pre-Christian culture.

To examine this hypothesis we can take a brief look at *Beowulf*, which is ideal for our purpose since the poem explores the jointure of the two cultures by concentrating on themes they share in common to some degree. Among these common themes is certainly the apocalypse—or more precisely, a Christianized form of the hopeless Germanic eschatology.

Like heroic literature everywhere, *Beowulf* takes place in an age set between myth and history. Heroes, the founders of civilization, are descended from the gods, as we are in turn descended from the heroes. The Heroic Age mediates temporally between this world and the other. A culture projects into its Heroic Age its own ideal forms, against which it can measure itself, and the hero is an ideal type against whom men can measure their behavior—although by this measure cultures and men will always be found deficient. The Heroic Age always reveals the fallen nature of the present age by contrast.

Heroes are unlike gods, whose cultural functions are much more complex—as a rule, the gods are not embodiments of cultural ideals or models of human behavior. Although the heroic world is symbolic it is not mythical, because it shades imperceptibly into the historical,

whereas myth remains transcendent; so in the heroic world mythological themes can be explored in human-historical terms, and in this
regard a Heroic Age resembles sacred history. If the mythical world
is separate from the historical, the heroic world fills the gap between
the two.

The heroic world of *Beowulf* occupies this intermediate zone between myth and history. The poem opens with the mythical foundation of civilization itself, in the few generations beginning with the
mysterious arrival of the good king Scyld Scefing and culminating in
the building of the ideal hall Heorot; and it concludes in the relatively
clear light of history, with the events surrounding the destruction
of the Geats, in the detailed account of their wars with the Swedes.
Further, it is hard to avoid the impression that this final destruction
is meant as an appropriate conclusion to the creation that opens the
poem. The fall of the Geats is symbolic of the death of civilization,
just as the founding of Denmark is symbolic of its birth. When the
hero dies, civilization as we see it in the poem will die with him.
The poem's vision is as total and self-enclosed as that of the *Vǫluspá*,
though it is less mythical and more historical.

Just as myth accounts for the absence of its world in the themes
of loss, fall, exile, decay, and so on, our poem accounts for the fact
that the heroic world, historical as it is, is definitely past. *Beowulf*
focuses on the collapse of the heroic world, a collapse that results in
the world of history as we know it and at the same time displays the
essential nature of history as collapsing, falling, eschatological.

This eschatology is not genuinely apocalyptic, however. Nothing
is revealed in this destruction except the nature of history, the world,
and human life. No hidden world is disclosed. We might be tempted
to say, then, that *Beowulf*'s eschatology is essentially northern and
not Christian; but there are two Christian components in it. First,
Beowulf takes the myth of the eschaton from native belief and his-
toricizes it the way Christianity does, by removing it from a world
of mythical symbols like Ragnarök and setting it into the historical
world as a statement about human history. *Beowulf* is not just a parable abstractly illustrating the theme of the transience of human life
and culture, like the episode we call the Lay of the Last Survivor (ll.
2231–70). Rather, it is a statement of these themes drawn from the
patterns of history itself, as Christian-historical as Augustine's presentation of the fall of Rome, or Gildas's and Wulfstan's analyses of

the fall of Britain and the Viking devastations of England. If north-ern myth declares that existence is transitory and eschatological, *Beowulf* is Christian enough to ground this belief in history.

So in *Beowulf* Christianity appropriates the mythic eschatology of the Germans by historicizing it. In the process, the myth tends to blunt the apocalyptic theme with its starker eschatological ana-logue, stressing transience, death, doom—that is, judgment—rather than redemption, salvation, and revelation. The result is part of that peculiar contribution of the Anglo-Saxons to Christianity, that grim Christian realism so attractive to us in retrospect.

The second Christian component in *Beowulf*'s eschatology is the poem's very motivation. The world destroyed at the end of the poem is the heroic world, that pre-Christian world which in many respects had to be renounced by the Anglo-Saxons with the coming of Chris-tianity. The poem is in large part a lament for those losses; and pre-cisely a lament, for in the poem Anglo-Saxon culture seems to be mourning for its lost past. Mourning epitomizes the normal, healthy process of relinquishing the past and coming to terms with its ab-sence. To the reader of *Beowulf* it need hardly be argued that a culture can mourn for its past as an individual can. Mourning is in fact com-monly experienced collectively.

The question is often raised, why is *Beowulf* an Anglo-Saxon epic at all, since it is set in Scandinavia and the hero does not belong to the English national past? It is no accident that Beowulf belongs to a tribe famous for its heroes but equally noteworthy for its com-plete disappearance from history long before the composition of the poem. This striking fact points to one of the chief themes of the poem, which does not so much describe and praise the heroic world generally as focus on its disappearance in particular. The collapse of Beowulf's world at the end of the poem is presented as an inescap-able necessity, as ineluctable as death. *Beowulf* begins and ends with funerals and is mournful throughout; when it is not meditating on the necessity of death, it is demonstrating it in a sequence of mourn-ing figures—the Danish people, Hildeburh, Hrothgar, Hrethel, the old father, the last survivor, Wiglaf, and the Geats. The poem ends with the passing of Beowulf, the passing of his nation, and the pass-ing of the heroic world altogether, and mourns all these losses. It is a poem of mourning, an act of cultural mourning.

The distinctive psychology of mourning, with its blend of love, devotion, obsessive memory, guilt, self-mortification, anger, renunciation, and relief, might account for the poem's complex tone better than the more conventional theory of cultural nostalgia. The poem's ambivalence toward the past may be illogical, admiring it and renouncing it at the same time, but that is only typical of mourning. The destruction of the heroic world at the end of the poem represents a renunciation, but also an appropriate self-punishment, left hanging forever in the future, for the guilt that such a loss inevitably inspires.

Chapter 2

Transformations of Chaos

The Anglo-Saxons were among the least Romanized of the bar-
barians when Christian missionaries arrived in 597. Their many war-
ring tribal kingdoms were gradually converted in the course of the
seventh century and, due partly to the unifying force of Christian
doctrine and ecclesiastical structure, emerged in the eighth as a fairly
unified English culture, and in the ninth as a nation. This new culture, like most in the European Middle Ages, was Christian in a very
full sense, and its literature is almost entirely concerned with religious
themes. Most of it is written by monks, and most of it is in Latin; but
much is written in Old English, including some thirty thousand lines
of poetry—the earliest European vernacular literature—in which the
Anglo-Saxons expressed a Christian faith peculiar to their culture.

Anglo-Latin literature of the same period is distinguished by its
own styles and themes, but it does not differ dramatically from the
rest of European Latin literature in anything so fundamental as its
conception of God or the human condition. In Old English, however, where a native poetic tradition extended back into the oral
period before the conversion, and where perhaps the ancient oral
poetic tradition still throve, Christianity's ideal vision found itself in
direct contact with the fibrous reality of a culture whose language,
customs, institutions, and social structures had not been formed
along Christian lines and whose values retained for centuries the in-
eradicable stamp of tenaciously conservative prehistorical traditions,

many of them common to the other branches of the Germanic family tree. With these traditions the Church had to make accommodation, as it must in the conversion of any vigorous culture. Though Latin was spoken *ex cathedra* and within the monastery, Old English remained the language of the court, the hall, and the hut; and as the mother tongue, it could hardly be dislodged as first language even inside the Church.

The two literatures in the two languages do not exactly represent two worlds, though. Most of the vernacular poetry that comes down to us is learned, written by the same men who wrote and conversed in Latin every day. Much of it, in fact, is translated from Latin, such as Bible stories, the Psalms, saints' lives, and the meters of Boethius's *Consolation of Philosophy*. Even so, in this poetry we see the Anglo-Saxon conception of God in a striking way, as educated and sophisticated Anglo-Saxons saw him through the medium of their own poetic language and the unshakable bias of their native cultural heritage. This vision is Anglo-Saxon in the same sense that we say Saint Matthew's is Jewish, or Saint John's Greek.

Analysis of this vision depends upon understanding how the immemorial traditions of the Anglo-Saxons, embedded in the language and the religious beliefs they brought from their original homelands on the North Sea, reciprocally shaped the newer faith imported from the Mediterranean, even as that faith reshaped their traditions. *Beowulf*, like Anglo-Saxon culture generally, strikes the reader as a peculiar blend of these two traditions, resulting in a Christianity that is dark, realistic, anxious, and violent—in short, heroic, and oddly modern.

The complex relationship between these Christian and Germanic traditions in the poems and in the culture that gave birth to them has always structured literary study of the period. An important difficulty is that while early Christianity is extremely well documented, almost nothing is known about the native religious belief of the Anglo-Saxons, which we can detect only in the shadows that it cast on the Christian belief that supplanted it. Anglo-Saxon paganism is commonly reconstructed indirectly, from Tacitus's first-century account in the *Germania* and from twelfth-century Scandinavian sources, which give a plausible but by no means certain interpretation, and from the mute, always uncertain evidence of archaeology, especially grave goods (see Arnold, pp. 123–41). Since E. G. Stanley's influential caveat, *The Search for Anglo-Saxon Paganism*, historians have grown scrupulous in this regard, so I will focus on Anglo-Saxon sources, scanty as they are.

Fortunately, we have one brilliant testimony on the subject of Anglo-Saxon paganism, a short account in Bede's *Ecclesiastical History of the English People*, written in 731 by a native churchman within living memory of the conversion. I will outline the themes in this story that are explored in the vernacular poetry; then before coming to *Beowulf*, the most difficult by far of all our poems to interpret, I will briefly survey three shorter poems (like most Old English poems anonymous, undatable, and untitled), chosen to represent the wide range of genre and religious expression in the literature.

The Parable of the Sparrow

As Bede tells the story, an Italian missionary named Paulinus traveled to the north of England around the year 625 to convert the Northumbrian king Edwin. When the king was finally prepared to convert he called a conference of his chief men and counselors "so that if they agreed with him, they might all be consecrated together in the waters of life" (p. 183). Bede summarizes the conference in two short speeches that express economically how the new faith must have appeared to the wise men of old. In the first speech Coifi, the chief priest, addresses the king:

> I frankly admit that, for my part, I have found that the religion which we have hitherto held has no virtue or profit in it. None of your followers has devoted himself more earnestly than I have to the worship of our gods, but nevertheless there are many who receive greater benefits and greater honor from you than I do and are more successful in their undertakings. If the gods had any power they would have helped me more readily, seeing that I have always served them with greater zeal. So it follows that if, on examination, these new doctrines which have now been explained to us are found to be any better or more effectual [*meliora et fortiora*], let us accept them at once without delay. (p. 183)

This speech is remarkable for its mixture of cynicism and naïveté, a strangely rationalized tribalism. It is not so much an argument as a grudging personal complaint to the king. The high priest is so grieved by his social status that he is prepared to renounce his tribal religion, as if the king's favor were equivalent to the gods'. He has stumbled into a right position, though for the wrong reason — "from sense of injured merit," as Milton would say — and with almost comically inappropriate expectations. It is clearly implied that whereas the old gods did not reward the devotee's service through the king, the new one will.

Christianity hardly promises material prosperity and worldly honor, however; the example of Christ, imitated in the lives of the saints, shows (in the seventh century, at least) that these are probably inversely proportional to one's faith. Such worldly standards are irrelevant, if not perverse, in Christian terms. But they are not comical or irrelevant here, because all personal relations in Anglo-Saxon society are profoundly materialistic, and it is assumed that virtue, however it is defined, will be rewarded materially. How else could one's worth be known? Besides, practically speaking, the king has already decided to convert, and there are clear material advantages to be had from following his lead. Thus Coifi embraces Christianity, though on decidedly non-Christian terms.

One detects here as well a social-political crisis in the old religion, which other evidence tells us was once intimately bound up with kingship itself; the chief priest has not been enjoying the king's favor, which his religion requires. Like primitive religions everywhere, this one embodies and reinforces the predominant social values — wealth and the honor that wealth symbolizes, won by absolute loyalty to the king and to the social order. Somehow, in the turmoil of the recent migrations to England and the subsequent transformation from tribe to state, the native religion has become something of an anachronism and has lost its power, which the Church is in fact destined to recoup. The Church will rapidly become powerful and rich in Anglo-Saxon terms — land, treasure, and even an extremely honorable *wergild* ("man-price") for its priests and bishops. In general, Coifi's priestly successors at the king's side will have less reason to complain. The Anglo-Saxon Church will come to terms with Anglo-Saxon materialism.

The second speech, the most famous passage in all of Anglo-Latin literature, is delivered by an unnamed counselor — indicating perhaps that here Bede is either inventing freely or adapting a familiar metaphor to his use.

> This is how the present life of man on earth, King, appears to me in comparison with that time which is unknown to us. You are sitting feasting with your ealdormen and thegns in winter time; the fire is burning on the hearth in the middle of the hall and all inside is warm, while outside the wintry storms of rain and snow are raging; and a sparrow flies swiftly through the hall. It enters in at one door and quickly flies out through the other. For the few moments it is inside, the storm and wintry tempest cannot touch it, but after the briefest moment of calm, it flits from your sight, out of the wintry storm and into it again. So this life of man appears but for a moment; what follows or indeed what went before, we know not at all. If this new doctrine brings us more certain information [*certius aliquid attulit*], it seems right that we should accept it. (pp. 183–85)

As the first argument was ethical, this one is metaphysical. The worldview portrayed here is consonant with everything we know about Germanic religion; the world is only an oasis of order in a universe essentially chaotic, at best indifferent to man, and from his point of view even hostile. In northern mythology this chaos is symbolized by the worlds of giants and other dark forces that surround this middle-earth and will finally destroy it. The gods themselves are warriors, like Edwin's thegns, who occupy a hall—Valhalla—and defend against this impinging chaos, and ultimately perish in the effort. We will see this worldview again in *Beowulf*, where the great hall Heorot is surrounded by the awful landscape of fens and monsters against which the hero defends it with his life.

The counselor as much as admits that the question "What lies beyond?" has previously not been an issue. The secular agnosticism of his speech recalls the casual worldliness of the previous speech, reinforcing our suspicion of a religious crisis. Christianity has raised the question, thereby revealing the limits of traditional thought. Yet the traditional image of the hall frustrates any answer, because it is so conspicuously *enclosed*—the hall does not even have windows. Man's point of view remains inside the hall, and he experiences what lies outside only as the border where the immanent meets chaos and the unknown. Snow may blow in the door, light may penetrate a few feet into the dark, a sparrow may enter and depart, but the storm is described phenomenologically. In this image the border is distinctly ominous, even terrifying, though life in the hall remains comfortable and happy.

What can Christianity do with such an image? The symbol itself is intractable, its meaning determined in large part by its phenomenology and its cultural associations. The attitude toward knowledge might be changed, and a description of the unknown be accepted on faith; but the hall as a symbol, and the warrior life that is lived there, will always bring with them a certain secularity of vision, as in the parable and in *Beowulf* too. The hall implies the worldly limits of vision itself, and an anxious concern with the border.

In the parable the traditional image of the hall has already been adapted somewhat by being cast in temporal terms: the hall is not a place, it is man's life, a fleeting moment of warmth in a cold, dark, violent eternity. This temporal twist to the image is distinctly Christian. The winter storm which traditionally represents the forces of chaos on the borders of the immanent—death and the unknown—thus becomes a symbol of a transcendent otherworld stretching to eternity, and the hall becomes a symbol of time—and not time as the Germans conceived it (see Bauschatz). Understood in the new terms of Christian philosophy (the problem of time and eternity), the myth is suddenly unendurable. Man's life is revealed as a meaningless momentary waste. Clearly the counselor has already discovered his fallenness. He is ripe for conversion. Surprisingly, however, the last stage of his implied argument is omitted, for a Christian like Bede should not accept the image of the winter storm as a symbol of the transcendent at all. The Christian otherworld is nothing like a winter storm.

The counselor's insight is very restrained. His sublime diminution of the world in the image is congenial to a Christian vision, as is his sudden humility before the mystery of transcendence; but his corollary that *other than this we know nothing at all* effectively maintains the world, fleeting as it is, as the absolute foundation of man's life—it is the immanent world that constitutes his ultimate reality and meaning. Does the counselor see beyond this? He does not renounce the image of his parable in favor of a more appropriate and comforting image from the Christian tradition—the orderly, earth-centered Ptolemaic universe, for example, or the Neoplatonic fall of the soul into the temporal world and its return to an ideal eternity. The image of the sparrow entering and leaving the hall could have suggested the soul and body to a Christian interpreter, but Bede declines the invitation. From a Christian perspective, the counselor's image remains inverted, for in Christian thought it is this world that is fallen and chaotic, and the other that provides ultimate reality and meaning. All he seeks from the new religion is "something more certain" about what lies outside the hall, a light in the storm; he wants more knowledge, but nowhere is it implied that human life is other than as he has characterized it, as simply shelter from the storm.

Both speakers ask very little of the new religion, actually. They seek a religion that will fulfill their material expectations, and clarify, without really changing, their dark, realistic picture of the universe. We might be tempted to attribute the limitations in these arguments to the limitations of the pagan spokesmen and not to Bede himself—perhaps he has given us only a brilliant portrayal of an intermediate stage in the conversion, half-pagan, half-Christian—except that Bede nowhere disavows or corrects their materialistic and realistic bias. In fact, he calls the speeches "divinely prompted" (*divinus admoniti*). Though his own belief is certainly orthodox, he seems to understand the parable of the sparrow with the instinctive sympathy of an Anglo-Saxon. He accepts the familiar arguments of the counselors, who are men of his own culture, in their own terms.

Though Coifi's warrior cult had disappeared by Bede's time, England was still governed by a warrior class that had adapted Christianity to the violent and defensive attitude toward the world that the old cult embodied. We expect to find such an attitude in any warrior society, since the job of a warrior class is to create and maintain order out of potential chaos and to guard the borders against encroaching enemies. After the conversion this ruling class stressed in its traditional poetic forms those features of Christianity that it could harmonize with the dark worldview of Edwin's court: God is king, Christ lord, the world is fleeting, falling, and soon to be destroyed; life is a losing battle against death, and fate is inexorable; never retreat or surrender, but die for your lord like a hero, so his fame (his glory) will live forever. This stark existential theology finds poignant expression in poems like "The Seafarer."

"The Seafarer"

"The Seafarer" is one of several poems commonly grouped as the Old English "elegies." These are dramatic monologues in which the speaker's experience and frame of mind are presented in realistic fine detail, though the situations giving rise to them are left relatively obscure, resulting in an almost riddling style which makes interpretation uncertain. The poems focus particularly on feelings of loss and decay. They elevate the pain of the transitoriness of happiness, life, and the world to a first principle, against which is sometimes balanced the Christian hope for salvation in a better world after death.

In this case the poet assumes the voice of a seafarer, who evokes a powerful sustained image of the hardship of the seafaring life—the physical pain, the loneliness of exile, and the affliction he feels at the memory of lost pleasures, especially the memory of feasting in the lord's hall with his companions.

> He knows not,
> he who lives happily on land,
> how sorrowing I on the icecold sea
> spent winters on the paths of exile,
> bereft of family and all friends,
> hung with icicles when hailstorms flew.
> No sound there but the sea's roar,
> icecold waves and the swan's song,
> the gannet's cry for entertainment,
> the curlew's call for men's laughter,
> and the seagull's song for mead-drink.
> Storms beat the cliffs there, birds cried,
> icy-feathered.   (ll. 12–24)

Though he has no hall, he says "In the hold I have known the halls of sorrow" (l. 5). In short, "Who goes to sea is full of longing" (l. 47). But this longing is ambiguous, for the Seafarer, like seafarers traditionally, has a perverse voluntary addiction to this way of life. He desires it, and he willfully renounces what he considers the illusory pleasures of the land dweller.

Halfway through the poem, after 64 lines, we are given to understand that this image bears a Christian meaning; like the winter hall of Bede's parable, it is in fact an image of life itself. The lord we

long for in life's lonely exile is the Lord God; suffering is our path
to wisdom and salvation; our wanderings in this transitory world
will bring us back to our true homeland at death, when we will join
our companions at the eternal banquet in the Lord's great hall. In a
strangely negative doxology, Christian and Germanic images reflect
each other openly:

> I do not believe
> that the wealth of the earth remains forever.
> Always, everywhere, one of three things
> will bring you doubt about your deathday,
> sickness or age or the edge of the sword
> will rob the life of the fated departing.
> For every man then the best memorial
> is praise of the living, those who come after.
> Let him perform before he depart
> bravely against the attack of enemies
> bold deeds on earth against the devil,
> so the sons of men will praise him afterwards.
> Then his glory will live among the angels
> forever and ever, eternal bliss,
> joy with his companions.   (ll. 66–80)

"Companions" here translates *duguð*, the Old English word for a
band of warriors, more commonly called by the Latin term Tacitus
used to describe it, the *comitatus*. The men of the *duguð* share in the
communal life of their lord's hall, where they swear absolute vows
to him. In return for his support—weapons, gold rings, land—they
vow in their banqueting before his high seat to fight and die for him.
"Furthermore," Tacitus says in his famous formula, "it is shocking
and disgraceful for all of one's life to have survived one's chieftain
and left the battle: the prime obligation of the *comitatus*'s allegiance
is to protect and guard him and to credit their own brave deeds to
his glory: the chieftains fight for victory, the *comitatus* for the chieftain" (p. 47).

During the pre-Christian period, this was the central institution of
the warrior class and the most visible and powerful institution in the
society. Kept alive in heroic poetry, it remained a tradition throughout Anglo-Saxon history, through centuries of change, long after
tribal life and the warrior cult had given way to a complex national

government and the Church. These heroic terms could symbolize the values and social bonds of the aristocracy and of the Church— much as the chivalry of King Arthur's court could symbolize the aristocratic ideals of the later Middle Ages, or the Homeric world embody the *paideia* of the Greek Golden Age, or as today the life of the pioneer-frontiersman remains a symbol of American individualism.

In this case, the Seafarer has turned from the joys of the earthly *duguð* only to embrace those of its transcendental analogue. This rich metaphor implies its own theology: God is presented as a lord who rules over a company of men who bind themselves to him by a voluntary contract in which they exchange their free wills and ultimately their lives for his greater glory and his generous sustenance, from which they may derive honor and fame. Like an earthly lord, God renders meaningful and palliates to some extent the horrors of life, which experience and traditional wisdom tell us is always as tenuous and fatal as the warrior's. God exacts absolute commitments which allow man to accept necessity, loss, constant struggle, and death— that is, his fate.

There is nothing here exactly to scandalize Augustine, but the image is stark even by his standards. The warrior life has been a natural metaphor for Christian life since Saint Paul told the Ephesians to "put on the whole armor of God"—the breastplate of righteousness, the sword of the Spirit, the helmet of salvation, the shield of faith (Eph. 6: 10–17). The Romans too understood the ideal of the soldier's loyalty unto death, but even they were in awe of the absolute commitment of the Germanic *comitatus* and its centrality in Germanic life. Compared to orthodox doctrines of faith and grace, this Anglo-Saxon expression of God's lordship is pretty harrowing.

The Seafarer's commitment to the heavenly *duguð* naturally estranges him from his worldly *duguð*. Since his real homeland is elsewhere, he is an alien in the world, a man for whom life itself is an exile. This idea too would have been familiar to Augustine, who saw the Christian as a citizen of the City of God and thus an alien, a foreigner in the City of Man. Here Augustine's spiritual metaphor joins with the traditional imagery of Anglo-Saxon poetry. The exile is a stock figure in the heroic world, as indeed he was in Anglo-Saxon social life; but in a Christian context his suffering takes on new meaning. Because the life of the exile enacts literally the spiritual truth of the human condition, it assumes a religious quality, especially when chosen.

The Anglo-Saxons liked to literalize the Augustinian metaphor of alienation. Beyond the traditional symbolic modes of the priestly, monastic, and hermetic lives, there was also the literal act of simply leaving one's homeland, either going as a missionary abroad or, at the furthest extreme, setting out to sea with no purpose other than to commit one's life into God's hands. Such voluntary exiles were well known if not common in Anglo-Saxon England. They were known as *peregrini pro amore Dei*, pilgrims for the love of God.

The prevailing interpretation of "The Seafarer," first propounded by Whitelock in 1950, argues that the Seafarer himself is such a *peregrinus*. The first part of the poem is therefore a literal and realistic description rather than an allegory of the Christian life. On the other hand, Stanley replied in 1955, Old English poetic diction is such that the factual and the figurative are especially difficult to distinguish. In addition, we might add now, the life of such a *peregrinus*, actual as it is, is itself allegorical by nearly any definition of that word. The poem is in fact symbolic and realistic at the same time—no mean feat in the early Middle Ages, when literary symbolism is generally abstract and calculated, and literature generally idealistic, viewing the world through the refining lens of theology. The lives of the saints, for instance (an extreme example, but the most popular literary genre of the period), are as flat and static, lacking in shadows and realistic personal detail, as their painted icons. To appreciate the realistic detail of "The Seafarer" we need only compare it with this contemporary Irish poem, also about the hermetic life:

> Alone in my little cell,
> no paltry man for company—
> this were my chosen pilgrimage
> before trysting with death.
>
> Let bitter wailing reach
> up to yon heaven of clouds;
> be sins confessed in piety
> with free and copious tears.
>
> Little food, and tasteless too,
> and the mind but set on learning;

farewell to strife and company,
welcome calm and quiet mind.

Be the earth that covers me
hallowed earth of monastery,
a tiny place with gleaming tombs,
I lying there alone.

(Bieler, pp. 57–58)

Not since Augustine's *Confessions* and not again until Abelard and Eloise and Dante do we find such respect for the validity and meaningfulness of psychological and sensual experience as we find in Old English poems such as "The Seafarer," where religious symbolism is rooted deeply in the world of experience.

The Seafarer, like Ishmael, is the vehicle of a certain vision, a certain wisdom. His personal experience is gradually generalized in the second half of the poem, quickly intersecting with the reader's. Not only is he alone, but his *duguð* has perished; the age of heroes is past; all men die; mankind itself is growing old; the whole world seems weak and pale; nothing lasts. This mounting horror at the emptiness and impermanence of worldly life finally merges into highly generalized (and prosaic) gnomic wisdom, where ultimate reality and meaning are finally located:

Great is the terror of the Lord,
    it makes the world turn aside.
He established the firm ground,
    The wide earth and the heavens.
Foolish he who dreads not the Lord,
    death comes to him unprepared.
Blessed he who humbly loves,
    to him grace comes from heaven.
The Lord establishes his spirit,
    because he believes in His might.
A man must steer with a strong mind,
    hold firm to that foundation,
Be true to his promises, pure in his ways.

(ll. 103–10)

This is Christian wisdom as Coifi and his fellow-counselors, King Edwin's *duguð*, came to understand it in their own language, a blend of the old wisdom and the new. The immanent world is as fleeting as ever, though it now has a foundation, a "firm ground"; though a man is wise to love humbly, he requires a strong mind to steer him through the world; and characteristically God's grace is given to him who respects God's might, dreads his terror.

In the first part of the poem Christian ideas barely intrude into the realistic depiction of the Seafarer's life. If the poem were to end at line 64, as it does in Ezra Pound's famous translation, we could argue whether it is Christian at all. Of course the conclusion tells us that it is. This is very like the case of *Beowulf*, except that that poem does not settle the question for us so clearly. On the other hand, the concluding gnomic verses of "The Seafarer" need not be attached to a dramatic character; they could be developed more systematically, as they are in our next poem, "Maxims I, Part 1." Here we see explicitly Christian philosophizing woven tightly into the most conventional native wisdom—so conventional, in fact, that two of the gnomic sayings we have just quoted from "The Seafarer" appear in this poem as well.

"Maxims I, Part 1"

The image of the winter storm has much the same value in "The Seafarer" as in Bede's parable. In the poem, of course, the storm represents the chaos and instability of *this* world, as opposed to the firm foundation of the other, whereas in the parable these are reversed; but it would be misleading to draw too sharp a distinction. The point of the parable, reinforced in the poem, is that these two visions are oddly harmonious—that given belief in the one, belief in the other follows easily enough. Both agree that life is brief and fatal, and both agree on the need for a strong stoic response. How meaningful is it to insist that the sparrow's brief interlude is happy while the Seafarer's is miserable? For both, existence is governed by a terrible tension, not so much between good and evil, but between order and chaos; to achieve the one, man heroically defends himself against the other.

"Maxims I, Part 1" is one of many gnomic wisdom poems in Old English. In general they articulate the order of the world created by God and maintained by right behavior. This particular poem is neither heroic nor monastic, and the world it refers to seems to be the real world of the poet. Though the end of the poem describes court life in familiar terms, with its gold-giver, oaths, councils, and wars, the tone throughout is not the familiar one. The poet reveals himself as a man working quietly out of sight behind the great cultural fantasies of the *scop*, not a great poet or a genius, but like those of us who might find ourselves studying his work a thousand years later, a decent intellectual nonetheless.

The poem dwells especially on the benefits of calm deliberation rather than heroic action. Wise men must talk together, avoid evil, subdue and educate the young, keep their women in line, maintain social order, and obey the king—but primarily, in this poem, they must talk together.

> Question me with words of wisdom,
> > do not leave your spirit hidden,
> the mysteries you know most deeply.
> > I will not reveal my secrets
> if you conceal your intelligence from me,
> > and the thoughts of your heart.
> Wise men should exchange ideas.
>
> > > (ll. 1–4)

God is introduced as the creator of man's tentative existence:

> First and foremost we should praise
> God our Father, for first He created
> our life and brief joy—and He recalls His gift.
>
> > (ll. 4–6)

Our "brief joy" is *lænne willan*, brief in the sense that it is only *loaned*. Like Anglo-Saxon land (in England even today), or like the provisions a Germanic lord gave his men, the things of this world and the world itself are given to us only for our temporary use, then to revert to their real possessor—a concept that puts a distinctly prefeudal twist on Augustine's more familiar distinction between the use and enjoyment of things. In poetry the word *lænne* is used almost exclusively in this sense, opposed to the absoluteness of God and heaven and the permanence of his grace. It is usually translated *transitory*. *Lif is lænne* is perhaps the most familiar formula and theme to students of Old English poetry.

God's nature, on the other hand, is the inverse of man's lot:

> The Lord is in glory, man is on earth,
> the young grow old, but God is eternal,
> fate cannot change Him, nor anything harm Him,
> sickness or old age.   (ll. 7–10)

In a sense, Christian belief only throws into higher relief the Anglo-Saxons' traditional realistic picture of life. By offering a highly idealized otherworld, it sharpens by contrast the traditional dualism of order and chaos. Thus paradoxically this world and man's life appear all the more chaotic and miserable.

The storm and the ocean are conventional symbols of this chaos. (Others are the ruined hall, the fen, and the battlefield.) What exactly is the meaning of such symbols? What in the world (besides the English weather) could arouse such gloom and terror in the Anglo-Saxon worldview, that an ocean storm could serve as a metaphor for life? One answer helpful in understanding both "The Seafarer" and *Beowulf* is provided in these lines from the "Maxims," in which the ocean storm is given a purely secular interpretation:

> A man steers with a strong mind: the storm stirs up the ocean,
>> in fierce weather the sea rushes in dark waves furiously
>> from afar toward the shore to discover its strength,
>> and the walls must withstand both wind and water.
>>> As the sea is calm
>>> when the wind does not waken it,
>> the people are peaceful when men have deliberated.
> They sit in council together, and among companions bold men
>> hold power naturally. The king wants to rule alone.
>> Holding land he is hated, giving much he is much loved.
>> Glory is with the proud, power with the strong,
>> and both together will wage war quickly.   (ll. 50–61)

The storm, a symbol we know from Bede and "The Seafarer" to have rich religious meanings, is here analyzed by a Dark Age Durkheim in purely psycho-sociological terms. The object of social life is peace (though that does not exclude war, which is required to establish and maintain it). Peace demands mental strength of the individual, the deliberation of men, and political power determined by a system of natural virtues—wisdom, boldness, generosity, pride, and strength, all embodied in the king. The ocean storm represents the world in which this complex of social controls is loosened. The threat is cosmic. We wonder even, How strong is the shore? Will the walls hold? There is nothing like a storm to remind us that there are terrifying cosmic forces against which we can defend ourselves only with tremendous effort.

The poet, like King Lear, realizes that these forces rage inside as well as outside man. They are psychological—a strong mind is our seawall, our shoreline; they are social—the people are an ocean, and only calm deliberation and orderly governance can prevent their stormy unrest. The image is drawn from the *Aeneid*, but also from Gregory the Great's *Pastoral Care*, which King Alfred translated into Old English: "The untrained steersman can steer easily enough on a calm sea, but the trained one does not trust him in rough seas or a great storm. What is power and rulership but the mind's storm, always tossing the ship of the heart on the waves of thoughts?" (p. 58). The psychological, social, natural, and theological meanings of this image were perhaps barely distinguishable in the early Middle Ages, but from our perspective we sense that what is being elevated to a metaphysical principle in these lines from the "Maxims" is primarily social order. Because man's world is so tentative, so *lœne*, its order is fragile and in constant need of repair. This task falls to the ruling warrior class, which has cultivated the vernacular poetic tradition as a vehicle for expressing precisely these values.

This profound concern for social order is not unwarranted, either; it is a response to two social contradictions common in Germanic society that constantly undermine it. The first of these is the nature of Germanic law, which is founded on the kin-feud; we will explore this contradiction in *Beowulf* later. The second is the economics of Germanic kingship, summarized in the line above, "Holding land he is hated, giving much he is much loved." Lordship is above all generous; but where does the land and wealth come from, with which a lord rewards his followers? Tacitus saw the problem back in the first century: "One could not maintain a large retinue except by violence and war; for they claim from the generosity of their chieftain that glorious war horse, that renowned *framea* which will be bloodied and victorious; for banquets and provisions, not luxurious but abundant, serve as pay. The wherewithal for generosity is obtained through war and plunder" (p. 47). In the more advanced politics of the eighth and ninth centuries, land had become the most important such gift, and Anglo-Saxon political life was often motivated by the king's need for new lands, when he had distributed too much of what he already possessed (see Campbell, pp. 124–55).

Social order

Despite the poem's lengthy discussion of God, then, "Maxims I, Part 1" is a remarkably secular poem, in which traditional worldly values are nested comfortably inside a transcendent Christian context. Like Bede's parable and "The Seafarer," it expresses essentially a realistic attitude. Social order may indeed be an image of the transcendent world, but it is also an end in itself. Thus in the concluding lines of the poem the kingship of God is imagined in strikingly materialistic terms, hardly as the Gospels would have suggested:

> Eager he who receives gold which abounds at the high seat,
> rewarded if he not be false to Him who gives us favor.

> (ll. 69–70)

"Christ I"

"The Seafarer" and "Maxims I, Part 1" are both contained in the *Exeter Book*, a richly various anthology of Old English poems compiled in the tenth century. "Christ I" is the first poem in this manuscript, and deservedly so. It is perhaps the most intellectually brilliant poem in Old English, a dazzling performance by a gifted poet and an inspired Christian thinker. It is a sequence of a dozen hymns (probably fifteen before the first leaf of the book was lost), each twenty to forty lines long, freely elaborating a sequence of one-sentence Latin antiphons from the Advent liturgy.

Unlike "The Seafarer" and "Maxims," "Christ I" is a poem unambiguously of the clerical-monastic world, deeply informed by Christian theology and biblical exegesis, a learned meditation on the Incarnation, a *lectio divina* for monks and clergy. Yet the poet exploits the traditional imagery of Germanic poetry too and strongly vernacularizes the Incarnation. So "Christ I" is a test case of the reach, tenacity, and flexibility of such imagery in a Christian context. Because the poem is in the form of a prayer, a direct address from this world to the other, and because it is an Advent prayer especially, a plea for the transcendent to reveal itself immanently, images of the immanent and the transcendent worlds such as we have been examining abound and are drawn with great clarity. In fact, the poem is a virtual catalog of such images, shifting rapidly and piling up in surreal display. The poet draws every available tradition into his meditation.

This protean symbolism is an aspect of the poem's meditative style. Neither narrative nor argument structures "Christ I." Instead there is an erudite free association of ideas and images, organized not only by the underlying antiphons but by the traditional symbolic associations woven from the Bible into the commentaries of the church fathers. The poem resembles nothing more than a biblical commentary, like Augustine's *Exposition of the Psalms* or Gregory's *Morals on Job*, in which the expositor plunges deep into his private concordance of the Bible and theological ideas and weaves a web of references and reflections around each verse of his text. Other than this arbitrary structure, there is hardly any movement in such a work except accumulation, gradually yielding a greater depth and completeness of vision. The whole meaning, however, is complete from the beginning. A happy result of this style for our purpose is that we may read the poem in the same way: touch any part, and the whole web shakes. We can examine only the first two sections here without misrepresenting the whole poem.

The first 17 lines are the incomplete first section, based on the antiphon "*O King of nations, and their desired one, and the cornerstone that makes both one: come and save man, whom you formed from dirt.*"

> . . . the King.
> Thou art the wallstone the workers once
> rejected from the work. Now it is right
> that you be head of the great hall,
> join together the wide walls,
> fast together, flint unbroken,
> so all on earth with eyes to see
> will wonder forever at the Lord of Glory.
> Skillfully manifest your own work,
> truthfast victorious, now let stand
> wall against wall. There is need of the work
> that the Craftsman come and the King Himself,
> and make better what now lies broken,
> house under roof. He created the body,

the limbs from clay. Now the Lord of Life
shall deliver from evil this wretched people,
the miserable from fear, as He often has.

(ll. 1–17)

This prayer is addressed to Christ by those awaiting his coming.
These are first of all, literally, worshipers in the Advent season looking forward to Christmas; but they are also the Old Testament world,
Israel, awaiting the Incarnation; those waiting in hell for Christ to
deliver them by his descent; and those of the last times awaiting the
Second Coming and Judgment. All four of these voices can be heard
in the poem's chorus. The central image is the building of the Temple,
which the poet calls the "great hall." It remains incomplete without
its cornerstone, which is Christ (Psalm 118: "The stone which the
workers rejected has become the cornerstone," echoed by Christ in
the Gospels). But it is also the Church, the spiritual body of which
Christ is the head; as well as the heavenly church, which will finally
be completed at the end of the world when the Jews and Gentiles
will be united (Ephesians 2: 20: "You form a building which rises on
the foundation of the apostles and the prophets, with Jesus Christ
himself as the main cornerstone").

Halfway through these lines, however, the image changes. The
hall under construction becomes a ruined hall awaiting repairs, and
this new image is immediately identified with the human body. The
image is perhaps drawn from Augustine's prayer beginning the *Confessions*, "My soul's house is too narrow for you to enter, let it be
enlarged by Thee. It is in ruins, repair it" (see Hill, *Notes*). It may also
echo the words of Christ: "'Destroy this temple and in three days I
will raise it up.' They retorted, 'This temple took forty-six years to
build, and you are going to raise it up in three days!' Actually he
was talking about the temple of his body" (John 2: 19–21). But for
a reader of Old English poetry the image resonates first of all in the
native tradition: the poet portrays mankind inhabiting a ruined hall,
calling out to God to reveal himself, to restore the hall and transform
it into the great hall of heaven. The antiphon supplied only the image
of the cornerstone, which the poet has elaborated further and further in a direction familiar to his Anglo-Saxon audience. The Temple
of the one tradition may be under construction, but the hall of the

other is in ruins. There is no mistaking that the ruined hall is the immanent world, Bede's winter-hall, now in ruins from the Christian
viewpoint; and no mistaking the materialistic emphasis on the clay
of the body. In the end, the ruined hall is a symbol with many meanings: the Temple, the Advent season, hell, the soul's house, the body,
the body of Christ, the Church, and the world—a comprehensive
symbol of immanence, of human being itself, the human condition.

The second section of the poem paraphrases the antiphon *"O Key
of David, and scepter of the house of Israel, who opens and no one closes, who
closes and no one opens: come, and lead the captive from the prison-house,
sitting in darkness and the shadow of death."*

> O thou Ruler and Thou Right King
> who holdest the lock and openest life,
> the ascent of the blessed, deniest another
> the beautiful way if his work avail not:
> for need truly we speak these words
> mindful of Him who created man:
> do not let the case of the sorrowful
> come to nothing; we in prison
> sit sorrowing, awaiting the sun,
> when Life's Lord will open the light:
> be to our spirits lord and protector,
> enfold our feeble thoughts in glory,
> worthy of the glory that He forsook,
> we who humbly had to wander
> to this narrow land, deprived of home.
>
> (ll. 18–32)

Here the world is portrayed not as a ruined hall but as a dark
prison in a foreign land. Man cries out to God, who is at once jailer,
judge, and *mundbora*—a lord protector in Anglo-Saxon law—to protect him, to hear his case, to leave his own homeland and come to
the prison himself, to open it with his own light. In the succeeding
sections of the poem the poet will identify these prison doors as the
gates of Paradise through which man entered the world, and also the
Virgin's maidenhead through which Christ followed to rescue him.
They are the doors that lock us away from the transcendent. Since
the prison is a traditional image of hell, here the Advent worshipers
are identified most strongly with those awaiting Christ's descent and

harrowing, though other voices from the first section are implied as well, and some new ones too—Israel in bondage in Egypt and Babylon. This theme of exile in the final lines gives a familiar Anglo-Saxon turn to the antiphon.

The image of exile in a prison house shut away from the light (that is, from the transcendent) has its deepest roots not in the Bible and its exegesis but in ancient philosophy, as a symbol of the Orphic, Pythagorean, Platonic, and Neoplatonic doctrine of the fall of the soul into the world. Man's soul has fallen into the prison of the body and the exile of worldly experience. It longs to escape and return to its true spiritual homeland, which it glimpses in dreams and visions, in ecstasy, and in truth and wisdom. Ricoeur calls this complex of ideas and images "the myth of the exiled soul and salvation through knowledge" (*Symbolism of Evil*, p. 279). It entered Western theology through Augustine, who effectively attached it to the quite distinct "Adamic myth," in which man falls through his own fault, his sin— the world is good but man is guilty. But Old English poems revive the exiled soul theme in surprisingly unalloyed form. Man's alienation from the transcendent is penal, but guilt is less an issue here than the simple givenness and inescapability of the dialectic of immanence and transcendence, the dualism of body and soul, the stubborn necessity of existing in the material world.

Augustine notwithstanding, we should not overestimate the importance of this theme in early Christian thought. It is probably no more than a distant and subliminal influence on the imagery of poems like "Christ I." It flourishes in these poems independently, because it is the profoundest philosophical expression of the Anglo-Saxon view of the world that is at least compatible with Christianity, if uneasily. It is something of a compromise, really, between the Adamic myth and the parable of the sparrow-flight, stressing the wretchedness of man's condition more than his sinfulness.

The imagery of bondage and release, most conspicuous in the symbolism of the harrowing of hell, is unusually pervasive in Old English poetry. In the long poem *Andreas*, for example, the imprisonment and liberation of Saint Matthew is narrated in these terms, and in *Elene* the raising of a dead man, and in *Exodus* the crossing of the Red Sea, to name only a few. A more philosophical example is

"The Wanderer," a companion elegy to "The Seafarer" in which the lonely exile portrays himself and the world in bondage:

> I know for a fact
> in an earl it is always a noble habit
> to bind fast the breast's locker,
> the heart's coffer, think what he may.
> The weary mind cannot withstand fate,
> or a troubled spirit be of assistance.
> Eager for glory then, often the dreary
> he binds fast in his breast's coffer,
> as I in misery my own spirit,
> deprived of home and far from kin,
> must often seal with chains of sorrow,
> since years ago in the dark earth
> I enfolded my gold-friend, and hence went
> winter-sorrowing over bound waves,
> seeking, hall-weary, near and far,
> a giver of treasures.   (ll. 11–26)

Not only this, but the winter storm binds the earth in snow, and the Wanderer is bound by sleep and sorrow together, as the Seafarer is bound in fetters of cold; and the body is variously a house, a locker, a coffer of the spirit, the mind, and life. In bondage in the land of exile, the Wanderer and the Seafarer call out like the chorus of voices in "Christ I." Because they embody the image of the fallen soul trapped in the world, their salvation lies in dreams and visions in which the soul leaves the body (both poems contain this motif), and in the gnomic wisdom that concludes both poems. The image of the ruined hall also dominates "The Wanderer."

What does the prison share with the ruined hall, the winter hall, and the storm at sea as symbols of immanence? No matter what the transcendent promises, the immanent world is chaotic and too intractable to idealize. Our experience of it cannot be denied or made to appear innocent. This view is an odd sort of Manichaeism, in which the material and spiritual worlds comprise a dualism; but the former is not necessarily evil, it is just necessarily *there*. It is the *grund*, the simple ground, which in Old English is also the bottom, the foundation, the abyss, and the depths, on which man walks, builds, and thinks, in which God and man plant, and the spirit grows. It is the *grund* that Christ visits in "Christ I" (ll. 42, 145), and the *grund* that Beowulf inhabits so fully.

Beowulf

Beowulf is a dense, crowded narrative in which the poet seldom relaxes his grip on the language, maintaining a poetic intensity for an incredibly long performance of 3,182 lines, keeping the reader's attention satisfied and alert by rapid shifts in tone and direction. The main plot, the hero's three monster-fights, moves along at a deceptively leisurely pace, with deceptive simplicity, but is framed, explained, supported, enhanced, and often ironically undermined by richly detailed digressions—historical, legendary, histrionic, meditative—that give the world of the poem a sense of completeness as well as monumentality. The poem's fullness of vision and its heroic cast lead most readers to consider it epic; but even this simple attempt to characterize the poem can provoke hostilities among critics.

Beowulf is perhaps uniquely resistant to conventional modes of literary criticism, partly because its relation to the rest of Anglo-Saxon culture is impossible to determine. But most of all, the critic is transfixed by the problem of the poem's inscrutable religious tone. It is a Christian poem about pagans with only minimal reference to Christianity or paganism; it is a Christian poem but secular. We have almost no precedents for interpreting the poem's thematic intentions. Is it, like the first half of "The Seafarer," open to a Christian reading? If so, how would an Anglo-Saxon audience (*what* audience?) have read it? For convenience scholars conventionally locate the poem at the Northumbrian court of Bede's day. Though we do not want to accede to this traditional date, or any date, juxtaposing the poem with Bede's brilliantly learned writing does remind us of their startling incongruous differences, and how little we really know of the Anglo-Saxon world outside the monastery from poetic evidence. Different as they are, though, it is Bede who provides our first clue for interpreting the poem.

Beowulf opens with a poetic variation on Bede's parable of the sparrow in the story of the Danish patriarch Scyld Scefing. He arrives from nowhere with no possessions, creates peace with heroic deeds, is honored as a good king, bears a noble son to succeed him, and dies—all in the first 25 lines. The ultimate meaning of his exemplary life is revealed in the next 27 lines, which recount his funeral:

> When Scyld departed at the appointed hour
> to pass strong into the Lord's power,
> they bore him down to the brimming tide,
> his own companions, as he requested
> when the Scylding lord, beloved king,
> long possessed the wielding of words.
> There in the harbor stood the ring-necked
> icy and out-bound ship of the prince.
> Then they laid their beloved lord,
> giver of rings in the ship's breast,
> mighty by mast where much treasure,
> wealth brought from afar was laded.
> I never heard of a handsomer hold
> adorned with weapons and war-clothes,
> swords and burnies lay on his breast,
> many treasures destined to pass
> far with him into the flood's possession.
> They gave him none the less in gifts,
> people treasures, than did they
> who in the beginning sent him forth
> alone on the waves, only a boy.
> Then yet they set a golden sign
> above his head, let ocean hold him,
> gave him to the sea, sad in spirit,
> minds mourning. Men know not
> how to say truly, hall-counselors,
> heroes under heaven, who took that load.
>
> (ll. 26–52)

His departure is as mysterious as his arrival. As Edwin's counselor put it, "what follows, or indeed what went before, we know not at all." Though he arrived with nothing, however, he departs with a full display of his accumulated being in the world, symbolized by the treasures he won, the war gear he won them with, and the golden sign over his head. The brevity of his life and the certainty of his death do not rob him of his glorious existence—he did in fact achieve much. More than this we cannot say, however, because he sails back into the unknown ocean whence he came, shockingly diminished in the last line to no more than a "load" committed to an unknown destination. Shockingly too, his elaborate and moving funeral rites imply no religious belief, just a clear-eyed respect for the facts of life and death.

It was difficult enough to assess Bede's attitude toward this traditional native vision, though in his case at least we could see it in the context of his orthodoxy and thus measure his irony and ambivalence. But here the world of the parable is the world of the poem— a hall in a storm, besieged, promised to ruin, distinctly material, strongly determined, wholly immanent. Here the transcendent is simply unknown, everywhere bordering the world of the known as the ocean surrounds the earth.

But the unknown transcendent does influence the world in two ways. First, it is ontologically prior to the immanent, and so is assigned credit for the simple givenness of the world. As in Bede's parable, the formulation is temporal: the past is the foundation of the present. This givenness is experienced as the constant pressure of *nyd* and *wyrd*, necessity and fate, on events. These are closely linked to Germanic notions of history and custom, but to the Christian observer they seem to operate much like Boethius's concept of Providence. Like Providence, *wyrd* has a vaguely divine aspect, which shows itself in the character of the hero, whose virtue is that he always chooses to do what he must, what is right and necessary, and so seems to live under a divine protection, though his life is tragic. This complex of ideas and images is hardly a theology, however, and (like Boethius's *Consolation*) it contains no specifically Christian terms. Though one senses Christian belief in the poem's many references to God, the poet carefully avoids any explicit mention of Christianity or its doctrines. In the above passage, for example, "the Lord's keeping" is quickly downgraded to "the flood's possession," and then to the agnosticism of Edwin's counselor, "men know not," which makes the ocean symbolically equivalent to the winter storm of the parable.

Second, the unknown transcendent affects the world as the constant threat and incursion of chaos, like the ocean storms in "The Seafarer" and "Maxims." An aspect of *wyrd* and *nyd*, chaos is morally neutral or ambivalent, though a Christian mind accustomed to the dialectic of good and evil is likely to attach one or the other of these values to it when they seem appropriate. Many of the classic problems of interpreting *Beowulf* derive from the irregular correspondence of these two ways of interpreting the world, which the poet notes and which the modern critic vainly tries to harmonize.

In the poem's main plot the incursions of chaos are symbolized by the sequence of monsters Beowulf must face—Grendel and his mother when they attack Hrothgar's hall, and the dragon when it destroys his own. Until Tolkien's landmark essay of 1936, "*Beowulf*: The Monsters and the Critics," the monsters were understood as folktale elements more or less embarrassing to modern adult readers. But Tolkien argues they are rich in symbolic meaning and can be interpreted to discover the chief themes of the poem. He is impressed by the poet's decision to put the monsters center stage as representatives of the encompassing darkness of Germanic myth, and particularly impressed by his attempt to illuminate these dark forces with the Christian concept of evil, most conspicuously by making Grendel a descendent of Cain.

We can extend Tolkien's analysis by noting that the three monsters are three very distinct symbols of different forms chaos can take in the human world and by interpreting them individually. Grendel is the least elusive of these symbols. After Scyld's funeral the Danish royal genealogy rushes down to his great-grandson Hrothgar, whose own exemplary career is symbolized by the building of the great hall Heorot. The building of the hall is balanced against its destruction, and the song of creation is balanced against the first murder. As Grendel is associated with Cain, he is implicitly associated with the hall's destruction. He is introduced into the poem more as a principle, an aspect of the creation, than as a character. The peoples of the world gather to build a hall, and he simply appears in the surrounding darkness; inside they sing of the new creation, and outside we hear the story of Cain. It is the Anglo-Saxon version of Newton's third law: for every order there is an equal and opposite chaos, for every creation a destruction, for every good an evil, for every light a shadow. The hall is no sooner built than its burning is foretold. No matter how strong its walls or brilliant its life, we are always aware of its fragility and transience. Grendel is Heorot's shadow.

In the section of the poem that takes place in Denmark, it is sometimes possible to believe that this "dark death-shadow" can be confronted and defeated. After all, he *is* defeated—though the sudden appearance of his mother destroys the illusion of victory, and her defeat too is only another delaying tactic. Below the surface of the main plot, the Danish court is crumbling, unaware of its imminent fall. The great celebrations of the hero's success are riddled with reminders that the king is old, his succession uncertain; his sons are too young, and his wife campaigns against his plan to adopt Beowulf; his nephew is perhaps plotting, his adviser Unferth is vaguely criminal, and the betrothal of his daughter is the first step toward the inevitable war in which the hall will be burned. Shadows are everywhere. Something is rotten in the state of Denmark, and Grendel is its symbolic embodiment. He symbolizes the same chaos as the ocean storm in the "Maxims," loosed when the strong grip of social-political order is relaxed. Seen in this way, Grendel is not much of a moral force. No doubt he is evil; but we are repeatedly told that God could destroy Grendel if he wished, and that Hrothgar is a good king—so there is little sense that Grendel is his punishment for anything except being human and old. Grendel is a *nydwracu*, a *necessary punishment*. The poet has wound him tightly in the language of necessity.

Not so his mother, whose attack is more clearly motivated and understandable; she wreaks legally justifiable revenge for her son's death. That Beowulf was also justified in killing Grendel for revenge is not to the point in Germanic law, and when Grendel's mother kills Æschere, Beowulf is justified in pursuing revenge once again. A legal system that encourages such a chain reaction contains a terrible contradiction: though vengeance is intended to inhibit violence, once it breaks out it is almost impossible to contain until it has run its awful course. The episode of Grendel's mother is framed in the poem by the Finn and Heathobard digressions, which tell of kinfeuds no truce can settle. Whatever else Grendel's mother represents, she represents the violence Anglo-Saxon kingship was most at pains to control, and which Anglo-Saxon law struggled for centuries to limit, modify, and eliminate. Eliminating revenge is perhaps the first task of civilization.

Grendel's *father* would have been quite another symbol. The hall, the *comitatus*, and war are the province of men, but the hut, the family, and agriculture are—symbolically at least—the province of women. The women of Northern saga and epic, like the women of Greek tragedy, are famous for their thirst for blood revenge (see Jochens). Women are so closely identified with the interests of the kindred that in Old English the same words—*mæg* and *mægþ*—mean both kindred and woman. From the point of view of men trying to run a society with lordly and political authority, family ties are a constant source of conflict, and *Beowulf* is definitely written from this masculinist point of view. In the poem women and marriage are a disruptive influence on the civilizing work of men, and the kin-feud is a fundamental source of social chaos. This defensive male attitude is not uncommon in military life, and we would hardly want to endorse it; it puts the modern reader, especially the female reader, in a rather awkward position.

The dragon is the last and most controversial of these symbolic monsters, and the ultimate meaning of the poem rests heavily on him. On the one hand he resembles the apocalyptic world-serpent of Germanic tradition that Thor, like Beowulf, fights to a dead draw. This mythical beast has no moral weight at all, since the Germanic apocalypse is not a judgment upon man but only an inevitability, and Thor's heroism is only his determination in the ultimately hopeless struggle against chaos. On the other hand, Beowulf's dragon also resembles Christian representations of evil, *malitia*, drawn primarily from the dragon of the biblical apocalypse. In the context of this allegory, it is often argued, Beowulf's defeat is a moral judgment brought on by his own pride and avarice. The poet's silence on this issue gives us nothing but a web of associations in which the dragon's meaning can be caught.

The dragon guards the buried treasure of a race that perished completely from history. We never learn their name, and except for the treasure Beowulf is unaware even of their existence—they are as remote to him as the Geats are to us. As the first part of the poem opened with Scyld's funeral and the consignment of his treasures to the ocean, this part opens with the funeral of an entire race and the consignment of their treasures to the earth. The Last Survivor understands the transience of the world in the largest terms, as he faces the unknown, the winter storm outside the hall, in full knowledge that it is the final victor in the battle we wage against it.

> Hold now thou earth, now heroes may not,
> possessions of earls. O good men once
> discovered it in you. Death in battle,
> fierce life-evil, took each of the men

of my people, of those who gave up this life,
saw joy in the hall. I have none to bear sword,
polish the plated cup, precious vessel.
Companions are vanished.   (ll. 2247–54)

The dragon causes Beowulf's death and brings about the imminent destruction of the Geatish people too. The long, complicated
history of the Geats' war with Sweden over three generations is told
in a confusing, unchronological series of digressions in this part of
the poem, as a chaotic background to the dragon-fight. Beowulf's
death will release tremendous, deeply rooted forces waiting to engulf
his world. His successful kingship has only been a holding action
against this chaos. His people will perish like the previous owners of
the treasure. The profoundest theme of the poem is that we are ultimately powerless to control history, and history itself is as mortal as
we are. Nations and peoples die too. The poet's most brilliant stroke
on this immense canvas is to conclude the poem on the eve of the
fated apocalypse, leaving us, like the Last Survivor, with a heightened sense of the extreme perilousness of the existence of our world.
The end of the poem is as apocalyptic as the beginning was prime-
val, the death of Beowulf and the Geats balanced against the origins
of the Danes and the building of Heorot.

As a final hedge against this awesome, awful vision, however, the
poet performs a final transformation. As he played to the Christian
notion of evil with Grendel and the dragon, he now offers the barest
glimpse into the darkness Beowulf enters, the barest hint of the rich
theology he can assume in his audience. When Beowulf dies, "his soul
went from his breast / To seek the judgment of the just" (ll. 2819–20).
And though Beowulf's funeral is as devoid of religion as Scyld's was,
Wiglaf instructs the men to carry him to the pyre "where he shall long
endure in the Lord's protection" (ll. 3108–9). When he is burned,
"Heaven swallowed the smoke" (l. 3155). These few grudging references to the reader's belief, however, hardly compensate for the overwhelming sense of loss and more loss to come at the end of the poem.

It is difficult to say what relation this vision has to Anglo-Saxon
Christianity, or even to Anglo-Saxon culture as a whole. There is no
other statement quite like it, so metaphysically secular, so slightly
Christianized, its stoic reserve refusing to see beyond the surrounding, threatening borders of the immanent—except for the speech of

Edwin's counselor. But I imagine it is deeply expressive of Anglo-Saxon attitudes that remained relatively unaffected by the Church. It is a cliché of the history of the English language that Modern English has inherited its concrete nouns mostly from Old English, and its abstract nouns mostly from French and Latin. *Beowulf*, and much of the rest of Old English poetry, expresses the vision implicit in that stubbornly concrete language of the Anglo-Saxons.

Chapter 3

Oral-Literate: Two Case Histories

Oral tradition and oral poetry are currently a glamour area in Anglo-Saxon studies, but most Old English poems are in fact highly literate, even if they bear the earmarks of oral style. For all their repetition and formulaic diction, most are based on Latin originals and are suffused with Latin learning, and many others are demonstrably literate in conception or style. It is easy for a literate poet to imitate oral style and easy to compose a literate text for the purpose of oral performance. Except in rare cases we do not know the circumstances of our poems' composition. In such a context, what should we conclude from the signs of oral style we find in *Beowulf*?

Here I examine the only two Old English poets we know anything about, Caedmon and King Alfred. ("Bede's Death Song" is probably not by Bede, and we know nothing of Cynewulf but his name and disposition.) In these two cases the features of oral tradition are woven into highly literate form in quite different ways. Bede's account of the oral poet Caedmon is itself so crafted and learned that Caedmon's orality can only be understood in literary terms as a classic account of divine inspiration. King Alfred's poems may seem unsophisticated on the surface and even present themselves to the reader as if they were singing aloud like Anglo-Saxon *scops*; but this is a highly erudite, literate pretense of orality, a metaphor of the written text as a speaker of the divine *Logos*.

Katherine O'Brien O'Keeffe argues that both these cases represent a long transitional phase between oral and literate culture and should not be mistaken for either. She goes so far as to suggest that Alfred was not really literate—that he could not write (see pp. 84–85). Here I suggest a different definition of literacy: a literate text is one that does not yield profitably to the generalizing tendencies of oral-formulaic analysis but loses its interest instead; however, it yields much in a close critical reading. It is not enough to cite the features or images of orality to demonstrate that a poem has emerged from a living oral poetic tradition. In Anglo-Saxon England we are dealing with a highly learned literary culture whose texts come at us like so many curveballs, each with a calculated spin of oral style upon it.

The real difference between oral and literary criticism lies in the attitudes and assumptions of the critic. Foley asks,

> Instead of assuming a poetics that owes its existence and contribution only to the poet, so that everything depends on his or her *conferral* of meaning to the phrase, should we not consider the traditional meaning that *inheres* in that phrase? What can *tradition* possibly denote if we ascribe referentiality solely or chiefly to the individual composing the poem, for no matter how brilliant an artist he or she may be, the poetic tradition remains more than a silent partner in the artistic enterprise. ("Textualization," p. 42)

Everything Foley says here about traditions and traditional rules in oral poetry also applies to literate poetry—or scholarship, for that matter, or all of human behavior. We always and everywhere live in a vast web of traditions and inherited meanings. We can choose either to see the artist as defined and limited by these traditions, as their spokesperson, or as enabled by them to spin new threads in the web. The oralist chooses to study how poems express traditions and traditional rules rather than how they express their authors' will, originality, and creativity. The poet is seen as a conduit for traditions. Orality obscures human agency; it is another instance of the postmodern axiom which claims that we do not really speak language, but it speaks us instead.

I choose, on the other hand, to focus on the poet's originality, on the ways in which poems break with traditions and traditional rules; and on free will, individual human agency, which in medieval thinking is not negated by the divine will but contained within it. These attitudes need not be mutually exclusive: a glass half empty is also half full.

Transcribing Caedmon

Bede recounts the story of Caedmon in his *Ecclesiastical History*. His account is in the genre of miracle story, part of a saint's life—the saint in this case being Hild, abbess of Whitby, the miracle being an instance of divine inspiration at her abbey.

Caedmon is an unlettered Anglo-Saxon cowherd who excuses himself from the mead-hall whenever the harp comes his way and he is expected to sing. On this particular occasion he goes to the barn, where he falls asleep and is visited in a dream by someone (*quidam*) who inspires him to sing a brief hymn of God's creation in Old English. Afterward he seeks out the town reeve and to general astonishment sings his new song. Until this moment it seems no one had thought of adapting the vernacular tradition of oral verse to Christian use, though the Church had been working to convert the English for the better part of a century. Caedmon is an immediate sensation. He is whisked off to Hild's abbey, where for the rest of his life he is read the Bible by day, sleeps on it by night, and recites it back in Old English verse to Hild's copyists in the morning.

Bede includes a Latin translation of Caedmon's first divinely inspired hymn in his account, and in several Latin manuscripts the ostensible original is written in Old English in the margins. The poem also appears in the Old English translation of the *History*, no longer in the margins. It is still a matter of lively debate just how original this Old English version of the hymn is. In the nineteenth century it was commonly thought to be a translation of Bede's Latin (see Frantzen, *Desire for Origins*, p. 146; Kiernan, "Reading Caedmon's 'Hymn'"). It is always possible that Bede simply invented or freely embellished the story and/or the poem. Saints' lives, especially miracle stories, are notoriously unreliable as historical evidence. Most scholars now, however, accept Bede's account as more or less factual and the Old English poem as authentically Caedmon's.

The story of Caedmon has become richly encrusted with interpretation, since critics treat it as a primal scene, the very *fons et origo* of the Old English poetic tradition. The hymn is given pride of place as the first English poem, a talismanic symbol of Anglo-Saxon culture, a paradigmatic blend of two traditions, the moment when literacy emerged from orality and Christianity from paganism in England.

And Bede's account is the origin of our own field of study: he is the first historian and critic of Anglo-Saxon poetry. We are his heirs.

Naturally the hymn has also become the focus of attempts to re-think these conventional ideas. Kevin Kiernan and Allen Frantzen deconstruct Bede's account by relating the long history of its reception among editors, though they sidestep issues of orality and literary genre; Martin Irvine (see pp. 197–99) and Seth Lerer (see pp. 33–35, 42–48) take up these issues in different ways. O'Brien O'Keeffe shows that the Anglo-Saxons themselves recognized the importance of Caedmon and struggled with ways of registering that importance in their copies of the hymn, with punctuation, lineation, and so on. So the hymn still marks a point of origin, the foundation of a new way of recording Old English poetry, which was once merely song. One would think there is nothing left to say—but in the world of criticism there is always more to say. I will add a few words about the literary genre of Bede's account of a preliterate poet—a highly literary miracle story about divine inspiration.

With the discovery of oral-formulaic poetry 40 years ago Caedmon's story became doubly important, since it seems to be a rare case history of an actual oral poet. Since Francis Magoun's first oral-formulaic study of the hymn in 1955 ("Bede's Story of Caedmon: The Case History of an Anglo-Saxon Oral Singer"), Caedmon's inspiration has commonly been reduced to a case of spontaneous formulaic composition—good ad libbing. We live in an age unimpressed by miracles. Stanley Greenfield asks exactly what the miracle was and itemizes the possibilities:

> Was it the gift of traditional poetic language, "aristocratic" and heroic, to an illiterate for the expression of Christian ideas? Insight into Scripture, along with the gift of language? The gift of memory? The fact that God chose someone "unsullied by the trivial qualities of pre-Christian verse and a complete novice in composition" to herald "a clean break with the heathen past symbolized by all previous poetry"? (p. 230, citing Wrenn, Huppé, Fritz, and Orton)

As E. Talbot Donaldson puts it baldly, "The true miracle . . . was to apply the meter and language . . . of heroic verse, to Christian themes" (p. 18). This literary effect we call the Caedmonian turn.

From the viewpoint of the literary historian, that may indeed be

Caedmon's achievement; but Bede is not writing literary history, and for him technique is hardly the issue. For Bede it is a case of divine inspiration, a miracle; and the more we know about miracle stories as a genre the less likely we are to adopt them as evidence for any-thing—at least anything literal. The dream visitor does not symbolize the oral-formulaic word-hoard, proficiency in public performance, or language itself speaking through the poet. His visitation signals that Caedmon is unique rather than representative. Bede even says, "It is true that after him other Englishmen attempted to compose religious poems, but none could compare with him. For he did not learn the art of poetry from men nor through a man but he received the gift of holy song freely by the Grace of God" (p. 415). The gift of God's grace does not negate Caedmon's originality but validates it.

The story validates the Anglo-Saxon tradition of vernacular bib-lical poetry in Bede's day by recounting its divine origin. In this it resembles, for example, the story of Veronica's veil, which validates the iconography of Christ by claiming a miraculous origin for all images of his face. Just as the miraculously produced image on the original veil miraculously reproduces itself, so Caedmon becomes the fountainhead from which the whole tradition of Old English Chris-tian poetry flows. Bede lists the poetic genres Caedmon is said to have founded:

> He sang about the creation of the world, the origin of the human race, and the whole history of Genesis, of the departure of Israel from Egypt and the entry into the promised land and of many other of the stories taken from the sacred Scriptures: of the incarnation, passion, and res-urrection of the Lord, of His ascension into heaven, of the coming of the Holy Spirit and the teaching of the apostles. He also made songs about the terrors of future judgment, the horrors of the pains of hell, and the joys of the heavenly kingdom. In addition he composed many other songs about the divine mercies and judgments, in all of which he sought to turn his hearers away from delight in sin and arouse in them the love and practice of good works. (p. 419)

Students of Old English poetry will recognize in this list all the types of vernacular Christian poetry that have survived (except per-haps saints' lives). It sounds like a catalog of much of the corpus. When the first manuscript of Old English poems was discovered by Francis Junius in 1651 it was immediately called the *Caedmon Manu-*

script; but if Junius had stumbled upon the *Exeter Book* or the *Vercelli Book* instead, he might have had the same reaction: this must be Caedmon, the poet described by Bede! Perhaps the compilers of all these poetic codices had Bede's account of Caedmon in mind when they chose which poems to include. Maybe it is true what Bede says, that Caedmon founded a literary tradition, not just because others copied his technique but because Bede's account itself helped shape the corpus that survives.

Be that as it may, and divine inspiration notwithstanding, Caedmon gets credit for the whole tradition, all its genres and subgenres, and so comes to symbolize the tradition itself, poetic inspiration in its native Christian form. Bede's account is a Christian version of "Widsið," a monastic version of "Deor," a sober Roman version of the Celtic Taliesin poems. Its vulgar reincarnation in our time is "I write the songs that make the whole world sing," in which Barry Manilow claims to have written every song in the book.

Bede's story is beautifully Anglo-Saxon in its restraint, and Roman in its depiction of Caedmon in the pastoral tradition. It has Bede's touch: simple, Benedictine, monastic pastoralism. Caedmon is like the shepherds abiding in the field who first heard the *Gloria* sung by the angelic choir when Christ was born in a barn. That story is certainly the nearest typological analogue to the Caedmon story, along with the story that follows it in Luke's gospel, Simeon's inspired *nunc dimittis* when Jesus was brought to the Temple. The story is certainly not about oral poetry, as Bede goes out of his way to make clear. Reading Caedmon's hymn as a prototypic oral poem is like reading *King Lear* as a geriatric case history: it misses the point because Caedmon and Lear are such special cases. If Caedmon is typical at all, he is typical of the divinely inspired pastoral bard, an image with a long literary history from Hesiod and Virgil to Milton, Blake, and Wordsworth—not to mention Moses, Christ, and Peter. It is an epic as well as prophetic image. He is the Inspired Shepherd Poet in England.

Maybe it takes one to know one: Bede's meaning was clear enough to Milton, who in the 1640's noted the episode in his *Commonplace Book*—"A marvelous and very pleasing anecdote is told in Bede's History about an Englishman who suddenly by an act of God became a poet" (1: 318). Milton, of course, was to become Caedmon's greatest inheritor, the greatest in the line that Caedmon began, of

Englishmen made poets by act of God. Like Caedmon, Milton was a divinely inspired vernacular poet converting the heroic tradition to Christian themes, filling epic form with Christian content; he too was visited nightly by an inspiring/dictating muse and recited his inspired verses daily for transcription.

The story of Caedmon and the celebrated discovery of the *Caedmon Manuscript* were perhaps even instrumental in Milton's choice of Genesis as his epic matter. Listen to Milton describe his own Caedmonian turn, in the third invocation in *Paradise Lost*:

> Not less but more Heroic than the wrath
> Of stern Achilles on his Foe pursu'd
> Thrice fugitive about Troy Wall; or rage
> Of Turnus for Lavinia disespous'd,
> Or Neptune's ire or Juno's, that so long
> Perplex'd the Greek and Cytherea's Son;
> If answerable style I can obtain
> Of my Celestial Patroness, who deigns
> Her nightly visitation unimplor'd,
> And dictates to me slumb'ring, or inspires
> Easy my unpremeditated Verse:
> Since first this Subject for Heroic Song
> Pleased me long choosing, and beginning late.
>
> (III: 14–26)

It is hard to doubt he was influenced at least by Bede's account of Caedmon. I digress because Milton provides a strong corrective to the shallow response that modern readers—at least scholars of Old English literature—have had to the story. The imagery of Bede's account is both classical and biblical. Caedmon is no more an oral poet than Milton is a gentle swain.

As with his account of Edwin's council and the parable of the sparrow, Bede's account of Caedmon should be read in its context to reveal its real genre and meaning. Bede presents the conversion of Northumbria as a miracle associated with Paulinus and as the fulfillment of Edwin's prophetic vision; the divinely inspired speeches of the king's counselors, including the parable of the sparrow, are also a miracle story. Similarly, Caedmon's vision is associated with Hild. The fourth book of the *Historia*, in which the story is told, is "the woman's book"—connected histories and hagiographies of Anglo-

Saxon churchwomen of Barking, Ely, and Whitby. Hild, Bede tells us in the chapter preceding the Caedmon story, was a grandniece of Edwin, baptized with him by Paulinus when she was a child. Perhaps she was there at the council, when the parable of the sparrow was told; if not, she was outside awaiting the outcome. Her own life is told economically and contains only a few miracle stories. They are a sequence of dream visions—one by her mother, two by nuns at the moment of her death, and Caedmon's. Caedmon is one of the jewels in her crown. Only Lees and Overing have given her her due.

Reading through Bede's account, we are focused on Hild as the story of Caedmon begins, and she hovers in our thoughts throughout. Her role in the story complicates our response and our interpretation. She is as much a mediator between Caedmon's gift and the grace of God as the dream visitor is. Caedmon depends on Hild to reveal the significance of his story. Hild gives him his gift as much as that vague *quidam* does. Hild's role in the story, we might say, has been at least partly displaced onto the angel. Milton's case is a good deal clearer: he needs no Hild to mediate his gift, and openly identifies his inspiration as female, his "celestial patroness." But Bede obscures Hild's role in Caedmon's inspiration, rendering the muse's inspiration only vaguely, and as male. Bede was, after all, an eighth-century Anglo-Saxon monk.

Caedmon depends on Bede and the reader too, as readers of a story whose meaning will be evident only to the educated, the literate. In both of Bede's stories we see God's hand gently guiding the political-ecclesiastical life of England by means of nocturnal visitations—dreams or waking dreams. God inspires the Anglo-Saxons to embrace the faith—inspires the counselors, inspires Caedmon to the monastic life, inspires him as a poet, and "by his songs the minds of many were often inspired to despise the world and to long for the heavenly life" (p. 415).

His poetry no longer has that effect on those who read or study it, so its vital significance has been lost, and Bede's account of its significance has been much misunderstood. Only when we see Caedmon's hymn as a case of divine inspiration, as Milton saw it, can we appreciate the relevance of Bede's account to the rest of Old English poetry. In any case, it is not the case history of an Anglo-Saxon oral singer.

King Alfred's Talking Poems

King Alfred wrote several Old English poems of striking originality. Three of these poems—two metrical prologues and an epilogue to his translations of Gregory and Boethius—are of special
interest. They share a concept of textuality that is unique in medieval
(and other) literature, though perfectly consonant with Augustine's
theory of language and the Christian doctrine of the *Logos*, as well as
with modern and postmodern formulations of the same ideas. They
illustrate the complex literariness of Old English poetry, which is so
easily overlooked, and the artful use of oral style in literate poems.
Oddly, however, these fascinating poems by the most prominent historical personage of the period have long been dismissed as trivial,
or as not really Alfred's.

Frantzen remarks in his book *King Alfred* that "neither the epilogue nor the metrical prologue to Alfred's translation [of Gregory's
Pastoral Care] has been adequately studied" (p. 39). This goes for
all of Alfred's poetry. Though the canon of his works has now been
established (see pp. 7–10), Alfred is never considered with Caedmon,
Bede, and Cynewulf as one of our named Old English poets, probably out of embarrassment that his verse is so undistinguished, and
a lingering skepticism that poetry so undistinguished could really
be his. Henry Sweet called the *Pastoral Care* poems "curious dog-
gerel" and "dislocated prose" ("also the case with much of our modern blank verse," he adds), though he thought they were probably
Alfred's (p. 473). The most generous assessment to date has been
Kenneth Sisam's, in his consideration of Alfred's authorship: "Nor
does the poverty of the verse tell against Alfred," he concludes; "Had
[he] chosen a series of battle-pieces instead of a course of philosophical instruction, he would probably have . . . been better thought
of as a poet" (p. 297). That is, too bad he doesn't fit our canon of
heroic poems!

Only a few lines of Caedmon have survived; Bede's authorship
of the "Death Song" is dubious; and we know nothing of Cynewulf; so a substantial body of verse by a man as well known to us as
Alfred should tell us much about the making of Old English poetry.
Knowing that the poetry is Alfred's sharply raises its interest, if not

its quality—though in fact these are related. That is what recent arguments about the canon have been teaching, that our notions of quality are not disinterested.

After a century's debate, we now have no reason to doubt Alfred's authorship of the two poems of *The Pastoral Care*, the metrical proem to *The Meters of Boethius*, and the 31 *Meters* themselves. These texts themselves acknowledge Alfred as their author, and the gravest charge being made today is that Alfred might have had assistance in their composition—though there is no evidence to suggest even this. Greenfield and Calder, following Sisam, accept Alfred's authorship of the *Meters*, though they do not address the problem of the *Pastoral Care* poems (see pp. 245–47); Simon Keynes and Michael Lapidge, also following Sisam, accept Alfred's authorship of the *Pastoral Care* poems, though they do not address the problem of the *Meters* (see p. 126, n. 18). "Evidence from early sources is unusually explicit," summarizes Frantzen. "The authorship of the versified meters of the *Consolation* has been controversial," he adds, "but the controversy has been based entirely on suspicion rather than positive evidence" (*King Alfred*, p. 45). Even the uncontroversial prose proem to the *Consolation* claims that it was Alfred who wrote the poems: "and then he turned them into songs" (Sedgefield, p. 1).

Alfred's poems, then, fall into two groups: the *Meters*, translated from Boethius's Latin via the Old English prose version; and the other, wholly original poems, including the proem to the *Meters* and the prologue and epilogue to the *Pastoral Care*. (The first meter, which Bruce Mitchell and Fred Robinson have canonized in their *Guide to Old English*, is something of a middle case, being a verse development of a wholly original prose version not based on Boethius. It is the one battle poem Alfred did write, and so—à la Sisam—the easiest to canonize.) I would like to reassess the poems in the second group, calling attention to their originality and literateness, notwithstanding all their pronounced oral features, and to explore how their literateness involves the reader with the Christian *Logos*.

These three poems (a total of 56 lines) are marked by a very strong style—unmistakably Alfredian, very much like his arresting prose preface to Augustine's *Soliloquies*, with its extended metaphor of gathering wood and building a house for the act of writing the book. They are certainly not failed attempts to imitate heroic or gnomic style, but along with a few other Old English poems constitute a distinct genre, or subgenre: a type of colophon, an address to the reader, in which an elevated, highly learned, poetically "metaphysical" concept is wedded to a plain, highly formulaic style.

I begin with the least studied of these poems (Frantzen does not even mention its existence), the ten-line proem to the *Meters*. One can use it to define this genre and in the process extend Benson's statement of its literary (as opposed to oral) qualities. It will help this time if I quote the Old English:

> Ðus Ælfred us   ealdspell reahte,
> cyning Westsexna,   cræft meldode,
> leoðwyrhta list.   Him wæs lust micel
> ðæt he ðiossum leodum   leoð spellode,
> monnum myrgen,   mislice cwidas,
> þy læs ælinge   ut adrife
> selflicne secg,   þonne he swelces lyt
> gymð for his gilpe.   Ic sceal giet sprecan,
> fon on fitte,   folccuðne ræd
> hæleðum secgean.   Hliste se þe wille!
>
> (Krapp, p. 153)

> Thus Alfred us old tales told,
> king of Westsaxons skill displayed,
> art of the poet, his pleasure great
> proclaiming poems to this people,
> delight to men in different speech,
> lest weariness should drive away
> the selfish man when little such
> he ponders for pride. I shall pronounce,
> put into poetry public counsel,
> announce to men—listen who will!

These lines invite us to believe it was Alfred who composed the *Meters* that follow; but it is often remarked that the use of the third person for Alfred in the first sentence, which then changes to the first person in the final sentence, casts some doubt on his composition of this poem itself. As opinion has tended to accept it as Alfred's, though, the use of the third person has come to be interpreted as conventional. George Krapp says, "The change of person at the end of the Proem might raise a question. This, however, may be nothing more than the usual convention of Anglo-Saxon style. Although . . .

Alfred is mentioned in the third person, this is by no means a certain indication that Alfred did not write [it]. The word *us* in the
first line . . . may mean nothing more than "for his people" (p. xv).
He probably has in mind cases like the prose preface to the *Pastoral
Care*, and Aelfric's preface to Genesis, where a switch from third to
first person occurs right after the formal greeting: "Alfric the monk
greets Athelwaerd the eldorman humbly. You bade me, dear one. . . ."
This convention is not Anglo-Saxon, however; it simply reflects the
formal greeting of Latin letters. The case of the poem, then, which is
not such a formal greeting, remains puzzling.

A solution to this little conundrum requires attention to other
features of the poem. Though Benson is surely right that this poem,
as the proem to a book, is intended to be read rather than heard, its
diction is distinctly oral: *ealdspell, meldode, spellode, cwidas, sprecan, sec-
gean, hliste* all imply oral presentation—and if Opland is right (see
p. 248), so do *leoð* and *leoðwyrhta*, as well as, I might add, *fitte*. Another
convention? The famous inertia of oral diction, or an imitation of
oral style? Perhaps it is just a hint of the dramatic structure of the *Consolation of Philosophy*, in which the meters, though literary (we cannot
imagine Boethius composing them orally, like a *guslar*) are presented
as if composed spontaneously in conversation and sung aloud by
the two conversants. That is a fiction of the *Consolation of Philosophy*
(and its translation) that requires a willing suspension of disbelief.

This calculated illusion of orality notwithstanding, the most problematical word in Alfred's poem, *ælinge*, is not even a poetic word;
it occurs only two other times (both times as an adjective), both in
prose. Bosworth glosses it "burning" or "ardor," and Toller as the
exact opposite, "tedium." The latter seems righter in this case, since
here the word is drawn from a passage late in the *Consolation* itself,
in which Wisdom apologizes for using tedious prose rather than her
more entertaining verse: "these long speeches will seem too *ælinge* to
you, since songs now please you" (Sedgefield, p. 127). The middle
sentence of the poem, then, offers verse as an antidote to the tedium
of prose, a means of holding the attention of the *selflic* reader—
"proud" in a Christian sense, though not really "selfish" in the modern sense; just incapable, for human reasons, of rising above himself
to attend to the truth; disposed toward himself fallen.

Now let us return to the problem of the first and third persons.

Another clue lies in Alfred's other prologue-poem, the prologue to
the *Pastoral Care*. Sisam notes that in that poem "the book itself
speaks" (p. 141); Benson further argues ("Literary Character," p. 335)
that it "was undoubtedly intended for readers and almost certainly
composed in writing, since the poem itself is made to say, in the style
of the Riddles,"

> Then into English Alfred the King
> turned each word, and to his writers
> sent me south and north.

It would hardly be surprising to find the same conceit in the
Boethius proem. If we attribute the two first-person pronouns in
that poem to the book itself, we would then read the first line "Thus
Alfred us, old tales, told." The *Meters* speak in the plural; but at the
end of the poem the book speaks in the singular: "Now I must speak."
There is little if any discontinuity in the switch of person; a book of
poems can speak comfortably in the singular or plural or both. This
is certainly a more comfortable reading than Krapp's, in which Alfred
begins by referring to himself in the third person, and then switches
to the first person toward the end of the poem. Besides, the conceit
also accounts for the oral diction: the poem speaks, the reader listens.
It is an exaggerated, literalized instance of Foley's characterization of
oral poetry generally, "Texts That Speak to Readers Who Hear."
   Benson's comparison of this conceit to the riddles, however, is a
little misleading. In the twenty years since his article, we have become
supremely sensitive to what might have then seemed a fine distinction. This is not just a poem in which an object like an inkwell or an
onion is made to address the reader directly; here the speaking object
is the text itself. The text as text addresses the reader in the first person. Among the riddles, number 26 ("Book") is the nearest analogy,
but there the book speaks more as an object than as a text, and the
book that speaks is not the particular book we are reading but the
concept of the book, or a hypothetical book. A much nearer analogy
is the sort of inscription commonly found on weapons—"Weland
made me," for example, or on Alfred's jewel, "Alfred had me made."
The inscriptions on the Ruthwell and Brussels Crosses have much
the same effect. The work speaks directly to us: "Rood is my name."
   But perhaps the nearest analogy of all is the astonishing portrait of

Saint John in *The Book of Kells*, in which the page itself is given limbs, as if the book were the incarnate *Logos*. Here is Saint John, author of the text the reader is holding, holding in his one hand that same text, and in the other the quill he wrote it with. The text in question, of course, is the one that begins on the next page of the manuscript, "In the beginning was the Word, and the Word was with God, and the Word was God." *Verbum est Deus*: the portrait fairly echoes with the idea. The page is Christ, the Word; *et Verbum caro factum est*, the Word is made flesh. This book is not just an object, but a person—a Person; the *Logos* speaks, the reader listens. Saint John is here being portrayed, we might say, in the Second Person.

Texts that address us directly as readers—texts that themselves speak in the first person, to us in the second, of the author in the third—invite us to meditate on their textuality. The gesture is obviously related to the later medieval convention of the *envoi*, in which the author speaks in the first person, to the text in the second, of the reader in the third: "Go, little song, to my lady."

Together, these two gestures frame the text. They conceive it as an independent intelligence, mediating between the author and the reader. They emphasize the distance between the author and the reader—the combined distances between author and text, and text and reader. Only the text can attempt to cross this distance, though it too is prey to the vicissitudes of life and language. The reader may be too weary or too proud to listen, for example, or scribes may copy it badly, or it might be intercepted or lost. So the text must be carefully prepared to achieve its goal: in this case, "Alfred made us *poems*, so you won't get bored!"; or in the *envoi*, "Go *straight* to my lady!" Ultimately, of course, the text will always remain at the mercy of the reader's will: *Hliste se þe wille!* Understanding, interpreting, listening, reading: these are not passive processes, but involve the active will of the reader. Understanding is the collaborative work of the author, the text, the reader, and God. Bede was confident enough of these connections that he felt no need to problematize them; but Alfred labors to make them explicit in his metaphor of a text pleading for the reader's attention.

This is not a simple or obvious poetic conceit. Outside Old English I know of no exact examples of it, and only four cases resemble

Book of Kells, portrait of St. John. (Courtesy The Board of Trinity College Dublin)

it at all. Ernst Robert Curtius, in his essay "The Book as Symbol," cites a near-analogy from the Greek Anthology (p. 307); more pertinently, the Third Book of Ovid's *Tristia* is made to speak directly to its author; less pertinently, Washington Irving plays with the idea amusingly in a chapter of his *Sketchbook* called "The Mutability of Literature"; and less pertinently still, the device is exploited in a delightful novel, *Book*, by Robert Grudin. The most important thing to be said about the conceit is that it is inconceivable in oral tradition, since it depends upon the notion of a fixed text and the metaphor of writing for its effect. It is a highly intellectual and literate conception, consistent with the Christian theory of language deriving from Augustine, especially his early work *The Teacher*.

Christianity may be logocentrism par excellence, but it does not conceive the *Logos* to be embodied unfallen in language—*Logos* is not to be confused with language. For Augustine language is only a closed system of signs referring to each other, mediating between author and reader in the same manner as our poems claim to. Such a theory reflects a sharp respect for the power of language but also for its limitations, its freedom and its arbitrariness, its independence from those who use it and from truth. Augustine says, "we learn nothing from signs which we call words" (*Teacher*, p. 48); we do not learn from words, but from the voice of reason they prompt within us, the Inner Master, Christ, the *Logos*. Thus the reader understands what he is reading because he is really listening to the voice of Christ. However, adds Augustine, "it reveals itself to each according to his capacity to grasp it by reason of the good or evil dispositions of his will" (*Teacher*, p. 51). *Hliste se þe wille.*

Readers of the *Confessions* will recall how central to this theory is the act of reading, and the written text—the sentence, the book, the psalm, the hymn, the Scriptures. In the concluding books of the *Confessions* Augustine explores the central paradox of reading, the elusiveness and multiplicity of meanings produced by what we now call the hermeneutic circle. He argues repeatedly that this multiplicity of meaning exemplifies the time-bound and space-bound qualities of human mentality, as opposed to God's perfect knowledge (see Vance, pp. 34–50). That is, language is fallen. One result of the gap between language and the *Logos* is the multiplicity of true interpretations—true, even if they are not intended by the author. The text overflows with meaning, and each reader takes from it what truth he can. "As a spring in a small place is very plentiful for many rivers . . . so your steward's narrative [Moses' account of the creation], written with few words, overflows for many preachers in watery streams of truth, in which everyone finds his own truth as well as he can, this one one, that one another" (*Confessions* XII.27).

In his prologue-poems, then, Alfred has adopted the conceit of the speaking text. Or we might say more sympathetically, he has recognized the fact of his text's own voice, the fact that the text is not him, and that he cannot speak through it directly to the reader once he has given it existence. He has recognized that writing is a risky business, that the transmission of the truth from one mind to another is indirect and uncertain, requiring a collaboration of the author and the reader, the text and God (Christ, the Inner Master, the *Logos*).

Readers of Jacques Derrida will have no problem applying a postmodern vocabulary to this conception. Even those suspicious of Derrida's influence on criticism generally might find his meditation in *Of Grammatology* on the relations between speaking and writing precisely relevant to this case. A brief reflection of this sort will clarify Alfred's strategy of animating the text by projecting his voice into it and then cutting that voice off from himself. This strategy calls attention to, even as it tries to erase, the literary objectivity of the text, the difference between speaking and writing. What I called before "this calculated illusion of orality," Derrida would call the illusion of presence, or "simulated immediacy" (p. 15). These poems, however, like the page from *The Book of Kells*, simulate not the author's voice (the usual strategy), or the voice of an Anglo-Saxon *scop*, but the voice of the *Logos* itself, in an attempt to redeem the fallenness of language (that is, writing) in Christian terms, by calling attention to the Word that underlies the text, here depicted as speaking writing. The writing speaks, but its speaking is only a metaphor for writing, and words are only metaphors for the Word. It is not simply a case of a written text imitating oral style, though oral style does become implicated in the metaphor.

At the same time, Alfred, by writing of himself in the third person, succeeds only in objectifying, naming, and calling attention to himself even as he tries to distance, hide, or cross himself out. This is a self-effacing (self-erasing) gesture, this lending of being to writing, but it is necessarily futile, because only what is written can be erased. It is futile to say "I did not write this!"

This reflection may even help us see what is distinctively Anglo-Saxon about such a gesture, why an Anglo-Saxon poet like Alfred might have invented it. First of all, in Alfred's day an oral tradition probably still underlay Old English poetic textuality generally, suggesting the metaphor's dynamics. Just as relevant, however, are the Anglo-Saxon habits of speaking itself, characterized by understatement, restraint, and silence. For Alfred to call attention to his absence from his own writing is only a more bookish version of the familiar paradox of Old English elegies like "The Wanderer" and "The Wife's Lament," in which the hoarding of language, that typical Anglo-Saxon silence, is overfilled and broken even as it is being described and affirmed. Those poems are statements out of silence, expressions of the inexpressibility of grief, contradictions of their own assertions. Alfred's poems share the elegies' lonely self-effacement but express it in a metaphor of writing.

Citing Curtius's essay in a brief discussion of the medieval concept of writing, Derrida says "there remains to be written a history of this metaphor, a metaphor that systematically contrasts divine or natural writing and the human and laborious, finite and artificial inscription. It remains to articulate rigorously the stages of that history" (p. 15). When such a history is written, it should include Alfred's poems as one of those stages. But we are being led further and further from our texts in this reflection, and our survey of Alfred's three poems is not even complete yet.

In the third poem, the epilogue to the *Pastoral Care*, we may not find the same conceit exactly, but we do find the same conception of textuality. Here Alfred makes a metaphor out of Augustine's simile of the overflowing spring, quoted above, developing from it his own elaborate logo-hydraulics. (The simile is ultimately drawn from John 4:10–14, "the well of living water," and has already been filtered by Alfred through the *Pastoral Care* itself [see Isaacs, pp. 87–88].) The *Logos* is here conceived as ever-living water, flowing from the hearts of those who believe in God; they receive it from those books through which God directs its stream,

> through holy books hither on earth,
> through minds of men variously.

Some hoard it up in reason's hold,
wisdom's stream, seal with lips,
so wastefully it won't flow out,
but the well dwells in a man's breast
by God's grace deep and still.
Some allow it out over the landscape
to run in rills, but it is unreasonable
that such clear water, loud and undeep,
overflow the fields, become a fen.

(Dobbie, *Minor Poems*, p. 111, ll. 11–21)

Here the doctrine of the superabundance of the *Logos* has been oddly harmonized with the Anglo-Saxon habit of hoarding language in silence. Not only can the overflowing *Logos* be contained in small speech, but Augustine's flowing rivers have been dammed up with restraint and silence, in a flood-control project to drain the fens of the spirit. That is a very Anglo-Saxon, very Alfredian turn on Augustine's image, by a king who knew what it meant to drain fenlands. After 21 lines of this elaborate metaphor, the reader is addressed directly and insistently with four second-person pronouns:

So draw you to drink, now God gave you
what Gregory has granted you
at your door, the Lord's well.   (ll. 22–24)

But who is speaking here? The first person, which might give us a clue, is used only once in the poem, in the very first line:

Þis is nu se wæterscipe   ðe us wereda god
to frofre gehet   foldbuendum.

Now these are the waters the God of Hosts
promised us as a comfort to earthdwellers.

Neil Isaacs does not ask who "us" are here, assuming it is *us*, appositive with *foldbuendum*; in which case the speaker of the poem is one of *us earthdwellers*, that is, the author. He does note, however, that the *wæterscipe* is the book itself, which is spoken of in the poem as "here" (*her*, l. 27)—that is, in the reader's hands, right before his eyes. "In this sense," he says, "the epilogue is like an envoy, and this sense seems to persist throughout the poem" (p. 84). In which case, we could construe the *us* in line one as an accusative or a dative (as in the first line of the Boethian proem above), roughly appositive with *se wæterscipe*. This may be one of those many Old English poetic sentences to which Mitchell and Robinson have sensitized us (see Mitchell, "Dangers," and *Old English Syntax* 2: 905–13; Robinson, *Appositive Style*, pp. 17–18), in which two grammatical and syntactic constructions overlap, *apo koinou*, along with an ambivalent usage of *ðe*, as either a relative pronoun or a particle/conjunction functioning with *nu* (Mitchell, *Old English Syntax*, 2: 325). So on the one hand, "This is now the well that the God of Hosts promised us . . ."; and on the other, ". . . the God of Hosts promised us as a comfort to earth-dwellers." In the second case the accusative *us* would be the *litterae* or *halga bec* for which *se wæterscipe* is being offered as a metaphor. So even in this poem, the book *may* be construed as speaking, offering us its watery streams of truth—though that is only one possible reading.

Alfred's prose prefaces to the *Soliloquies*, the *Pastoral Care*, and the *Consolation of Philosophy* handle many of these same themes—the nature of writing, the perils of transmission, and the problem of interpretation. It is a feature of the poems and not the prose, however, to develop this particular conceit and this concept of textuality.

Our willingness to read these poems in this way would be stronger if we knew that this animating gesture was conventional enough to have been recognized by readers of such prefaces as a feature of the genre. It is reassuring, then, that three other Old English poems, "Aldhelm," "Thureth," and the "Metrical Preface to Wærferth's Translation of Gregory's *Dialogues*," also belong to the genre. In fact, from these poems Keynes and Lapidge conclude that "the convention . . . of the book speaking in the first person by way of preface to what is to follow, is fairly common in Old English poetry" (p. 333, n. 1). Like Benson, Keynes and Lapidge see the origin of this convention in the riddles; it is certainly closer, however, to the colophon—an epilogue (often metrical) addressing the reader, appended to a manuscript by the scribe or sometimes the author, describing the contents or asking for prayers, and often referring to the facts of the book's production. Robinson considers "Thureth," an eleven-line poem that begins "I am a benedictional," to be just such a colophon (see "Old English Literature," p. 13). "Aldhelm," another "talking book" poem, is a seventeen-line fragment, a florid macaronic in Old English, Latin, and Greek, serving as preface to Aldhelm's *De virginitate*. It is so Aldhelmian in style that we might suspect it was written by Aldhelm himself (like Alfred referring to himself in the third person), except it does little but praise Aldhelm lavishly.

Of these poems, the most interesting in relation to the Alfred poems is the "Metrical Preface to Wærferth's Translation of Gregory's *Dialogues.*" The book this poem prefaces was once attributed to Alfred but is now considered Wærferth's contribution to the Alfredian project. The poem, which comes to us in only one late manuscript, may or may not be contemporary with Alfred, but it is certainly Alfredian in style and concept. However, though it expresses quite clearly many of the ideas I have been discussing, it is so straightforward that it only reveals by contrast the greater interest (and the greater quality) of Alfred's own poems:

> Who thinks to read me
> can find in me, if he much desires
> a sure sign of the spiritual life,
> that quite easily he can ascend
> to the heavenly home with hope and joy,
> bliss in the city for those who can see
> the Son of God with their own eyes.
> A man can reach that, he whose reason
> is perfect, then through his inner will
> he may believe in the help of these saints,
> and follow their example, as this book says. . . .
> Bishop Wulfstan had me written,
>   . . . who begot this book
> which you in your hands now hold and examine.
>
> (Dobbie, *Minor Poems*, p. 112, ll. 1–12, 16–17)

The reader can receive the overflowing Word only if he much desires it, if his thinking is perfect, and if his inner will is to believe and to imitate the saints. Christian reading is active, willful, intentional, and collaborative. For all of Wærferth's intellectual clarity, however, the poem is not Alfredian. Alfred's brevity, subtlety, style, and wit—in his use of oral diction, for example, or the extended metaphors—are missing in the flat intelligence of this poem, which then goes on to beg the reader's prayers not only for its author (in the third person, of course), but also for that better poet, King Alfred, "who set him this example" (or perhaps "who sent him this exemplar")—*þe him ðas bysene forgeaf* (l. 21).

Chapter 4

Beowulf and the Men's Hall

This is the first of three chapters testing the usefulness of psycho-analytic anthropology as an approach to *Beowulf*. It began as an attempt to explain the persistence of wooden architecture in Anglo-Saxon England by analyzing the hall as a symbol and a ritual space. This seemingly innocent topic, however, clung tightly to several others; it quickly merged with the themes of the preceding chapters and finally grew into a psychoanalytic overview of *Beowulf*'s relationship to a wide array of Anglo-Saxon customs and institutions. It was published in *Psychiatry* magazine in 1983, before I was reborn as a nominalist and promised to stop generalizing so much.

In retrospect it is easy to see that the analysis is essentially structuralist and so bears the mark of structural anthropology generally: it appears to make clear and simple binary oppositions out of what are in reality vague, complex, ambiguous, overdetermined, and ambivalent social relations. That is, it idealizes history. However, *Beowulf* also idealizes history. The ethnographic model I develop here will seem less reductive if we keep M. I. Finley's method in *The World of Odysseus* in mind: it is an ethnography of the world of the poem rather than of any historical reality the poem supposedly represents. That is to say, the model fits the poem better than it fits the infinite complexity of Anglo-Saxon England, though it is sometimes difficult to separate these in our minds.

Subsequently, this first overview prompted new and more precise psychoanalytic questions about the relation of the reader to the poem—this reader, as well as the Anglo-Saxon reader. The next chapter grapples with two of these psychoanalytic questions—Freud's theory of identification, and the relation of Freudian to Christian psychology. That chapter does not deal with *Beowulf* directly but is essential for the final chapter, which explores the reader's complex identifications with the hero, the hero's followers, the author, and the Anglo-Saxon world.

Armchair Anthropology

To explore the meaning of the hall as a ritual space, I focus particularly on the ritual functions of poetry in the hall, the same poetry that is our major evidence regarding the hall, especially *Beowulf*. I think of the hall as a cultural institution and redefine the native poetic tradition in relation to the hall's varied ritual life, with which the poetry is so concerned.

Though the argument focuses on the hall, it includes a framework of theoretical concerns. Early Anglo-Saxon culture is of anthropological interest chiefly because of its rapid and dramatic emergence from Germanic tribal prehistory into a leading role in the civilization of Christian Europe. The conquest of Britain by the Anglo-Saxons in the fifth and sixth centuries, and their conversion soon afterward, is a case history of the transformations of a tribal society suddenly introduced to the special forces of civilization and the higher religions that control them. The Anglo-Saxons are fascinating in this regard because of the fortuitous developments that prepared for this transformation and made it so successful.

One of the questions this transformation suggests was posed by Freud at the conclusion of *Civilization and Its Discontents*: "The community, too, evolves a super-ego under whose influence cultural development proceeds. It would be a tempting task for anyone who has knowledge of human civilization to follow out this analogy in detail" (p. 141). If the aims of civilization can be advanced only "through an ever-increasing reinforcement of the sense of guilt" (p. 133), we can understand the role Christianity plays in this process more clearly in psychoanalytic terms. If the common distinctions between shame and guilt cultures—and between tribal and civilized (or traditional and modern) societies—are seen psychologically, a society's conversion from one to the other might display the coherence (or incoherence) of psychological development. Thus psychoanalytic theory might help clarify the origin of Anglo-Saxon civilization, which appears at first a puzzling historical case.

This tempting task of Freud's may seem remote from an analysis of the hall as ritual space but in fact grows directly out of it. The hall's ritual functions in the pre-Christian period parallel, in ways consonant with tribal organization, those of the Church afterward. In the century before the conversion, the aristocratic warrior class that the institution of the hall embodied had already undertaken to inhibit sexuality and violence in the society in the interest of its own power. Such inhibition began the dissolution of tribal structure and prepared for the reception of Christianity and the doctrine of guilt, which in turn secured these inhibitions and completed the transition to civilization. After the conversion, many of the traditional functions of the hall were transferred to the Church, and the hall and the Church operated together as twin institutions regulating social and cultural life. Thus the analysis of the hall is germane to the largest issues of cultural development.

These arguments require some introduction, after which successive sections will deal with the development of inhibitions on sexuality and violence in the kinship and lordship systems; the meanings of the hall in Anglo-Saxon life; and conversion, guilt, and the development of the cultural superego. The final section returns to the problem of England's unusually rapid and successful growth as a nation and examines the role that the hall and its poetry played in that development.

In the fifth century the Germanic tribes of northern Europe were migrating. Two of the less conspicuous and more primitive tribes from the Baltic shore and the Danish peninsula, the Angles and the Saxons, fell together in their movement westward along the coast of the North Sea. In the middle of the century they began an unorganized and gradual migration to Britain, where they ultimately devastated and supplanted what remained of that already declining Roman province. A century later, Roman missionaries arrived to convert the loose confederation of tribal nations they found there. The conversion was relatively rapid, native religion was largely eradicated, and letters, laws, and the other arts of Christian civilization were introduced. Within only a century, the Anglo-Saxons entered into a golden age of Christian learning and international influence, sending their own missionaries and scholars into a declining Europe. This astonishing transformation from primitive tribes to an advanced Christian-European state offers a compelling case history for the historian and anthropologist; but the whole period remains one of the darkest parts of the Dark Ages—so dark as to seem nearly impenetrable to those who study it.

The reasons for this darkness are not hard to find: since writing was introduced only with the Roman mission, there are no literary remains from the preconversion period; and since the early Anglo-Saxons built entirely in wood, there are virtually no archaeological remains from the period either. Given this dearth of hard evidence, the historian must be cautious. J. N. L. Myres, the greatest authority on the early period, for example, opens with this caveat: "It is not possible to discuss fully the complex and obscure history of the Teutonic peoples of North Germany in the Roman period, nor would it be relevant to the present purpose" (Collingwood and Myres, p. 335).

This caution is excessive. One of the peculiarities of English historiography is that it conventionally treats the history of the island rather than the peoples who settled it. Thus we study the Britons and the provincial Romans more than the Continental tribes who totally supplanted them. It is like writing the history of America in terms of native tribes and treating the previous history of the invading Europeans as irrelevant. Further, English history has naturally been dominated by the methods and aims of political history, which are useless in the study of preliterate tribal societies. Myres does not enter into the "history" of the Continental tribes, as if only the reconstruction of events could be historically significant. Until recently, Anglo-Saxonists have chosen to accept this attitude rather strictly, hesitating to generalize, hypothesize, or attempt a large reconstruction of cultural forms from the fragments we possess. Theory is only "imaginative surmise" (Whitelock, *Beginnings*, p. 9). Of course this ostensible refusal to theorize disguises an old model which is being taken entirely for granted (see Stafford, pp. 78–79).

The historian's fear of theoretical models was perhaps a response to the excesses of early Anglo-Saxon scholarship, which was dominated by German scholars who projected into their work a romantic image of Germanic prehistory. The result of this reaction, however, was a resistance to anthropology and the other social sciences that developed in the meantime—though literary scholars occasionally glanced sideways, such as Francis Magoun on *mana*, Charles Donahue on potlatch, and Jeff Opland on oral poetry.

But if Anglo-Saxonists have avoided anthropology, it is equally true that anthropologists have avoided Anglo-Saxon England. Interest in the origin and development of religion dominated the early years of anthropology and (hand in hand with classical archaeology, which did not extend to northern Europe) resulted in a wealth of new theory. This interest, however, gave way early in our century to patient and empirical fieldwork, warier of theory and unsuitable in any case for the study of ancient societies. Concern for evidence led to a fear of diachronic models, since the newer synchronic methods seemed so much stronger—more evidential and less theoretical. But it is impossible to study ancient societies like the Anglo-Saxons without a historical method, because lack of evidence prohibits sound ethnography. The problems that concern me here are the emergence of civilized England from its tribal origins and its conversion to Christianity; the relations between these two transformations can be seen only in the light of a historical anthropology.

When anthropologists abandoned the grand historical theories of Durkheim, Edward Tylor, Frazer, and the like, Freud's anthropology, which addressed the same problems, went too. His myth of the primal horde seemed to be a typical excess of the period. This is a nice case of throwing out the baby with the bathwater. Psychoanalytic theory does not stand or fall with the myth of the primal horde, and it remains the soundest basis we have for a historical anthropology. To make new use of psychoanalysis in anthropology, we must integrate it into synchronic study, as Victor Turner has done with his work on sublimation and projection in Ndembu ritual ("Encounter with Freud"); or, in the case of ancient societies, use it to reanimate historical method, as Girard has done in his work on sacrifice and Greek tragedy, which makes sense at last of Freud's theory of murder in the primal horde. Without some historical method like psychoanalysis, we would have to abandon the anthropological study of the past.

Actually, the old school of armchair theorizing about the origins of religion never entirely succumbed to ethnography. Frazer's comparative mythology, in which Germanic myth played a strong part, found support in Jung's theory of archetypes and has been pursued by specialists in comparative religion such as Erich Neumann, Mircea Eliade, and Joseph Campbell, who ground their comparative methods in archetypes. Although archetypes may reveal the common structures (and perhaps meanings) of myth, however, they are not easily integrated with historical evidence. Archetypes somehow embody and unite the mental functions of the individual and the collective symbols of religion—but how? Archetypal theory concentrates on the internal logic of mythical symbols, and not on their relation to other cultural phenomena. More simply, the universalizing tendency of archetypal analysis draws us away from particular historical problems. These shortcomings are illustrated in the first "psychohistorical" study of Anglo-Saxon culture known to me, Foley's study of *Beowulf*—though not in the more recent work of John Hill, whose psychoanalytic reading of Anglo-Saxon culture is largely harmonious with my own.

Just as comparative mythology is still with us, Durkheim's sociological analysis of myth also lives on. It gave rise to the work of Marcel Mauss, Jan de Vries, and Georges Dumézil (and his student Michel Foucault), whose comparative methods are grounded in the evolution of particular social forms. De Vries and Dumézil have given new life to the study of ancient Germanic culture, finding unity in its social and religious development by tracing its relations to other Indo-European societies, using linguistic and historical evidence. Thus the cults of the various gods, and their interrelations, can represent the various social classes and their relations to each other. The transformations of a figure like Othin from a god of war to a god of kingship and wisdom might reflect the changing role of the warrior class as Germanic society developed. But latter-day sociological theories of religion suffer from the same weaknesses as Durkheim's: social organization accounts for only a small portion of ritual and myth, which native informants tell us are always vastly overdetermined; and again, no psychological ground is offered for the collective representations of religion.

The role psychoanalysis might play in this impasse is easy to see. Freud's psychology, after all, is both universal and particular, synchronic and diachronic, directed as it is toward the analysis of the case history; and it is equally concerned with the whole range of individual and cultural phenomena and their relations. In the study of early Anglo-Saxon culture, a psychoanalytic approach is especially useful as a ground for constructing a model of the evolution from primitive tribe to civilized state, through the particular history of migration and conversion. With such a model we might be able to explain, at least in part, the extraordinary cultural energy that the conversion of England produced and the particular forms it took.

Virtually all interpretations of Anglo-Saxon culture have turned on a single problem, which has dominated the thinking of historians and literary scholars for the last century. Because all our literary evidence is from the Christian period and was produced and transmitted by the Church, we have hardly any evidence from the pagan period that has not been filtered through a Christian lens. In this literature Christian elements are blended in astonishing ways, more or less harmoniously, with older native elements. *Beowulf*, "The Seafarer," the Sutton Hoo treasures—all the surviving monuments of the culture abound in striking incongruities of religious sentiment and symbolism. It has seemed an inevitable duty of history and criticism to isolate the elements of the two cultures and to organize interpretations around their relationship. This method is essentialist, of course. It assumes that "Germanic" and "Christian" are unified concepts, referring to two separable realities competing for Anglo-Saxon society; but in the end the Anglo-Saxons created, however unlikely it may seem to modern eyes, a living synthesis of their traditional culture and their new religion.

Our response to this synthesis is determined in part by the awful imbalance in our knowledge of the two cultures. Our knowledge of early Christianity is finely detailed, but the culture the missionaries found when they came to England is shrouded in obscurity. Any interpretation of the synthesis of the two rests on an interpretation of the conversion, which in turn rests on knowing what kind of culture was being converted.

When Christianity came to the Indians of Brazil, it was met with indifference or hostility; brought to the Hindus, it was absorbed whole and inconspicuous into their existing beliefs; African slaves found in Christianity a consolation for their condition and an ethic

of subservience; the Chamulas of the Yucatan, considering themselves Catholics, still hold Mayan rites and worship Mayan gods in
the churchyard. Each of these cultures grasped Christianity in its own
terms and for its own purposes. So what was it in early Anglo-Saxon
culture that enabled it to find in Christianity the source of historical,
intellectual, and spiritual expansion?

Kinship and Kingship

Instead of beginning with the relation of native and Christian elements, then, I begin with an even more basic relation between two
distinct forms of social organization, one based on blood and the
other on oaths among men. The evolution of this relation through
the whole history of the Anglo-Saxons—during the thousand years
between Tacitus's ethnography of the North German tribes in the
first century and the Norman conquest—sheds light on the history
of many other cultural forms.

Even a cursory examination of Anglo-Saxon law and literature reveals the importance of the kinship system. The role of kinship in
the early period can hardly be exaggerated, since the tribe is a racial
unit and one's place in it is determined by birth. Conflicts that arise
in the system, between blood ties and marriage ties, or between kinship obligations and sworn obligations, have always been recognized
as one of the great themes in Anglo-Saxon and other Germanic literature—the unavoidable and unresolvable clash of loyalties that results in tragedy. Much of the fascination of northern literature lies
in the picture it presents of a society governed largely by the arcane
rules and complications of the kin-feud. Only recently, however, has
the kinship system even been studied seriously; only recently the
terms *cognate* and *affinal* were introduced into the Anglo-Saxonist's
vocabulary by an eminent historian who worried that the use of
anthropological terms might appear "trendy" to his colleagues (see
Bullough, pp. 17–18).

Discussions of Germanic kinship often assume or imply that the
kindred is an institution competing for power with political structures. The laws, however, show that the kinship system is bilateral
rather than agnatic; the nation is not a *patria*, a fatherland, but simply
a *cyn*, a family. A person's kindred consists of both paternal and ma-

ternal relations, much as in our own day, and each person's kindred is therefore unique. Though not at all vague in structure, kindreds are individualized and overlapping, so by their nature they can never take the form of institutions. In the Germanic world this system endows women and men with nearly equal legal rights. A woman leaves her kin but not her kindred when she marries, and her children belong to both her own kindred and her husband's; a woman has rights of divorce, inheritance, and ownership; and her kindred has the same obligations to support, defend, and revenge her as her male kin. As in many cultures, the mother's brother has a special role in the kindred; here his importance maintains a nearly equal balance between paternal and maternal claims on the individual. The terms most used to denote these kindreds in Old English are *mæg* and *mægð*, which not coincidentally are homonymous if not identical with the words for "woman." This identification of the kinship system with women figures prominently in the following argument.

A person's kindred serves him or her socially in three ways: first, being exogamous, it defines incest and regulates marriage; second, it supports him or her legally, and in certain circumstances economically; and third, it carries out revenge, providing a strong deterrence to violence. Germanic customary law does not really deal with individuals at all but with kindreds that share responsibility for their members' actions. A person's status in regard to this law, in fact membership in the community, depends upon a kindred traced to the fourth degree (see Jolliffe, pp. 2–6). The tribe as a whole is also called a kindred (*mægð* or *cyn*), and the king, who is elected from one preeminent kindred in the tribe, is called *cyning*—a son or descendant or a member of the *cyn*. The royal line is thought to descend from the founder of the tribe, and ultimately from the gods, and it rules over this interwoven social organization of kindreds.

In the Continental period before the migrations, however, the king (*rex*) is not the only ruler (see Tacitus, p. 43; James). The lord (*dux*) rules over a war-band bound to him by oaths of service rather than kinship. These bonds are as strong as kinship and constitute a tightly structured warrior class. Its members need not even be members of the tribe. The relation of these equal and complementary social orders includes a limited contradiction of loyalties, which gives rise to continuous but limited conflict in the society—that is, the social system is not perfect, but it is stable. Heroic literature, which ostensibly describes this period, gives the impression that the question of priority between the two modes of organization was not settled definitively and that practice varied widely. The literature focuses attention on the continual clash between them, as when a man violates his oath to his lord to fulfill his responsibility to his wife or kin, or (more often) when he violates kinship bonds in obedience to his lord. Late narratives like the *Volsungassaga* and *The Nibelungenlied* are still exploring these fault lines in heroic society. Because everyone in the *comitatus* has a kindred (except the special category of "kinless man"), conflict arises often enough to make it a central theme in myth, legend, and literature. The story of father and son, or brothers, compelled to fight each other by the contradictory exigencies of this dual order is conventional enough to remain a prominent motif as late as the Arthurian romances—though romance is more concerned with the new conflict between lordship and romantic love, rather than with kinship.

Kinship and lordship ties, then, distinguish two overlapping but clearly distinct social organizations: a privileged class of lords and their warriors, and the rest of society, whose primary responsibility is agriculture, organized into kindreds and ruled by a royal kindred. The first class is exclusively masculine, and the second is typically characterized by feminine symbols. The division and conflict between these two groups is evident in northern myth and religion, in which there are actually two communities of gods: the Vanir, agricultural fertility deities such as Freya and her brother-husband Frey, who are portrayed as prior in time but not in power; and the Aesir, the terrible gods of warfare, Thor and Othin. These latter are said to have come north and made peace with the older gods after a long dispute. Dumézil finds in this mythology, with its "higher" and "lower" cults, evidence of the typical structure of society found among all Indo-European peoples—distinct social classes dedicated to agriculture and war. These classes are characterized by the predominance in each of kinship or lordship structures.

The stability of this dual system, such as it was, seems to have been destroyed by the migration to Britain. The *comitatus*, which in the homeland had been a complementary and perhaps only an occasional social institution, the function of which was to wage war, in

England became by default the skeletal structure of an actual government. That Britain was already organized into kingdoms made such a transformation almost inevitable. As Anglo-Saxon colonists assumed power over their new territories, traditional Germanic lordship assumed new administrative functions. During the first century of Anglo-Saxon settlement, a new hierarchical class structure could crystallize around the new facts of lordship-as-political-system, with the lord as a warrior king.

As families exfoliated over several generations, the reassertion of old kindred structures came to be felt, but the newly powerful lordship structures resisted it peacefully. Here we see the beginning of a centuries-long conflict between these two competing social organizations, in which the newly legitimized political structure of warrior kingship attempted to retain and strengthen its power in the society. This competition is clearly visible in the laws, which document the solidification of political power and the gradual erosion of the rights and duties of kinship in legal matters.

The contradiction is not exactly a struggle between two groups, since many men belong to both the kinship and lordship systems. Rather, a new form of political authority was being defined vis-à-vis the ancient and natural demands of the reconstituted customary kinship system in the new country. The two corresponding religious cults of warfare and agriculture, meanwhile, would have continued to flourish complementarily, since they represented the class and economic divisions in the society; but their relation to each other as "higher" and "lower" must have been accentuated, since the warrior cult was now established as the religion of the ruling class.

Less than two centuries after the settlements began, as these two social orders were in the process of defining and limiting each other's rights and new contradictions between kinship and kingship were developing, Christianity arrived in England. The Anglo-Saxon kings adopted it with relative calm and rapidity, partly because it helped to solidify their new power structures within an even larger one at a time when their legitimacy was being questioned by custom. The Church became a partner to the state and grounded kingship in an international religion instead of in the indigenous warrior cult. It integrated the English kingdoms into the older order of European kingdoms, under the universal spiritual leadership of Rome and the Kingdom of God.

The transformations I have been tracing—from the tribal stage, where kinship and lordship ties were balanced complementarily in the figures of the king and the lord, to the more dynamic stage where lordship usurped kingship and set out to replace the functions of kinship with a hierarchical system of political bonds based on oaths among men—is in some ways paradigmatic of the origins of civilization. Civilization requires that the social order based on kinship be subordinated to a political order, which aims to unite the largest possible groups. The primary allegiance of each individual to the nation rather than to the family can be achieved only by eliminating the self-perpetuating internal violence that in tribal organization is controlled by the kin-feud; and this can be achieved only by a central legal authority that guarantees vengeance in the name of the state rather than the kindred. Of course the conflict between the two did not end, and never will—the relation of the family to the state is still a crucial issue for us—but it was an even greater problem in the early stages of civilization.

The Anglo-Saxon case is paradigmatic especially because the antagonists in this struggle were not just the kindred and the state, but the state as embodied in a ruling warrior class. The antagonists, then, were—originally, at least—the social forms of instinctual love and aggression, the family and the army; and we can analyze the evolution of their relationship throughout the period in terms of civilization's need to repress and control the twin instincts of sexuality and violence. Here I am adapting Freud's theory that such repression and control are the *sine qua non* of civilization, and that "the evolution of civilization . . . must present the struggle between Eros and Death, between the instinct of life and the instinct of destruction" (*Civilization*, p. 122). The kindred and the *comitatus* are the clearest possible social embodiments of these two conflicting instincts.

The first step in this analysis will be to explore the relation between women and the kindred—both denoted by the words *mæg/ mægð*—and the status the kinship system gives to feminine power. This relation might be said to support Freud's jaundiced view of women as the antagonists of civilization: "Women represent the interests of the family and of sexual life. The work of civilization has become increasingly the business of men, it confronts them with ever more difficult tasks and compels them to carry out instinctual sublimations of which women are little capable. . . . Thus the woman finds herself forced into the background by the claims of civilization and she adopts a hostile attitude towards it" (*Civilization*, pp. 103–4). As with many of Freud's most Victorian pronouncements, this only requires a sensible translation into contemporary terms to retain its usefulness. In a society where women are generally excluded from the formal structures of male power, it is not surprising if men see the claims of the family as subversive. Freud lived in such a society, and so do we, to judge from debates on a wide range of public issues today. In the Anglo-Saxon case, as the rights of the kindred are diminished, so too are the rights of women. Thus throughout the Anglo-Saxon period the traditionally strong position of women in Germanic society gradually erodes, until women are finally set under the lordship of their husbands.

Our second step will be to define the relationship of lordship and aggression. It would be wrong to claim that the warrior class, even in its original form, is simply institutionalized aggression, for the aggression it focuses on the enemy outside the tribe allows close male bonding within it. War, like sacrifice, is a means of harnessing aggression and deflecting it away from the group. Those who join in violence together are bound to each other by their shared guilt for breaking normal taboos against such behavior. Warriors are thus justified to some extent in seeing themselves as the guardians of social order. In fact, the rituals of the old warrior cult, carried over into the rituals of kingship, strictly forbid internal violence in a set of elaborately defined taboos. The most exotic of these is known as the peace (*grið*) of the king, a carefully measured precinct surrounding the king and his hall, in which all violence and threat of violence, even the carrying of weapons, is prohibited and punished. "Thus far shall be the king's peace, from his burh-gate where he resides, in all four directions, three miles and three furlongs and three lineal acres and nine feet and nine sceafta-munda and nine barley-corns" (Chaney, pp. 155–56). A breach of the king's peace is not just a crime but, as the form of the prohibition indicates, a violation of sacred space.

The warrior class could see itself, then, as devoted to peace rather than aggression and ironically—but rightly—claim that the prime source of internal violence was the kinship system. In this way it justified its sustained attack on the powers of the kindred. Lordship's most dramatic and visible success in its long struggle to undermine the power of kinship was the virtual eradication of vengeance as the mechanism of the kin-feud. Of course vengeance originally functioned as an inhibitor of violence, not its cause. From the kindred's point of view vengeance is always directed outward and serves to protect its security; it serves the same function for the kindred that war does for the tribe. But as the social group grows in size, members are required to identify first with the state rather than their kindreds, and violence between kindreds becomes intolerable. Thus law tends to undermine the claims of the family.

The attack on the rights of the kindred can be traced in the development of Anglo-Saxon law. The early laws encourage a payment of money (*wergild*, man-price) in place of vengeance. The king is involved in more and more of these penalties—so much to be paid to the victim or his kindred, so much to the king. Later laws allow a kindred to disclaim one of its members and to refuse to support his claims. Still later, the kindred is replaced by a group of neighbors or associates (*gegildan*) who are bound together for purely legal and economic purposes—an early form of the guild. In the end, every citizen is related to the workings of the law through the protection of a lord, rather than his kindred, in a system that resembles feudalism.

But despite the military state's understanding of itself as peace-keeper and its belief that violence originates either from outside or from the kindreds within, it is after all a martial institution, draped in the symbols of warfare and dedicated to social control. Opposed by nature to the forms of natural self-regulation found in tribal customary law, it absorbs and centralizes powers that were before diffused in the workings of kinship. We can hardly overlook that this growth of legal authority is the most comprehensive form of aggression in social life.

The establishment of governmental power at the expense of kindred-rights and individual freedom is the social equivalent of the individual's early renunciation of instinct from fear of authority and is in fact bound up with it. In individual development, the renunciation of sexual and aggressive pleasures precedes the internalization of authority in the form of the superego; it is involuntary, and it is not aggression directed back against the self in the form of guilt. It is felt simply as aggression against the self by an authority, as a call to obedience under a threat of punishment. At the cultural level, this call to obedience replaces customary law's call to conformity with the whole group, reinforced by shame, and it precedes the call of morality and guilt that Christianity introduces.

As in individual development, the transition from one stage to the next is often traumatic. Most primitive societies come into civilization as conquests or colonies, dragged forcibly out of their ways. In the Anglo-Saxon case, the authority that accomplished this transition was not imposed from without but gradually evolved as the society's own institutions responded to historical developments. This is what England shares with a few other ancient civilizations, such as Greece: by one means or another they brought themselves out of their own tribal origins, which meant that their cultures escaped being destroyed in the process. The circumstances of the migration to Britain had already forced social development before the arrival of the Church, which could destroy native cultures as effectively in the early Middle Ages as it would later in America and Africa.

The Hall and the Hut

When the Anglo-Saxons invaded Britain, they settled in scattered villages instead of cities, and they built their houses of wood instead of stone—an apparent regress from the Romano-British civilization they supplanted. Whitelock attributes this regress to the technological backwardness of the invaders (*Beginnings*, p. 15); even in the tenth and eleventh centuries, however, not only rural settlements but great houses were still being made of wood, and they still resembled the villages and halls of the settlers five centuries earlier. The tenth-century royal manor at Cheddar, Somerset (see Rahtz), strongly evokes the world of *Beowulf*, except for the stone chapel which stands next to the hall. After the conversion churches were regularly made of stone and had windows, often of glass, though halls continued to be made of wood and remained windowless.

The stubborn preservation of this ancient form of building is related to the hall's symbolism. Originally, the hall was not primarily

a form of habitation; it was a *meðelstede*, a formal place. In its traditional form and usages the hall defined and structured a traditional
way of life. It preserved a constellation of values and distinctions
essential to the culture and therefore was not to be exchanged lightly
for some more "advanced" form, such as the city, the villa, the castle,
or the palace.

The symbolism of traditional dwellings is an anthropological commonplace, from the Greek *polis* (see Fustel de Coulanges) to the
Indonesian Atoni house (see Cunningham). Dwellings are cosmic
symbols, guiding the behavior, belief, and thought of those who
dwell in them by organizing their notion of the world. To understand the meanings and functions of the hall, then, is to understand
one of the most basic, pervasive, and persistent structures in the
world of the Anglo-Saxons. Perhaps the survival of the traditional
hall in architecture, social life, and literature was vital to England's
rapid and successful development after the conversion.

The cosmic symbolism of the hall is revealed in the parable of the
sparrow in Bede's *Ecclesiastical History*. As a symbol for the world of
human existence, the hall in winter perfectly suits Germanic religion
and the culture fitted to it. In northern mythology the ordered universe is created out of chaos, which is always threatening to engulf it
again. The imperative of both the religious and heroic life is to maintain order by holding off the forces of chaos—enemies of the tribe
and also internal violence, symbolized by giants, ogres, dwarves,
monsters, dragons, the world-serpent, and the Wolf.

The hall symbolizes not only this world but the other one too.
The only clear image of an afterlife we find in northern myth is Valhalla, the hall of the slain. This otherworldly hall is also specific to
the warrior class—it is inhabited by those who have died in battle.
It serves the same function in the mythic world that the hall does
in society: it is from Valhalla that the heroes venture out against the
forces of chaos at Ragnarök, the final battle.

Beowulf provides the most detailed picture we have of the cosmic
hall. The building of the great hall Heorot is a metaphor for the birth
of civilization in the poem; it is celebrated with a hymn of God's
creation. The whole poem takes place in a world defined by the hall.
Fully alive in language, *Beowulf* seems to throw a bright light into the
darkest corner of Anglo-Saxon history, illuminating the hall as the

vital center of the human world. It is such a detailed and compelling picture (and so much other evidence seems to confirm it) that only the most committed skeptic could deny it is a credible representation of the early Anglo-Saxon world before the advent of Christianity and civilization, of a tribal society dominated by a warrior class whose world was the hall.

However, although the hall is a credible world in a limited sense (as when we speak of the "academic world," "sports world," or "business world"), it is inconceivable as a whole historical world: for it is a world without agriculture, without women, and without economic or domestic life of any sort. Even if we say the hall is only the world of the warrior class, or of just the lord, it is still only a partial picture. In *Beowulf* the hall is a house, but it is not exactly a home—men drink and talk there, but they do not live there; they do not eat there (a feast is a *gebeorscip*, a beer-drinking, or a *symbel*, a ceremonial feast, and there is no mention of food), and for the most part they do not sleep there. The hall is a *meðelstede*, a formal place, a ceremonial place, a primitive form of court.

The peculiarity of the world of *Beowulf*, then, lies in what is not there. Except for a few casual references to the *burs* where men go to sleep, we hear nothing of the village or the people outside the hall. We need not doubt the accuracy of the picture of the hall in *Beowulf* once we understand its perspective and its limitations, however. The poem shows us the world of the hall from the inside and seems totally indifferent to the rest of the human world outside; this is because poetry itself, like other forms of *meðelworda* (formal words), is one of the traditional ceremonial activities of the hall. The functions of the hall include the functions of poetry, and poetry serves the hall. By elucidating these functions, we can see the relationship of the world of *Beowulf* (and the world of native traditional poetry generally) to the historical world that created it and account for some of the characteristics of the poetry.

The best evidence we have for understanding early Germanic society is *Beowulf* itself, but its vision is idealized, archaic, anachronistic, and only partial. As for other evidence, only recently have methods been developed for discovering and excavating sites from the settlement period. These sites show that the hall was typically the center of a small village (or *tun*) composed of numerous buildings.

Most of these were small huts, dug one or two feet into the ground and covered with a simple thatch roof. They housed single families, or crafts such as weaving and pottery. Huts of this sort appear in rural England through the eighteenth century (see Hodgkin). The excavations at West Stow reveal three halls with at least forty-some huts (see West); all evidence of habitation, including food, utensils, and household and toilet articles, is found in the huts, not in the halls. Although the mundane life of the early Anglo-Saxons seems to have revolved around these huts, *Beowulf* and the other poems hardly suggest their existence—except perhaps for the "earth-pits" (*eorðscrafu*) of the "Wife's Lament" (see Harris). The large areas of life located in the hut, and which the hut symbolizes, are obscured by the *Beowulf* poet's silence.

The village as a whole suggests to the anthropologist a typical structure of tribal villages around the world (see Lévi-Strauss, pp. 31–38), consisting of numerous huts surrounding a men's ceremonial house that also serves as a bachelors' quarters—just what *Beowulf* suggests about the hall. The hall and the hut are symbols of two worlds, balanced complementarily, whose meanings and functions are defined in their relation to each other. This distinction is one of the most elemental in the culture.

Symbolically, the two dwellings correspond first of all to the two systems of social order: the hall is the locus of lordship, the hierarchical order based on oaths and gifts, while the everyday world of the huts is ordered by the traditional obligations of kinship. Second, the hall is a domain of men; and the huts, of women. Neither this distinction nor the first, of course, is mutually exclusive. Men bound by oaths in the hall still live in huts and remain obligated to their kindreds; they move back and forth between the two worlds as easily as we move between home and office. Likewise women—at least royal women—have a ceremonial function in the hall; but they are excluded from the *comitatus* and its oaths, and they are conspicuously absent in the world of poetry—though we know from laws, wills, and charters, and from Bede and other Latin sources that in the early period they enjoyed extraordinary freedom and influence outside the hall. The hall/hut distinction corresponds, then, to the two related distinctions, lordship/kinship and male/female.

Third, and perhaps most conspicuous, the hall was the domain of

Settlement village of West Stow, reconstruction. (From Randolph Swearer, Raymond Oliver, and Marijane Osborne, *'Beowulf': A Likeness*, New Haven, Conn.: Yale University Press, 1990; photo by R. Swearer; reprinted by permission)

a ruling warrior class and the huts were *de facto* the domain of the agricultural class. In addition, these two classes had complementary religious cults in the pre-Christian period: the hall was the precinct of the Aesir, while the huts were the precinct of the Vanir. The higher and lower religions correspond, then, to two domains of life, characterized by sex, class, occupation, and social relations, and are expressed most visibly in the cosmic symbolism of the two dwellings and the village structure that sets them in relation with each other.

These several oppositions may seem less than orderly, since easy logic reveals contradictions. How could the hut be the domain of women, for example, if men lived there as well? And how could it be the domain of agriculture, if warriors also lived there? But the relationships can be illustrated by a Venn diagram, in which *B* is a subset of *A*. If *A* comprises all those in the kinship system, and *B* all those in the system of oaths among men, we can see that the former includes the latter, but not the reverse; that is, everyone in *B* is also in *A*, but *B* excludes much of *A*. The distinction is sexual insofar as *B* contains men only, and not-*B* includes some men and all women. Similarly, *B* can represent the warrior class and its cult, and *not-B* the agricultural class and its cult.

There is no reason such a tribal structure could not remain stable while rulership resided in the whole set *A*, as it did originally. But after the migration, when it was transferred to *B* in the form of a warrior-king, *B*'s power to rule over *not-B* became a problem to be solved. In Dumézillian terms, *A* represents the kingly cult of the first function, *B* the warrior cult of the second, and *not-B* the agricultural cult of the third. But the power of *A* was usurped by *B*, resulting in a truncated and problematic structure. The conversion effectively solved the problem by restoring the autonomy of *A* in the form of the Church, thus restoring the ideal tripartite structure of Indo-European society. The resemblance of the diagram to an idealized village structure, where *B* is the hall and *not-B* the huts, is not too surprising.

I need only point out that the hall is (architecturally speaking, of course) an erection, and the hut is a hole in the ground, to suggest the psychological symbolism that underlies these distinctions. In *The Interpretation of Dreams* Freud discusses the house as a symbol of the body (pp. 225–26), and in Old English poetry the body is regularly described as the house of the mind or the soul. More interestingly, the hall is commonly used to depict states of mind—to be sad, for example, is to inhabit a sorrow-hall or a care-hall or a joyless hall (see Hume, pp. 69–71). The symbolism of modern houses opposes the cellar to the attic (see Bachelard, pp. 17–18)—the first a natural representation of the unconscious and the irrational, the second of consciousness and rationality. The hut and the hall correspond neatly to this distinction too. In the hut a man's relations to the earth are revealed directly: here the Anglo-Saxon man slept, here his woman lived and worked, and here he lay with her; here they brought the produce of their agriculture for her to cook, and here they ate. The hut is a symbolic form of space that we can characterize as telluric— a space containing women, kinship, fertility, sex, agriculture, food, sleep, and night. It is an earthen place, suited to our earthen natures, male and female.

The hall, on the other hand, is as cultural as the hut is natural.

The social relations celebrated in it are a social invention, distinct from blood. As we can see in such examples as Bede's parable of the sparrow-flight, in Valhalla and in Heorot, the hall symbolizes cosmic and social order, holding off the opposing forces of chaos, which are identified to some degree with nature. "The principle task of civilization," as Freud says, "its actual *raison d'être*, is to defend us against nature" (*Future*, p. 15). The ruling warrior class was dedicated to this defense, and its ceremonial life in the hall was directed toward that end. There were ceremonies of gift-giving, oaths, and boasts, which created and constantly reaffirmed social bonds; and then there were drinking and poetry. The ceremonial life of the hall may look like a fraternity party with a martial theme—rituals of fellowship and service, drinking, boasting, and singing—but the underlying meaning and unity of these activities can be seen best in their original cultic character, for Othin was not only the god of war and kingship but also the inventor of mead and poetry. Mead and poetry were not just Germanic society's ways of entertaining itself, then; they were ceremonial activities specifically of the warrior class in the hall, related to each other and to the larger symbolism of the hall itself.

Snorri Sturluson tells us that when the Aesir came to make peace with the Vanir, they all made a truce by spitting into a crock together. The Aesir, not wanting it to be lost, made the spittle into a man named Kvasir, who was so wise he could answer any question. But he was killed by dwarves, who put his blood into a pot and mixed it with honey—"and it became the mead which makes whoever drinks of it a poet or scholar." Othin stole the mead back from the dwarves and it became "his drink, his gift, and the drink of the Aesir" (p. 103), the gods of the warrior class—that is, the drink of the warrior class.

The religious use of intoxicants is common enough that we cannot be surprised if mead had cultic significance. The specific relation of mead to the hall is revealed in poetic compounds like "mead-hall," "mead-bench," and even "mead-path" (the path leading to the hall); in *Beowulf*, "he took away their mead-benches" is a metaphor for conquering a tribe. Opland has discussed the relation of drink to poetry, arguing that ritual drinking in the hall was part of the warrior's boast, a poetic form of ancestor veneration; and he also notes the compound *ealusceop*, "ale-poet" (see pp. 180–87). Neuman de Vegvar discusses the drinking-horn (like the one found at Sutton

Hoo) as a ritual instrument, something like a Germanic equivalent of the Native American peace pipe (see also Bauschatz, pp. 72–78).

I would not suggest that in historical times Anglo-Saxon poetry served anything like a cultic function, of course, since the cult in question was entirely supplanted by Christianity and is never referred to in the poems that survive. But the social structures that the old cult served, embodied in the hall/hut distinction, lived on; in fact, the rapidity and strength of the conversion were due in part to Pope Gregory's enlightened policy of not disrupting such structures if possible. The hall remained the locus of social-political (though not sacral) power and still embodied a heroic ethic, expressed in poetry in which idealized history shades imperceptibly into mythology. Poetry, as an essential component of hall life, remained a tradition of an Anglo-Saxon aristocracy that still considered itself, long after the conversion, as a warrior class.

To see poetry as a ceremonial activity of the hall would be to re-define its nature pretty sharply. We should not read *Beowulf* naively as the literary description—or even idealization—of the society that produced it, or of any past society either, but see instead the func-tions of such poetry within the society, and see its symbols in rela-tion to the larger system of symbols clustered around the hall. The hall is not so much an idea-complex in poetry, as Katherine Hume says (see p. 64), as poetry is first of all an idea-complex in the hall. The world depicted in the poems is an idealization of only one of the pre-Christian society's institutions, one of its classes, and one of its sexes—a projection of certain of its essential ideas and ideals into a quasi-mythical form.

We know that the poetry's vision is archaic and partial. Poetry is no more representative of the whole culture than are the saints' lives, which give an equally myopic vision of Anglo-Saxon England as seen from inside the monastery. The native poetic tradition—by which I mean the tradition that the Church found in England, and particu-larly heroic rather than gnomic poetry—was originally, of course, an oral tradition and as such a group phenomenon. It expressed group values and served the needs of the group, or the needs of individuals specifically in relation to the group. In the case of heroic poetry, the group in question was not the society as a whole, as is sometimes as-sumed, but the warrior class. This generalization can probably be extended to the heroic literature of other cultures, notably the Greeks. Among the Anglo-Saxons, poetry served the small groups of the warrior class not only by illustrating and defining the bonds that held them together but also by reinforcing them psychologically, by means of the figure of the hero.

In his book on group psychology, Freud analyzes the army as a typical group and draws from it his "scientific myth" of the ur-group, the primal horde. He discusses tribal society and the role of heroic poetry in it (*Group Psychology*, pp. 134–37). The epic hero, he says, is an "ego ideal" (an early version of the superego) who slays the primal father; this is the "heroic deed" that stirs the hearts of the fraternal group whenever it is told. It is unfortunate that the discussion of the ego ideal is so firmly tied to the myth of the horde, which can hardly be accepted in the form Freud gives it; but certain parts of the analysis can be recovered.

There is no reason to doubt that members of the group relate to the hero just as they relate to their lord, accepting him as an authority and identifying with each other by means of their common relation to him. The hero, like the lord, functions as an ego ideal for the members of the group. They do not identify their egos with him; they do not wish to be him, or even be like him, for nothing would destroy the group more quickly than such insubordinate identification. The warriors, rather, identify with each other by means of the hero as a shared ego ideal. The ideal is an unattainable narcissistic fantasy which is sharply distinguished from the ego itself and even critical toward it. In a war-band, the ego must submit slavishly to the ego ideal. As Tacitus puts it, the lord fights for honor, but his men fight for him (see p. 47); they attribute all their deeds to him and must perish in battle if he does. From this we can see how submissive the ego is to its ideal, as we would expect in a military group where obedience is so necessary.

Because the lord and the hero are ideals of this sort, they are free from judgment; they need not be exemplary to retain their authority. The endless debate over whether Beowulf behaves correctly at the end of the poem is thus beside the point. What matters in the context of the hall is how Beowulf's troops behave, which is why the faithful Wiglaf's speech chastising his unfaithful companions is not anticlimactic after Beowulf's death. Those who relate to the hero as an ego ideal do not pass judgment on him, just as they would not presume to judge their lord. Whether or not Byrhtnoth should have let the Vikings take position at the Battle of Maldon is similarly beside the point to the men who sacrifice themselves for him after he has been killed. They are not fighting for his cause, but according to their own speeches in the poem die out of duty to him as their lord. The group's common relation to the hero, then, reinforces their common relation to their lord and strengthens the members' identification with each other. This much can be said about the psychological function of heroic poetry in the hall without becoming involved in the myth of a primal horde.

Girard adds that Freud's myth is a symbolic statement about the role of ritualized violence (sacrifice) in inhibiting the self-perpetuating cycle of revenge, thus allowing for the development of civilization. This view clarifies certain themes in *Beowulf*. The figure of Grendel's mother reveals the antagonistic relation of the warrior class and its later transformations to the kindred and its system of revenge. Her symbolic meaning is certainly determined in part by the fact that she is a woman, a mother, and an avenger. The story would be very different if she were merely another monster, or even Grendel's father. His mother, we are told, is his only kin; his father is unknown. The figure of the avenging mother is sharply conceived and hardly arbitrary. Attempts to explain her specifically as a woman and mother have fallen back on Jung's Terrible Mother archetype and have seen in the succession of battles the working out of the hero's oedipal crisis (see Foley, "*Beowulf*").

But even from the point of view of the hall, Grendel and his mother are contrasting symbols: Grendel's violence is the spiteful response of a lordless man to his exclusion from the life of the hall, but his mother's is sheer vengeance for her kin. The figure of the avenging mother is natural enough (see Jochens), since kinship and the kin-feud belong to the world of women, the world of the huts, and are contrary to the interests of men and the hall. Beowulf clearly represents the world of men. Other women in the poem are similarly at the center of kinship struggles: the queen openly discourages her husband from choosing Beowulf as his successor instead of her sons, a political solution to the problem of succession that could prevent the dynastic struggle that will ultimately destroy Heorot; and their daughter will be the focus of a war with the Heathobards, as Hildeburh was the focus of the war with the Frisians. The world of women is seen as chaotic and intrusive, a problem men have to deal with. Women must be tamed, like the violent queen Thryth (or Modthryth).

Grendel's avenging mother, then—his *maeg*, his woman/kindred —represents among other things the threat that women and the ancient claims of the kindred pose to the civilizing work of men. The hostility toward civilization that Freud attributed to women was apparently noticed and returned by the men, at least in their poetic fantasies.

Thus, in reinforcing bonds among men that will be stronger than kinship, heroic poetry advances the aims of civilization. In overcoming the natural and primitive claims of kinship in favor of political order and civilization, the hall and its heroic values function like the Church: "Anyone who prefers father or mother to me is not worthy of me" (Matthew 10: 37); "If any man comes to me without hating his father, mother, wife, children, brothers, sisters, and yes his own life too, he cannot be my disciple" (Luke 14: 26). Now we can return to the question of how this model of early Anglo-Saxon society might help us understand the success of the conversion.

The Hall and the Church

When the Roman missionaries landed in Kent in 597 they were received hospitably by the King Æthelberht, whose Frankish wife was already a Christian, and allowed to preach. Their tolerant welcome indicates at least that the king did not see the new religion as a threat. There were practical considerations, of course—relations with Christian Europe, and the solidification of kingly power at home—but Christianity was probably not wholly incompatible with his society's traditional beliefs, especially if the old religion was in a state of decline or even atrophy. Religious beliefs are among the profoundest organizing principles of a society, or at least the profoundest expression of those principles. The mythology of a culture is so much a part of its social and mental organization that it can hardly be supplanted without a revolutionary reorganization, or the calculated attempt to adapt the new religion to existing cultural forms, or the fortuitous congruence of old forms to new ones. All these features were present to some degree in the Anglo-Saxon conversion.

The Anglo-Saxons, at least in the south, were not converted by a few daring spiritual athletes aggressively attacking the native religion. They were converted instead directly to Benedictine monasticism, and a short description by Bede suggests why the process went so smoothly: the natives were particularly impressed by the monks' communal life.

> As soon as they had entered the dwelling place allotted to them, they began to imitate the way of life of the apostles of the primitive church. They were constantly engaged in prayers, in vigils and fasts; they preached the word of life to as many as they could; they despised all worldly things as foreign to them; they accepted only the necessaries of life from those whom they taught; in all things they practiced what they preached and kept themselves prepared to endure adversities, even to the point of dying for the truths they proclaimed. To put it briefly, some, marvelling at their simple and innocent way of life and the sweetness of their heavenly doctrine, believed and were baptized. (pp. 76–77)

The monks, that is, inhabited a men's ceremonial house of their own and committed themselves by oath to a life of spiritual heroism for their Lord; they had renounced their kindred, their sexuality, and their aggression; their daily lives were a round of ceremonial song and feasting (though centered on wine rather than mead); they were engaged in spiritual warfare; they were the servants and army of a king, and they waged war on an invisible enemy who attacks the spirit. In these respects, the English ruling class had little difficulty identifying with the new religion, which was well suited to replace its own religion of military lordship by revealing new levels of meaning in its symbols.

The martial vocabulary of spiritual heroism and warfare had already been fully developed by the Church. It had functioned on the literal level in the age of persecution, as it would again in Christian wars against heathens and heretics, and the Church retained it as a system of metaphors for monastic spirituality when there were no physical enemies to combat. This vocabulary, translated into Old English, became the special hallmark of Anglo-Saxon Christianity. The easy commerce between the hall and the Church is a commonplace in Anglo-Saxon studies. In the vernacular poetry saints are depicted as spiritual warriors devoted to their Lord, and native heroes assume a Christian aura; Christ is the resolute young hero who leaps up to embrace his fate on the cross; Satan is the lordless man exiled for his betrayal; heaven is a great feasting-hall; the familiar form of the social-political exile becomes the lonely ascetic; Germanic fate shades into Christian providence; Christ and his disciples, or the saints, or the faithful, form a *comitatus* like any lord and his thegns. Every student of Old English learns to see these relations in each text he comes to and knows the double meanings of words like *dryhten* (lord/Lord), *dom* (fame/Judgment), *treow* (loyalty/faith), *wrecca* (exile/pilgrim), *lof* (praise/worship, fame/glory), and many others.

Even the initial identification of hall and Church in poetry was celebrated as a momentous event. The story of Caedmon is not just about the Christianization of secular poetry, since hall poetry was not exactly secular. It is not just that the Church found a surprisingly convenient and congenial vocabulary of lordship, doom, exile, and ethical ideals in the native heroic tradition; the Church also appropriated the social and religious functions of this poetry as an activity of the men's hall, already devoted to a kingly religion as a ceremonial activity of the warrior cult. The naturalness with which Caedmon moved from the hall to the Church is even implicit in the imagery of his short poem, in which he says of God, "He first shaped for sons of earth / Heaven as a roof, holy shaper," gracefully adapting the cosmic symbolism of the hall to its new Christian context.

It is commonly said that the conversion resulted in a spiritualization of the warrior life and that the heroic tradition is therefore treated as a system of metaphors for the religious life. A psychological view takes another step; the conversion resulted in an *internalization* of the warrior life, a refocusing of the aggression of warfare and rulership inward upon the self, where the real enemy has been relocated, resulting in guilt. The oaths and boasts that gave form to the militancy of the hall are transformed into vows of instinctual renunciation and acts of self-mortification. The story of Saint Guthlac is neatly symbolic of this conversion. Guthlac is an Anglo-Saxon warrior (his name means "war-play") who after his conversion first retires to the monastery and later to the fens in solitude to combat devils who are waiting there to assault him—transparent projections of his own inhibited desires, which become the very means of his self-punishment and his salvation.

This internalization, evidenced by the conformity of vernacular Christian poetry with the native heroic tradition, is an excellent example at the cultural level of Freud's assertion that the superego is formed by the internalization of aggression. The Church, which acts in the culture as the superego does in the individual, was established in England by the same mechanism through which the individual superego is formed—the turning back of aggression upon the self, in the internalization of the warrior life. This process, as unsociable as it is in an extreme case like Guthlac's, is in fact another giant step toward civilization. Even common sense tells us that mastery over our human nature is preliminary to the establishment of an orderly and moral society on any scale larger than the tribe and that order and morality consist in identifying the instincts and learning to control them.

Two objections might be raised at this point, however: first, that the hall did not *become* the Church, after all, but remained a separate institution—a distinction indicating some limitation to the possible internalization of energies. But even in individual development not all aggression is internalized as guilt, and we would hardly expect a complete renunciation at the cultural level either. Although the Church and the state remained identifiably separate, they were in effect the sacred and secular arms of government, joined legally, economically, politically, and by blood.

The second, more interesting objection is that the Anglo-Saxons already possessed a religion, which surely must have performed the functions of cultural superego that I am claiming originated in the Church. The lord and the hero functioned as shared ego ideals, which would seem tantamount to a cultural superego. But the hallmark of the superego is guilt—that is, self-aggression. Not every agency that regulates behavior critically can be said to act as a superego. The difference between primitive religions and Christianity is clear in this regard. Early Greek religion, for example, served a number of functions without promulgating a code that regulated behavior comprehensively. The Greek gods hardly embody a superego! Instead, primitive religion restricts its regulation of behavior to specific occasions, in specific times and places, when right behavior is rigorously determined and overseen by authority. These ritual occasions vary from culture to culture and can serve any number of functions.

The religion of the Anglo-Saxons regulated certain behavior relating to agriculture and war, but the Germanic gods were not moral any more than the Greek gods were, and they did not constitute a superego overseeing behavior generally. In traditional society most behavior is regulated not by religion directly but by habit and convention, the "way" of a culture, its ethics, which may be defined and illustrated in its mythology but not regulated by it. One is expected to conform to the behavior of the group and to obey whatever authority has the power to enforce these demands.

Christianity has been a major agent of expanding civilization partly because it not only regulates behavior comprehensively but also regulates desire, by means of a constant inhibition of sexual and aggressive instincts. The first of these is converted into ritual and moral (aim-inhibited) behavior, and the second is guilt, self-aggression that punishes the ego with anxiety for failure to live up to the demands of an internalized authority. These demands are so comprehensive that they are impossible to fulfill, and they often oppose the customary behavior of society, as the story of Jesus illustrates so dramatically.

In the individual the superego develops in the resolution of the child's relationship with the father. I would not want to insist too strictly or too finely on the analogy at the cultural level. In cultural development the parental drama is less clear than the role of doctrine: as long as the several developments prerequisite to guilt have prepared its way, guilt can simply be taught. The superego can be given as a baptismal gift to anyone or any culture ready to accept the necessity of inhibiting the instinctual life in the interest of the group. The ego's precarious hold on the instincts, which are now identified as the enemy of the common good, condemns it to self-hatred and self-punishment, all in the service of civilization. The social evolution that preceded the conversion of the Anglo-Saxons prepared for this development, and the ascendancy of England afterward is due at least in part to it.

The vocabulary of inhibition, guilt, and self-punishment does not imply a negative attitude toward civilization or Christianity, of course. The development that the migration and conversion brought about was as natural as individual growth, and in England it was especially smooth and successful. The resulting culture was a coherent and powerful blend of its two components. The conversion was so much an exchange of gifts that it can be described as either the Christianization of the Anglo-Saxons, or the Anglo-Saxoning of the Church. Christianity donated its civilization and its powerful influence upon the social and cultural development begun before its arrival; in return, the native culture donated to Christianity its characteristic spiritual realism, a return to the hard reality of human existence missing from Christian literature since the Gospels and not to be seen again so clearly until the twelfth century. The abstract and dogmatic vision of the human world in nearly all early medieval literature comes from the tendency of Christian thought to soar beyond the actual world of experience in metaphors increasingly distant from their literal sense, until history becomes the static and schematic structures of icons and saints' lives. But at its best, as in a poem like "The Seafarer," Anglo-Saxon literature presents a world where spiritual meanings reside in concrete reality itself, and spiritual truth does not simplify or deny the terrible complexities of human existence. The "spiritualization" of the life of the hall, then, was complemented by the "realization" of the Christian vision under the influence of the native traditions embodied in the hall.

Mourning the Past

The renunciation and internalization that result in superego formation at the cultural level suggest the analogy of individual development in terms I have so far avoided; but perhaps the inner unity of the many phenomena we are dealing with will be clearer if we finally confront the superego in its relation to the oedipal struggle. In the individual the renunciation of oedipal desires results in an internalization of the oedipal relationship and a consequent production of guilt. We learn to feel guilty in this renunciation: guilt is generated not only by the parental threat that first forces the renunciation, but by the feeling that such a renunciation, once effected, amounts to a turning away from the parents, a rejection of them, an abandonment, a loss which must be atoned for. In this model, psychic development

is a progressive separation from childhood and its oedipal identifications; a movement into mature individuation in which relations
can be successfully established only if the oedipal desires have been
internalized and transformed in the form of the superego. As a result, guilt comes to regulate social behavior within a large group by
means of an internalized authority that its individual members share.

Because this interpretation of the process focuses our attention
on the relation that the individual must establish with earlier stages
of his or her own growth, it provides an especially rich analogy with
cultural developments like the conversion, in which an earlier stage
is similarly being renounced, internalized, and transformed. The attitude that Anglo-Saxon culture struck toward its own renounced past
can help clarify this transformation, so we return to *Beowulf* again,
this time to consider the psychology of mourning that governs its
relation to the past.

The theory of oedipal resolution I have just outlined is in large
part that of Hans Loewald, who has linked the problem of separation
to the psychology of mourning (see pp. 384–404, 257–76). Mourning epitomizes the normal healthy process of relinquishing the past,
and since it normally involves feelings of guilt and self-mortification,
it epitomizes superego formation as well. Moreover, as Loewald has
noticed, Christianity intensifies this process:

> With the advent of Christianity, initiating the greatest intensification
> of internalization in Western civilization, the death of God as incar-
> nated in Christ moves into the center of religious experience. Christ is
> not only the ultimate love object, which the believer loses as an exter-
> nal object and regains by identification with Him as an ego ideal, He
> is, in His passion and sacrificial death, the exemplification of complete
> internalization and sublimation of all earthly relationships and needs.
> (p. 260)

At the level of cultural history too, we might add, the New Testament provides a powerful model for the renunciation and internalization of the past—the Old Testament—and encourages the formation of the cultural superego—the Church—as a means of preserving
that past in a transformed state as a model for the future. This way of
separating from the past is a model for both the reconstruction of the
ego after the resolution of the oedipal crisis and its reconstruction

after the acceptance of Christianity. Both can be seen in schematic form in the act of mourning for a lost love object.

In "Mourning and Melancholia," Freud defined mourning as "the reaction to the loss of a loved person, or to the loss of some abstraction which has taken the place of one, such as one's country, liberty, an ideal, and so on" (p. 243); this reaction is an internalization of the lost object, a withdrawal of libido from the object back into the ego by identification. Two features of this process are of special interest to us. First, there is a temporary clinging to the object through the medium of a "hallucinatory wishful psychosis," during which "each single one of the memories and expectations in which the libido is bound to the object is brought up and hypercathected [i.e., over-indulged], and detachment of the libido is accomplished in respect of it" (p. 245). Second, to the degree that the severed love is unconscious or ambivalent, its internalization is characterized by self-reproaches and a sense of worthlessness. That is, unresolved reproaches against the lost object are refocused upon the ego, which has now identified with it. These self-reproaches culminate in an illusional expectation of punishment, which finds satisfaction in an insistent self-exposure; thus the self-mortification characteristic of mourning. Loewald has elaborated this theory to include all the losses, separations, and re-nunciations of psychic life; but even in its simple form, it shows how a poem like *Beowulf* serves the process of mourning and how the psychology of mourning explains some of the poem's most problematic features.

I would not want students of literature to catch me calling *Beowulf* a "hallucinatory wishful psychosis" or a "libidinal hypercathexis," but heroic poetry generally does serve to prolong a culture's identification with a lost past while at the same time acknowledging that past as irretrievably lost. As an act of mourning, it fixes an image of what has been lost, organizing the disturbance brought about by that loss with an exacting and wholly absorbing review of the culture's relationship to it, until the object is internalized, and the loss is accepted and carried forward into the new possibilities that it has opened for the future. Heroic poetry is a creative assimilation of cultural loss, providing not only continuity with the past but emancipation from it by transforming it into art. *Beowulf*, like any successful act of mourning, both acknowledges the loss and assumes responsibility for it; it refuses to repress or deny the loss or the feelings of guilt it engenders. As Loewald explains, emancipation from the past requires a conscious mastery of guilt, not an evasion of it: "Bearing the burden of guilt makes it possible to master guilt, not in the hasty form of repression and punishment, but by achieving a reconciliation of conflicting strivings" (p. 391; see also pp. 257–76).

No cultural change as powerful as the conversion could be survived without such mourning. Without it, the old culture would simply be destroyed and replaced by a new one rather than internalized and transformed in healthy cultural growth. Christianity, of course, encourages this growth in a number of ways. First, the life of Christ is the fulfillment (that is, internalization) of Old Testament history and thus a model for the successful renunciation of the past; second, the death of Christ is the occasion for perpetual mourning in the Gospel narrative and the eucharist, where the loss is transformed in a celebration of his resurrection into the spiritual life (that is, internalization); and third, this history and its ritual reenactment are accompanied by the doctrine of guilt. All of this makes Christianity a religion ideally suited for guiding cultural transformation through conversion, by forming a cultural superego from the guilt generated in the act of mourning for the past that conversion renounces.

The transformations of heroic culture after the conversion have always been the primary focus of Anglo-Saxon studies. It is as if the heroic world were retained, but now as a system of metaphors for Christian life; thus the pervasive language of spiritual warfare, in which the enemy has been internalized and the battlefield is the soul. Christianity, with its doctrine of guilt, encourages the internalization of what has been renounced and reinforces the sense of guilt caused by the abandonment of the traditional culture.

In these terms we may be able to understand the ambivalent attitude *Beowulf* takes toward the pagan past, which has always seemed so puzzling in light of the poem's Christian—and even monastic—provenance. The tone of the poem is not nostalgic or confused and does not reflect a partial or even ambivalent Christianity. Rather, it is devoted to the task of mourning for the past, which demands both a full acknowledgment of the love that has been withdrawn from it and a clean detachment from it by accepting its death as absolute. We experience the same sort of ambivalence individually whenever we mourn for a loved one: we concentrate lovingly on our memories precisely as a way of accepting our loss as final so we can put it behind us.

Now we can better understand *Beowulf*'s awesome apocalyptic themes. The poem ends as Beowulf's world is about to be destroyed, with the Geats resigned and waiting for their inevitable doom, reviling themselves for abandoning their hero in his final trial. The acceptance of guilt brings about the expectation of—and the demand for—punishment, which is satisfied by this act of self-mortification in the literary imagination. The twin themes of guilt and punishment for the abandonment of the heroic past are characteristic of much Anglo-Saxon literature, certainly of the works commonly called heroic and elegiac, which are the most studied and are usually considered the most interesting and characteristic productions of the vernacular culture.

The whole complex of themes was traditional enough to have been revived in clear form during the Viking invasions centuries after the conversion. Wulfstan responds to the latter-day national calamity by chastising the English not so much for their sins as for the corruption of traditional social values, especially loyalty to kindred and lord. "The Battle of Maldon" also reproduces the seemingly contradictory attitudes of *Beowulf* by simultaneously praising and blaming —and openly accepting guilt for the death of—another abandoned hero, one who so fully embodies the ancient ethic that, paradoxically, he is as hopelessly fated to perish as Beowulf.

When we consider *Beowulf* as an act of cultural mourning, we can see to what use it puts the eschatological myth the culture inherited, under the influence of the apocalyptic myth it accepted with Christianity. The eschatological myth is historicized, according to the demands of the new religion, and is then used to depict the death of the old heroic world, thereby clarifying the culture's renunciation of its own pagan past. The past is internalized and transformed in a strong Anglo-Saxon Christian culture—all the stronger because the past has been mourned for properly, respectfully, and lovingly, and not just discarded.

When we consider *Beowulf* as an act of cultural mourning, we are perhaps also touching on the function of epic as a type of literature. There is good reason to believe that primary epic is not a traditional genre of oral poetry, even though it uses oral poetic techniques. More likely, it is the form in which the sort of comprehensive review of the heroic past that we see in *Beowulf* is made, during the transition to civilized life when rapid cultural change has already overwhelmed traditional culture. The study of modern oral traditions in Europe and Africa seems to support this interpretation, and Opland's survey of the Germanic evidence leads us to think that *Beowulf* too is not an example of a traditional genre but is very unlike the purely oral poetry of the early Anglo-Saxons. The long narrative poem of the heroic past in traditional style is a literary form invented as the culture's way of mourning the recent loss of its past. Mourning itself is a prominent theme not only in *Beowulf* but in epics as diverse as *Gilgamesh*, *The Iliad*, and *The Nibelungenlied*—the last of which is fully as apocalyptic/eschatological as *Beowulf*, depicting even more awesomely, perhaps, the collapse of the old Germanic world.

The process of mourning for a past state that must be renounced, then, is another way of describing the formation of the superego on the individual or the cultural level. The most important occasion of this process, the one that suggests its universality and thus its broad explanatory power, is the oedipal resolution. The development from tribal to civilized society involves a renunciation of the primacy of kinship ties, and their internalization and transformation into the many relations demanded by civilization under the guidance of the superego, just as mature object-relations can be developed only after the individual's analogous renunciation of the parents.

It may seem, however, that we have lost sight of the hall, the institution whose survival in its several transformations somehow served the Anglo-Saxons through this transition. Not only did the hall provide a model for political life and Christian spirituality, but it remained a great anachronism as well, preserving native traditions throughout the Christian period in architecture, social life, and poetry. "The Battle of Maldon" testifies as clearly as the royal manor at Cheddar to the persistence of the hall in its ancient form.

What purpose is served by such a survival? In the individual, Freud would call it a "residue." It is essential to his view of human nature that "in mental life nothing which has once been formed can perish" (*Civilization*, p. 69). The superego itself is "a residue of the punitive agency of our childhood" (p. 243). At the cultural level such residues are called traditions, and they, alas, are all too perishable. A culture that undergoes traumatic change, such as a primitive society pulled suddenly into the modern world, is likely to lose its traditions under the overwhelming impact of civilization. The least tragic solution to the problem of constructing a new culture out of the ashes of the old is usually full integration into the new culture. But Anglo-Saxon culture managed this transition without such devastation, and there is no doubt that its great vitality was in part due to the continuity of its development, the survival of traditions that made the difference between growth and just change.

A culture profits from growth as an individual does. Its customs and institutions have a rationale in history and do not seem arbitrary or disconnected. Just as important, the residues of the past provide a repertory of attitudes and responses that can be brought to everyday experience. In the individual there is a normal fluctuation of mental attitudes, controlled by an appropriate range of regressions, as we move from erotic to parental, political, religious, aesthetic, imaginative, or other responses the world calls for. It is easy to see the analogous repertory of cultural responses preserved in the traditions of our own culture. Attitudes, values, and ideals associated with Native American, European, English, Puritan, revolutionary, frontier, and other and more recent stages in our history, as mutually exclusive as some of them are, constitute a rich and coherent repertory for us and are evoked in our political, domestic, sexual, religious, scientific, artistic, commercial, and other experiences. Such a repertory—preserved in institutions, customs, play, education, and especially literature and the other arts—is an adaptive feature in a culture. Perhaps the creativity often associated with regression in the individual is analogous to the genius and vitality of a culture, measured by its ability to adapt to changing circumstances in the present by evoking its past.

The case in point is not America, of course, but Anglo-Saxon England, and the tradition in point is the hall. Throughout Anglo-Saxon history the hall served as an adaptive and creative focus of cultural regression. Its self-evident anachronism and its transformation into systems of metaphors in the religious, political, and literary life of Christian England do not signal loss but preservation. The world of the warrior class described by Tacitus and the heroic world described in *Beowulf* evolved in several directions, transformed and preserved in the metaphors of art, ritual, and social life.

The residues of history stored in the metaphors of cultural life are not unlike those encountered in the liminal, or transitional, phase of ritual, which Victor Turner calls "a cultural means of generating variability, as well as of ensuring the continuity of proved values and norms," "a repertoire of variant deep cultural models" ("Process," pp. 69, 70). The hall was just such a model, which proved adaptive in the drastically changed historical and cultural conditions of the Anglo-Saxons' migration and conversion.

Chapter 5

Two Psychoanalytic Excursions

Between the previous chapter and the next one I would like to pose two psychoanalytic questions not directly focused on *Beowulf*. The first concerns the psychoanalytic understanding of the hero, in society but especially in a literary text: What can Freud's concept of identification tell us about catharsis? The second concerns the relationship of psychoanalysis to Christian (that is, Augustinian) psychology: What can Freud's concept of the superego tell us about Christian guilt? Each of these questions has to do with superego formation, first in heroic society and literature, and second in its specifically Christian form. After these excursions the discussion of superego formation in the Anglo-Saxon conversion and in the reading of *Beowulf* can proceed on firmer footing.

I have already suggested that the epic's role in the evolution of culture depends upon the dynamics of the audience's (or the reader's) identification with the hero and that this identification is modeled on our individual and collective identifications with various voices of authority, such as parent, lord, king, and God. These interrelated identifications are complex enough to deserve their own discussion. They are in fact a classic problem in psychoanalytic theory. Beginning with Freud's first thoughts on the subject, identification and superego formation have always been discussed in relation to the tragic hero rather than the epic hero; so now our focus shifts back to ancient Greece.

Identification with the Hero

The Greek tragedies were public religious and civic performances, and Aristotle assumed they illustrated moral principles—*hamartia* in essentially good characters. Their powerful effect on the audience can hardly be explained in moral terms, however—except perhaps that they simply outrage all our common notions of morality and justice. Public as the plays are, and Aristotle notwithstanding, there is little agreement about the moral principles operating in *Oedipus* and *Prometheus Bound*. It is just as hard to imagine an Athenian audience as a modern one leaving the theater murmuring to each other, "Well, *that* made sense!" and "Yes, he certainly deserved *that*!" Rather, our response to the plays is individual, emotional, and psychological. Everyone responds to *Oedipus* in his or her own way, though Aristotle suspected that underlying our various responses there are principles to be described. I bring to this ancient problem the psychoanalytic theory of identification, a concept unknown to Aristotle, who speaks instead of imitation, sympathy, and catharsis. What might identification be able to tell us about catharsis? And how relevant might these concepts be to the epic?

Our response to tragedy is more obviously a concern of psychoanalysis than of literary theory or philosophy, for several reasons. First, tragedy is acted out rather than expounded, because, as Ricoeur says, its essential themes are unspeakable (see *Symbolism of Evil*, pp. 211–31)—which is to say, I think, that they are repressed, in the audience as well as in the play. To make them conscious requires the sort of analysis best suited to unconscious ideas. Second, though Shakespeare may have known well enough the value of the drama as a metaphor for life, it has assumed new value after Freud, because we now understand how our own characters and roles in life are acted out largely under unconscious direction. "Character is fate" has a new depth of meaning in an age when it is understood, as Freud says, that "the ego is not the master of his own house." Richard Rorty explains how different this new image of the self is from the pre-Freudian picture of the intellect under the sway of the passions. The drama provides a perfect explanatory model for identification. Richard Wolheim's discussion of identification, for example, adopts the dramatic model by dividing the self into author, character, actor, and spectator.

Third, and more to my own point, the tragedy resembles in essential respects psychoanalysis itself: it is a strictly delimited, intense psychological process, which, if Aristotle is right, results in the particular therapeutic effect he calls catharsis. In both cases, this effect proceeds from an identification (with the hero or the analyst) that is highly disruptive psychologically but ultimately resolved. Freud himself, in his early work with Josef Breuer, performed what he called "cathartic analysis." Though he never discusses the relation of his use of this term to Aristotle's, we can follow his terminological clue and discuss our identification with the hero on the analogy of the psychoanalytic drama of identification called transference and the termination of analysis. Then perhaps we can apply this dramatic model to the epic—or at least to *Beowulf*, an epic with a distinctly tragic tone.

It was in regard to the epic, in fact, that identification with the hero was first discussed by Plato. Socrates asks Ion, who is a rhapsode, a reciter of Homer,

> When you produce the greatest effect upon the audience in the recitation of some striking passage, such as the apparition of Odysseus leaping forth on the floor, recognized by the suitors and shaking out his arrows at his feet, or the descriptions of Achilles springing upon Hector, or the sorrows of Andromache, Hecuba, or Priam—are you in your right mind? Are you not carried out of yourself, and does not your soul seem to be among the persons or places of which you are speaking, whether they are in Ithaca or in Troy or whatever may be the scene of the poem? (pp. 18–19)

"Are you in your right mind?" *Sympatheia* and *ecstasis* so undermine reason that poetry is exiled from the Republic. The poet, after all, "has been inspired and is out of his senses, and reason is no longer in him" (p. 18), and the reader's identification with the hero, though Plato does not exactly call it that, is too much like madness to suit the philosopher.

Aristotle's approach is more psychological. The theory of catharsis is presented quite clinically in the *Politics*:

> An emotion which strongly affects some souls is present in all to a varying degree, for example pity and fear, and also ecstasy. To this last some people are particularly liable, and we see that under the influence of religious music and songs which drive the soul to frenzy, they calm down as if they had been medically treated and purged. People

who are given to pity and fear, and emotional people generally, and others to the extent that they have similar emotions, must be affected in the same way; for all of them must experience a kind of purgation [catharsis] and pleasurable relief. (pp. xv–xvi)

In his definition of tragedy in the *Poetics*, Aristotle says simply "through pity and fear, [tragedy] achieves the purgation of such emotions" (p. 12). So if Plato believes that poetry causes madness, Aristotle believes that it cures it. The theory assumes, of course, that the audience is already emotionally disturbed, unbalanced, overemotional, blocked up, and that, as with physical ailments, a laxative is the obvious treatment. Not everyone has the problem—certainly not philosophers; but as Aristotle sees it, it is endemic in the lower classes, who should be given regular doses of tragedy and cathartic songs to keep them calm.

Paradoxically, then, the unbalanced, manic audience is not given a model of sanity to identify with, but by way of inoculation and immunization is presented with madness to exhaust them: terrifying plots, and characters driven to insanity by the gods. And not only tragic heroes are mad, according to Aristotle; Achilles is also mad, in the sense that he is angry, and anger too is a form of possession, an unbalancing, a loss of *sophrosyné* and reason. Madness, therefore, in the Greek sense, is actually a requirement of a good plot, tragic or epic. A good plot will enter the irrational so squarely that even in summary it will evoke terror and pity: "The story should be so constructed that the events make anyone who hears the story shudder and feel pity even without seeing the play. The story of Oedipus has this effect" (pp. 26–27). The unbalancing of the emotions is thus a *sine qua non* of good narrative art and has a therapeutic effect on emotional disturbances in the audience.

Except for this medical metaphor of purgation, however, Aristotle does not explain why this treatment should work, though he knows from observation that it does. If he is right, and the unbalancing performance does somehow relieve common emotional disturbances, then one should be able to describe the process psychoanalytically.

There has been a continuous and ever-widening stream of commentary upon Aristotle's few sketchy remarks about catharsis, and every age has had its own understanding of the process. Pedro Laín Entralgo comments:

It would not be difficult to compose a history of European feeling and thought following the thread of this immense philological and exegetical hodgepodge. The Renaissance commentators were accustomed to interpret the favorable effect of tragic catharsis as a hardening to the vicissitudes of life produced by familiarity with spectacles that fill us with fear and compassion. The French preceptors and playwrights of the seventeenth century, more devout, extend the cathartic process to all the passions and interpret it as a purification of the individual. (p. 186)

Goethe dismisses the problem altogether by taking catharsis as a feature of the play itself rather than the mind of the spectator, though to do so he has to claim that the discussion in the *Politics* is irrelevant to the *Poetics* (see Eissler, p. 545). The distinctively modern interpretation, on the other hand, understands *catharsis* as a term borrowed from Greek medicine. Jacob Bernays speaks of it as "a designation transferred from the somatic to the affective in order to designate to the treatment of a sufferer a treatment with which the endeavor is not made to transform or repress the aggrieving element but to excite and foster it in order thus to bring about the relief of the sufferer" (quoted in Laín Entralgo, p. 187).

Bernays was an eminent Viennese classicist whose *Zwei Abhandlungen über die Aristotelische Theorie des Drama* was published in Berlin in 1880. According to Laín Entralgo, "Hardly had the study by Bernays been published than it gave rise to no less than one hundred and fifty works for or against it" (p. 186). Widespread interest in the subject extended to the Viennese salons, where Josef Breuer's first patient in cathartic analysis, Bertha Pappenheim (Anna O.), heard of it and so was able to help Breuer rediscover catharsis as a medical treatment in his treatment of her during the years 1880 through 1882 (see Dalma). In 1882, Freud became engaged to Jacob Bernays's niece Martha, and Freud's sister Anna later married Martha's brother, Eli Bernays. It is not hard to conclude from these connections that Aristotle's theory, as understood by Bernays, was not just "in the air" but was a strong influence on Freud and Breuer's development of the "cathartic method," the subject of their joint volume *Studies in Hysteria* in 1895.

The cathartic method treated hysterical symptoms by encouraging the patient to recall the traumatic events that had triggered them and to release the repressed emotions attached to those memories. The socially appropriate response to a traumatic event, like the death of a parent or loved one, often prohibits an adequate affective reaction. In cathartic analysis these events are reexperienced in the relative security of the therapeutic setting and an "abreaction" provoked, resulting in relief. Freud soon decided, however, that although the cure worked, its effects proved temporary, and he abandoned it. Breuer had already abandoned it in a panic after Anna O., his only patient, fell in love with him during treatment. In the final pages of *Studies in Hysteria*, Freud speculates briefly on this first case of transference, which he was quick to recognize as an inevitable hazard of the method, but which at this early stage he describes simply as a "false connection" (see pp. 301–4). He was only beginning to understand the complexities of the analyst's role in the patient's shifting identifications during the analytic process.

Though Freud abandoned the cathartic method, it does have elements of permanent value. It remains as a residue in Freud's later work and in fact still persists in various forms today, from the fully psychoanalytic "re-grief therapy" of Vamik Volkan and the cathartic psychotherapy of Michael Nichols and Melvin Zax, to the California pop therapy of Thomas Scheff. What does cathartic therapy, as Freud and these latter-day exponents practice it, have to tell us about tragic catharsis, if anything?

It would seem to suggest that tragedy reexposes the audience to commonly repressed traumas and that the resulting catharsis is a sort of collective abreaction to universal features of psychic life. Perhaps (if we elaborate this idea freely with elements from Freud's later work), tragedy briefly reawakens the oedipal crisis, or the other losses and humiliations suffered in growing up—the repression of instinctual love and violence that constitutes the discontent of a civilized audience; perhaps the tragic hero, like the epic or folk hero Freud discusses in *Group Psychology and the Analysis of the Ego*, is reenacting the murder of the primal father: "Hearers understand the poet, and in virtue of their having the same relation of longing toward the primal father, they can identify themselves with the hero" (p. 137).

Perhaps; but we will reject this whole train of thought as too simple, just as Freud rejected the cathartic method. It is veering too sharply into the universal and neglecting the clinical variety we should expect in individuals. It could only be a blunt instrument of analysis. Besides, although the great tragedies clearly do concern

these themes, their heroes are of a special sort. The tragic hero is destroyed for what Aristotle assumes is his *hamartia*, his fault, which
complicates our identification with him considerably. If he represents
an ego ideal, it is a distinctly guilty one; if he is a wish fulfillment, it
is at least partially the fulfillment of a death wish.

Does *Beowulf* share these tragic dynamics? Recently when I read a
comic-book version of it to my six-year-old son, he leapt about with
his sword, clearly identifying with the hero; but he was mortified
when the hero died. He stared at me in disbelief: "He *dies?*" Tragedy
is not for children, and neither is *Beowulf*. The hero's death ruins their
identification, and it surely complicates it for most adults. It is not
likely that everyone will identify with the hero in the same way, and
considering the hero's tragic end, it is not likely that anyone's identification can be maintained in a simple way throughout the play or
the epic. So our first simple thoughts about catharsis and cathartic
method will appear only as residues in our own conclusions.

The term *identification* was introduced into literary criticism by
Shelley, who elegantly expresses the modern, commonsense attitude
toward the hero:

> Homer embodies the ideal perfection of his age in human character;
> nor can we doubt that those who read his verses were awakened to an
> ambition of becoming like to Achilles, Hector, and Ulysses. . . . The
> sentiments of the auditors must have been refined and enlarged by a
> sympathy with such great and lovely impersonations, until from ad-
> miring they imitated, and from imitation they identified themselves
> with the objects of their admiration. Nor let it be objected that these
> characters are remote from moral perfection, and that they can by
> no means be considered as edifying patterns for general imitation.
> (p. 486)

But that is precisely our objection. No one in his right mind would
choose to be Achilles—not to mention Oedipus, Hamlet, or Lear.
No one would want to shoulder their agonies outside the text.

We do identify with the hero, of course; but Freud taught us there
are forms of identification that do not stem from admiration and imitation. The tragic hero, a figure of towering proportions and often
terrifying features whose character is idiosyncratic and flawed, whose
story is after all tragic, is an ideal we identify with only indirectly,
or in a highly specialized sense. Our identification is complicated by

unconscious factors; for example, the hero is likely to inspire guilt in us for our own inadequacy. ("No! I am not Prince Hamlet, nor was meant to be," as Eliot's Prufrock says—though Prufrock's guilt-ridden, hesitating ambivalence is the one quality he does share with Hamlet, whose madness, like that of many tragic heroes, eases our temporary mad identifications with them.) In short, our relations to these heroes have some of the murky complexities of our every-day relations to parents, priests, teachers, political leaders, doctors, gangsters, and all the other authority figures stalking about in the superego. As ego ideals they are critical, fearsome, and bound up with our guilt.

Notice how Shelley shifts the focus of the analysis from plot to character. Whereas Aristotle says "the plot is the first essential and the soul of a tragedy; character comes second" (p. 14), for Shelley it is the hero who bears the meaning. Perhaps that misconception leads to his other errors. Psychoanalysis, however, will refocus our attention on plot; Freud's interest in character notwithstanding, he never treats it as other than a narrative, a case history. Identification too is a development, an act with a structure—a beginning, middle, and end. Among psychoanalytic concepts, the dramatic structure of identification is especially well understood, because it is at the heart of the psychoanalytic relationship itself, in which the development of the patient's identification with the analyst, his or her transference, is used as a route to cure. So analysis is a drama of sorts, too, a thera-peutic drama of identification with a beginning, middle, and end.

Pope says the audience at a tragedy will "live o'er each scene, and be what they behold," which is not wholly true, since we identify only with certain characters, especially the hero. To observe charac-ters, even to sympathize with them, is not necessarily to identify with them in the psychoanalytic sense. In our personal relations, even to love someone is not necessarily to identify with him or her. A child may love both parents, for example, and identify with only one. Not every strong attachment is an identification, which I will define here preliminarily as simply an extension of the self that fails or refuses to distinguish itself from an object. Such identification is in fact gen-erally incommensurate with mature object-love, since it denies the object its own being. It is immature in the sense that it is regressive, because in identifying with the object the ego recaptures some of its own infantile narcissism, that first stage of mental development in which the world was not yet clearly distinguished from the self.

This is a highly simplified definition of identification. As with so many of Freud's original concepts, which are always elegantly simple, a subsequent half-century of clinical practice has revealed number-less forms of identification and has generated theoretical distinctions to account for them, culminating in Roy Schafer's "Identification: A Comprehensive and Flexible Definition." The near-Byzantine com-plexity of the concept in the post-Freudian literature is due to the fact that any part of the self (id, ego, or superego) may identify with any or all aspects of the object (desired, feared, or even hated, for example), resulting in a wide array of effects and disorders. In gen-eral, primary-process and *in toto* identifications tend to be neurotic in adults (see Smith, "Identification Styles"), although the most fun-damental of all primary-process identifications, the formation of the superego during childhood, is paradigmatic of later identifications and is especially useful in understanding the mechanics of the trans-ference. It is these latter forms that concern us here, and to describe them I adopt a simple model for relatively normal adults, similar to Loewald's.

In normal development, identification takes a number of forms in a sequence beginning with infantile narcissism. At this early stage, the two complementary types of identification that are to emerge later, *projection* and *internalization*, cannot usefully be distinguished (Smith, "Identification Styles"). The first to evolve is probably pro-jection, in which aspects of the self are projected into the world and attached to objects. A little girl may identify with a doll in this way, as if it were herself, or herself as she wishes to be. As the ego slowly learns to distinguish its own states from those of others, it comes to accept the separateness and objectivity of others and the world: the doll is only a doll, so you need not cry if your brother sticks his tongue out at it. But to the unconscious the world remains a playhouse, and projection remains active in many forms in adults. A familiar example is paranoia, in which the fearful, guilty ego finds the world's most innocent gestures threatening. Lovers routinely dis-cover to their dismay that the beloved's encouraging gestures were only projections of their own desire. Our sense of bodily violation when our home is broken into or our car wrecked also bespeaks the ease of our projective identifications, even with inanimate objects.

Of special interest to us are the temporary narcissistic fantasies that come into play in art, such as our daring identifications with the hero, which can also be a type of projection. We may identify with a character as an externalization of some aspect of our own ego, a projection of our desire, or a figure of ourselves as we would like to be, or imagine ourselves to be, or fear we are: I am Tarzan, Clint Eastwood, Oedipus, King Lear. In works of art, which occupy the psychological middle ground of "transitional objects" between clearly subjective and clearly objective worlds, we can venture into identifications without fear of the chastisement, disillusionment, and loss that inevitably attended our infantile identifications, which we had to renounce more or less unwillingly as we discovered that our dolls—and parents too—were not merely extensions of ourselves, not merely parts of our private worlds.

If, as adults, we are to be chastised or disillusioned for identifying with a literary hero, it must happen in the literary work itself, since normally such an identification lasts only so long as we are engaged with it. Don Quixote and Walter Mitty are examples of pathological identification, exceptions to prove the rule: as readers of romances, their identifications become a form of madness when carried beyond the act of reading. As heroes themselves in their own romances their madness is only typical and is the basis of our own identification with them, mad readers that we are. We identify with these heroes, whose madness is that they identify with heroes in the same way. Their humiliations are their chastisement, and ours too. But the book comes to an end, or we put it down, and unlike them we can terminate our madness. We are not crazy after all.

We are taught this danger early, in stories like *Alice in Wonderland*, *The Wizard of Oz*, and *Peter Pan*: we must return to reality and deal with our real father, bastard that he is, after we have projected our murderous rage for him onto Captain Hook and made him walk the plank; we cannot remain in Peter's world of infantile wish fulfillment, painful though it is to leave. It is our fate to grow up. The inferior forms of art we call escapism are perhaps distinguished by the conspicuous absence of this theme, inviting us to form identifications that are then not resolved within the work. At the other extreme is tragedy, in which our projective identification is both guilt-laden and very conspicuously terminated within the work by the humiliation and destruction of the hero, thus forcing *internalization* on us—the last act in the drama of our identification.

Narcissistic projections outside of art are usually pathological and laden with guilt, since the infantile desires we fulfill in this regressive way are usually unattainable in reality and illicit to boot. As these projections are broken, as reality forces us to renounce our narcissistic demands that the world serve, reflect, and embody us, this idealized past is then internalized. Internalization (or introjection) is something of a reverse projection, in which our relations to renounced or otherwise lost objects, our repressed desires, are retained as ego structures, as relations among components of the self. The grandest identifications of this sort occur in the internalization of our oedipal relations, by which the superego is formed. The awesome, idealized parents of our infancy become inner agencies, ideals by which the ego is constantly being measured and found wanting. The consequent guilt is normal and socially useful: it makes us moral and self-critical.

Calling internalization a form of identification is perhaps misleading, though, because unlike projection it is not regressive and narcissistic. "The ideal outcome of internalization is identity in the sense of self-sameness as an individual, and not identification and identity with objects" (Loewald, pp. 84–85). It is by internalization that our inner world is constituted and distinguished from the external world; it is the only road to normal, healthy object-relations. New identifications and new internalizations are always forcing psychic reorganization to some degree, as the inner world grows and shifts its relations into new patterns of coherence. Psychoanalysis and tragedy (as well as religion and epic) are calculated means of such growth and reorganization.

Projection, relinquishment, internalization: this is the normal drama of identification, the beginning, middle, and end of the oedipal, as well as the analytic and tragic cures. Childhood, analysis, and the tragedy must all come to an end; the parents, the analyst, and the hero must be relinquished, our relations with them internalized along with all our other demons.

So the audience does not simply identify with the hero and then

live through the plot with him; the form of our identification changes
as the plot develops toward its inevitable end—just as our identification with parents develops, or the analytic transference, or any other
narcissistic bond that reality forces us to relinquish. Lear must die.
We will learn nothing from his death except that it is inevitable. But
that is hard enough to learn. It is a maturing thought.

Others have noticed that our relation to the hero changes during
the course of the tragedy. The change is usually described in terms
of the two emotions Aristotle repeatedly links, terror and pity: our
terror turns to pity as the play progresses. This is a commonsense interpretation, which itself implies a shift in identification. Suppose we
see an old lady being beaten with a tire iron on the street: we feel
terror, identifying with her. But when it is over, her attacker fled, she
stunned and dying, our terror turns to pity as we stop identifying
with her and come to see her objectively as a woman who has been
injured and needs our help. Simon Lesser suggests a similar shift in
the tragedy; at the end of the play we are led to a point of detachment, when we identify no longer with the hero but with the cosmic
order that has punished him, and our terror with him turns to pity
for him. However, I am not so sure we can identify with such an abstraction unless a clear image of it is provided, such as Tiresias, into
whom we can project ourselves.

Be that as it may, it is surely not enough to say that our identification with the hero has simply been terminated. Identification
with someone who is guilty and is being punished so extravagantly
involves us in a drama of the superego, which cannot be so cleanly
resolved just by shifting our identification to the punishing agency.
At best we would end up saying "Yes, I certainly deserve *that*!" We
cannot speak of relinquishing a powerful identification without internalization, which is best understood in the mechanism of superego formation. Loewald's analysis of the oedipal process adopts the
termination of analysis as an especially illuminating analogue, because "experiences purposefully and often painfully made explicit in
analysis usually remain implicit in ordinary life."

> Analysis, understood as the working out of the transference neurosis,
> changes the inner relations which had constituted the patient's charac-
> ter by promoting the partial externalization of these internal relation-
> ships, thus making them available for recognition, exploration, and

reintegration. By partial externalization, psychic structures in their inner organization are projected onto a plane of reality where they become three-dimensional, as it were. However, the analyst, as was the case with the original parental figures, is only a temporary external object in important respects. The relation with the analyst, like that with parental figures in earlier ego development, has to become partially internalized. . . . The pressure of the impending separation helps to accelerate this renewed internalization. (pp. 259–60)

Projection, relinquishment, internalization: Loewald sees in this process a general law of mental life, which will bring us back to tragedy.

Emancipation as a process of separation from external objects . . . goes hand in hand with the work of internalization, which reduces or abolishes the sense of external deprivation and loss. Whether separation from a love object is experienced as deprivation and loss or as emancipation and mastery will depend, in part, on the achievement of the work of internalization. Speaking in terms of affect, the road leads from depression through mourning to elation. (p. 263)

As in analysis, so in tragedy: the hero too is a temporary object promoting the partial externalization of internal relationships, thus making them available for recognition, exploration, and reintegration. The temporary nature of our relation to the hero is important to note. The plot comes to an end, and so does the hero. The pressure of his fated destruction accelerates the reinternalization of what we have projected upon him.

From depression through mourning to elation: this is to speak of the process, as Loewald says, in terms of affect. This is the clue to an achieved understanding of catharsis in tragedy and in psychoanalysis that encompasses far more than Aristotle, Bernays, Anna O., Breuer, or the early Freud conceptualized. Catharsis, if it is to be more than a transient cure, is not simply the unlocking and venting of pent-up emotion. Instead it is participation in a drama of recognition, exploration, and reintegration that I take to be the highest mode of identification. The affective concomitants bear witness to the underlying structural changes in process.

The early idea that curative catharsis was merely the release of emotion is related to Freud's early understanding of anxiety as the consequence of repressed libido. Cure was simply un-repression. The understanding of catharsis he subsequently achieved is the product of his revised theory of anxiety in *Inhibitions, Symptoms, and Anxiety* (1926), where anxiety is taken to be a response to danger. He also came to a deeper understanding of the dynamics of structural change, of which the drama of identification is the central theme. It is more than fortuitous that in 1897 Freud first glimpsed his model for the drama of superego formation in *Oedipus* and *Hamlet* (see *Letters to Fliess*, pp. 272–73): tragic drama bears the significant plot in which our evolving identification with the hero recapitulates our most private dramas. Catharsis is a successful working out of the complex. It is psychologically therapeutic, as Aristotle realized, although not exactly like a laxative. It took Freud thirty years to understand the process.

I have at last to consider the *content* of our identification with the hero. The foregoing discussion has centered on plot, not character, following Aristotle's dictum that plot is more important. But who *is* the hero we identify with? If he is an ego ideal, why is he flawed? And why does he suffer so? What can identification tell us about *hamartia*?

Hamartia is notoriously difficult to define or translate and often difficult even to find, much less analyze, in the plays themselves. Is it a flaw, an error, or a misstep? And what *hamartia* do we see in Oedipus, Prometheus, Hamlet, or even Lear? Does not criticism usually reveal them as powerful but enigmatic characters crushed ruthlessly and unjustly by the gods? Is not their fault really only our feeling that they must be guilty of something if they suffer such punishment, or the projection of our own guilt upon them? For all his power, is not the hero's character really a cipher?

Do not all these questions apply equally to *Beowulf*? Many critics seem to ask how we can account for Beowulf's death if he didn't do something wrong. The case can be argued, but the evidence is all circumstantial. What did he do to deserve his death? (What did Hrothgar do to deserve Grendel, except grow old?) What after all can we say about Beowulf's *character*?

Perhaps the clue to character in the tragedies is that mysterious tragic mask. It is as blank as the imperturbable face of the analyst, as blank a screen for our projections, our transference. As for *Beowulf*, how many times have I found myself staring into the blank eye sockets of the Sutton Hoo helmet, which adorns the editions of our poem, or at the empty York helmet?

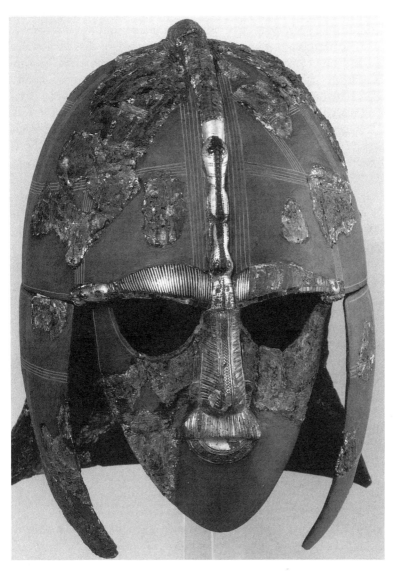

Sutton Hoo helmet. (Copyright British Museum)

Catharsis, we should never forget, is a matter of plot, not character. The hero is a blank. Think of Hamlet, as rich a character as any
tragic hero, yet paradoxically as enigmatic as any blank mask. To Kurt
Eissler (see pp. 22, 47) this radical ambiguity is the essential feature
of *Hamlet* and the source of its power. Sane or mad, moral, devi-
ous, incapable, young or old, male or female, even—anyone can play
Hamlet, anyone can identify with him; there are any number of interpretations of his character, because he is the perfect object of our
temporary transference. Likewise, there is no end to the interpretations of *Beowulf*.

But each of us must finally relinquish his or her narcissistic oedipal fantasies and internalize them. The play, the poem, must have an
end. Tragedy, and literature generally, helps us master this process,
which repeats itself endlessly in our psychic lives by inviting us to
enter into a drama of controlled regression and development.

Freud and Augustine

Many readers (including myself) feel an understandable discom-
fort when we bring the vocabulary and concepts of psychoanalysis to
bear on topics in medieval Christianity such as conversion. So here I
would like to think about the relation between these two systems of
thought in a philosophical language common to them both.

Freud's aggressive atheism is well known. "If the application of
the psycho-analytic method makes it possible to find a new argument
against the truths of religion, *tant pis* for religion," he says (*Future*,
p. 36). Jacques Lacan is just as blunt: "It is one or the other. If religion triumphs, it will be a sign that psychoanalysis has failed" (p. 7).
However, there is a surprisingly accommodating tradition that explores the relation of these two discourses by allowing each to inform the other (the work of Walter Lowe, W. W. Meissner, and Hans
Küng, for example). In literary studies, the most notable work of
this sort is William Kerrigan's landmark study of Milton's theology,
The Sacred Complex. Just as Milton's theology easily submits to "the
secular verdict of oedipal interpretation," so "psychoanalytic readers
engaging his epic have the opportunity to submit their theory of the
superego to the intelligence and sublimity of Milton's faith" (p. 6).
The title of Kerrigan's book refers to the way in which Christian be-

lief and doctrine encourage a distinctively religious resolution of the oedipus complex.

I have a mind to illustrate some of the relations between religion and psychoanalysis by a brief consideration of Saint Augustine rather than Milton. By choosing Augustine I define my concern as primarily theoretical. Most people, Freud included, approach religion primarily as behavior, ritual, spirituality, or belief; but Augustine is a theologian, a Christian philosopher, and we want to know how the religion of the philosopher might speak to the psychoanalyst. I will leave to others the job of psychoanalyzing Christian ritual and its symbology if they like, and I leave to others the attempt to put Augustine on the couch. My topic is not the psychoanalysis *of* religion but the relation between psychoanalysis *and* religion.

Augustine's understanding of religion is fully as theoretical as Freud's, and I wonder if Freud didn't perhaps prejudge religion by not assessing its philosophical component seriously enough. Freud objected to any attempt "to rescue the God of religion by replacing him by an impersonal, shadowy and abstract principle" (*Civilization*, p. 74). From a theological perspective, Freud's attack on naive, literalistic religion is perhaps just a necessary and healthy challenge to religion to rise above the terms of the attack (see Miller; Smith, "Stories of Childhood").

This is how a philosopher might try to mediate the dispute. This is the shape of the table. We are open to the possibility that psychoanalysis might illuminate Augustine's religion—open to the fact that it has; and also open to the possibility that Augustinian theology might just illuminate psychoanalytic theory—especially, as in the case of Miltonic theology, the theory of the superego. Thus we might be able to add an Augustinian chapter to Kerrigan's theory of the sacred complex.

Augustine offers himself to many psychoanalytic approaches, for many reasons: first, because we know him so well personally from his own self-analysis, the *Confessions*; second, because he is the premiere theoretician of human fallenness and free will; third, because his theology takes the form of a theory of knowledge and a hermeneutic—he considers God to be Truth as well as Being, a light illuminating the soul and an authoritative voice he calls "the Inner Master"; and fourth, because he considers the triune God to be revealed immanently in the tripartite structures of the soul—an identification that links theology to psychology as well as philosophy. Of course the psychology of his *De Trinitate* is not like modern psychology; but then again neither is psychoanalysis. Once Freud abandoned biologism, his definition of the mind's agencies became as much a faculty psychology as Augustine's: the mind's faculties are revealed in experience but are not necessarily grounded empirically as "things." Rather, both men's observations of mental process were gained in large part from profound introspection and are in consequence largely phenomenological. We should not be surprised if their descriptions of mental structure have much in common, and we will expect to learn much about the philosophy of each by noting their essential disagreements.

If I had to choose a mediating team in these negotiations, it would be led by Edmund Husserl. Husserl inherited Augustine's most lasting philosophical contributions through Descartes; and he sat in class with Freud, as their common teacher Franz Brentano dismantled nineteenth-century psychologism, opening the way for each of them to develop new theories of the self freed from empirical psychology. His sympathy for Augustine is signaled by the fact that his own philosophizing led him to convert to Christianity, if only on his deathbed. His phenomenological "egology" is a modern, secularized version of Augustine's analysis of the soul, and his concept of the transcendental ego occupies a variant middle ground between Augustine's Inner Master and Freud's superego. Freud's relation to Augustine, in short, is very like his relation to Husserl, so Husserl can serve as something of a translator.

The rest of the team should consist of Paul Ricoeur and Etienne Gilson, the former for his appreciation of the theological relations of both Husserl and Freud, and the latter for his willingness to read Augustine as a philosopher. But I would like Kerrigan at the table too, as a representative of the present generation who can speak several philosophical languages and see their affinities to psychoanalysis—as he has shown in his essays on Kierkegaard, Husserl, Lacan, and Derrida, among others. Husserl cannot have the last word today.

Training the searchlight of psychoanalysis on the *Confessions* might seem sacrilegious even to the unreligious, not because of Freud's atheism but because Augustine's self-analysis is so brilliant in his own terms that we feel a loss when we translate it into any others. We do not need a gloss to understand what he means by sin, God, or love, because his explanations are so clear. His introspection is not a modern nightmare begging for a cure, but a rational examination of his life, character, and mind. Anyone who wants to know about Augustine is better advised to read the *Confessions* than any attempt to analyze him in modern terms. But in that case, as in any good reading, Augustine's searchlight will be trained on us as well—as in Kerrigan's reading of Milton. With that in mind, we can think about what Augustine says about his life and his soul.

Augustine's sensitive reading of his own life in the *Confessions* builds immediate trust in the psychoanalytic reader. He seems to know what is important in his own psychic development. A nice example is the episode of his departure for Rome in Book V, the occasion for his finally flying from his mother's protective arms. "She loved having me with her, like a mother, but much more than many." He sneaks aboard ship at night, leaving her at a shrine weeping and praying that he won't leave her; when he sets sail in the morning, "the shore fell from our sight, where she raged with grief and complaint, filling your ears with sighs" (V.8). The shore is Carthage, so we cannot miss the analogy of Aeneas and Dido—especially since the account of his education had lingered over that story (I.13). Surprisingly, however, he does not call attention to it here, not even with a verbal echo. The mythic parallel lends its weight to the event, but negatively, by calling attention to the differences between them; for Augustine is leaving his mother, while Aeneas was leaving Dido in order to *return* to his mother—remember the oracle that compelled him:

> "The self-same land
> That bore you from your primal parent stock
> Will take you to her fertile breast again.
> Look for your mother old. . . ."
>   . . . But everyone
> Inquired what and where that place should be
> To which the god summoned us wanderers
> And called it a return.   (III.94–101)

These are two radically different actions, the one mythological, denoting the return to origins as a destiny, the completion of a cycle, the other a linear psychological development, the renunciation of oedipal ties as a requisite of psychic maturity. We may be tempted to equate them, since Augustine's destiny in Rome is in fact "our mother the Church," and he is going to renounce sex in the process; but *he* clearly sees the difference. The one is couched in regressive language, a fulfillment of the oedipal fantasy; the other is an adult resolution of it, an example of the sacred complex. In both cases there is a conflict, but Virgil and Augustine understand it differently. To Virgil it is caused by the eternal strife of the gods, particularly Jupiter and his wife; Augustine does not project it onto such mythical parents but understands it as internal ("my inner house, which I greatly stirred up against my soul, in our chamber, my heart" [VIII.8]), between himself and God, who lives within him as the *a priori* truth. He analyzes the conflict in his development as inherent in his fallen nature, seen both from within and from the viewpoint of a perfectly rational God.

Of course Augustine's analysis, like Milton's, is sometimes carried out in terms of "our grand parents" Adam and Eve, but Augustine can interpret these figures as psychological abstractions, as the intellect and the senses; so the Fall is internal to the soul, reenacted endlessly in every sin of an essentially sinful creature. In the *Confessions* his fallenness is a feature of his very existence, but it is not announced and analyzed until he re-enacts the original sin by stealing some pears in Book II, an act he then analyzes to discover its quintessentially irrational (that is, sinful) nature (II.4–10). In the *Aeneid* we are in the grip of symbols; in the *Confessions* Augustine is patiently analyzing these symbols for us. Freud and Jung might disagree as to whether Augustine's rational attitude represents genuine psychic progress, but there should be no dispute among philosophers.

What I have just called "the viewpoint of a perfectly rational God" is very like a transcendental ego, insofar as it is experienced as a psychic agency. But let us look at it in action before considering it abstractly. Augustine subjects the whole episode with his mother to this agency of truth, and it not only describes, it also criticizes. It is a corrective viewpoint, exposing the self's errors and misunderstandings. In this case it is especially critical of his mother: "Through my own desires you [God] rushed me to the loss of those same desires; and justly you punished her with the whip of sorrows, because of her car-

nal affection for me. . . . She wept and lamented, thereby proving herself by those tortures to be guilty of the inheritance of Eve, seeking
in sorrow what she bore in sorrow" (V.8). (Are we putting Augustine on the couch? No, he has put himself on the couch. God is the
analyst; we are just listening.) He is as sensitive to his mother's conflict as to his own, but he is unsparing in his demand (unconscious
at the time, though conscious on reflection) that their relationship
resolve into an adult form. He does not underestimate or sentimen-
talize either of their conflicts. After all, Christ was just as unsparing:
"Anyone who prefers father or mother to me is not worthy of me"
(Matt. 10: 37).

Here and in the rest of the autobiographical portion of the *Confessions* this transcendent point of view is felt as the voice of the mature,
converted Augustine, who can look back at his own thought and behavior (and his mother's) and see through its confused motivations
to divine God's hidden intentions—that is, the deepest true structure
of his life. (All this, by the way, is part of the "literal" level of interpretation.) However, even in the immediately introspective Book X,
this point of view is still with us, and there we can examine its function as a vigilant psychic agency, the Inner Master guiding Augustine
always through his errors toward true knowledge—that is, to God.
To know God, we learn in Book X, is to know the truth of the self,
because God is immanent in the soul in the person of Christ, the
Word and the Light, who speaks the truth and illuminates our being,
inspecting cognition and rendering self-deception and disguise pur-
poseless by their transparency. Christ is the Inner Master.

At this point in his confession, Augustine, like Milton, turns to
Genesis to find fit subjects of pure thought, and he concludes with
three books on eternity, infinity, and the creation of the universe,
interpreting Scripture in the same way as he has interpreted his life
and soul.

The theory of the Inner Master is developed most systematically
in Augustine's early dialogue *The Teacher*, where it is wedded to a
corollary theme regarding language. Language, he argues, cannot
teach the truth as the Inner Master can, because language is only
analogous to the Word; it is only a system of signs signifying each
other. (Those at the table nod knowingly, but the postmodern press
corps, accustomed to associate this idea with Saussure and Wittgen-

stein, Lévi-Strauss, Lacan, and Derrida, stir with anticipation.) The Inner Master is transcendent to language but has a psychological role to play. How does it fit into the large psychological schemes of *De Trinitate*? Is it a form of the superego?

In *De Trinitate* Augustine searches for God by contemplating man as His image, noting the many likenesses of the Trinity to be found in the soul. It is the grandest possible attack on dualistic metaphysics. Gilson writes that "the Augustinian universe derives its metaphysical structure from a complex participation in the nature of the divine being, a participation which is based on the transcendental relations of the divine Persons to one another" (p. 214). Beginning with the act of perception, all knowledge is conceived as a series of dualisms—creator/created—each mediated by a third party, an act of will or love. Two trinities of trinities are offered, one describing the relation of the soul to the world (knowledge gained through the senses), and the other describing the relation of the soul to God (knowledge gained through self-analysis guided by reason). If the three trinities of each of the two sets are combined, these composites appear:

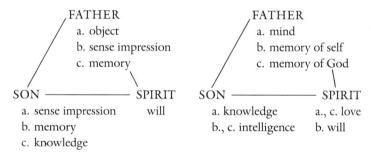

The first trinity is actually a detail of the Second Person of the second, where God reveals Himself in the soul's inner relations.

I realize it is an annoying interruption of the reading process, but a patient examination of these trinities will be required to glimpse the dynamics of Christian psychology. The reader is advised to stop reading and to study these charts and to refer to them when reading what follows. You will see that the world is drawn through successive loops of human understanding toward God, the three members of the Trinity exchanging places constantly in the process. Everywhere we turn in thought as well as in perception we find a relation of creator/created, mediated and animated by an active third term (or Person). This theological analysis of the mind has a built-in concern for language, since Christ is the Word, the *Logos*; a built-in psychological concern, since the will (or desire, *voluntas*) is an element in every relation in the soul; and also a special built-in psychoanalytic concern, since the father-son relation is the whole scheme's most fundamental metaphor.

Because the Son became man, we understand that he stands in our place on the chart. From this position it is easy to see that the presence of the First Person in the Second is the Inner Master in ourselves—which is attended to, when we are at our best, by the will.

Given these relations and the highly dramatic nature of Christ's relation to the Father in the Gospel narrative, psychoanalytic analogies loudly suggest themselves. At the very least we can say that there are many psychological metaphors for the Trinity, and one of them is psychoanalytic: if you understand your relation to your father, you understand something about yourself and about God. And it is a good bet that in this trinity—for it must be a trinity—the role of the mother will appear in the spiritualized Third Person, as a mediating animative force.

The Inner Master serves many of the functions of a Freudian superego (and ego ideal). But it is a vastly enlarged superego, a supreme rationality in itself unconflicted though always at odds with our fallen nature, a conflict conveniently symbolized in sensory and especially sexual terms, such as Adam and Eve. The Inner Master is the result of a specifically religious form of oedipal resolution, the sacred complex. It is religion's distinctive gift to human psychology and also to philosophy—remember Husserl, as well as Augustine.

We would be overhasty, however, sacred complex or no, simply to identify the Father as the superego. The Trinitarian presentation is dedicated to paradox and consubstantiality, and its terms are always in motion. When the Father's place is occupied by memory, for example, we note that Augustinian memory is very like the Freudian unconscious—and is therefore distinct from the superego, though related to it. The Second Person corresponds somewhat more harmoniously with our notion of the ego. The Son is a consciousness illuminated from above as having a phenomenological structure, noesis and noema unified by the intentionality of the will. At least that is the ideal from which the sinful soul, fueled by desire, in thrall to the senses, and irrationally deaf to the voice of its Inner Master, has fallen, and to which it is called to return.

The route of return is through the memory, as in Book X of the *Confessions*. Husserl calls it a "universal self-examination," and he cites the authority of Augustine to conclude his *Cartesian Meditations*: "Do not wish to go out; return into yourself, for Truth dwells inside man" (p. 157). Husserl's phenomenology, carried out by the transcendental ego, is from Augustine's point of view the psychology of unfallen man, the psychology of Adam, available to the philosopher in rare moments of illumination. It is a very ancient program. Ricoeur writes that "the fully declared philosophical decision animating the intentional analysis would be a modern version of the ancient theme of reminiscence" (*Freud and Philosophy*, p. 30).

What bearing can these abstruse reflections have on our discussion of Anglo-Saxon England and *Beowulf*? First, when we consider the process of conversion we must not imagine it as the simple substitution of one belief for another, one allegiance for another. Christian conversion involves the installation of the Augustinian Inner Master in the individual, a Christian superego, and the production of guilt. In addition, it is important to remember that this Christian superego not only oversees self-analysis in the individual, it also creates a community by installing the same transcendental ego, the same Inner Master, in every member of a Christian society. Furthermore, the language of psychoanalysis is surprisingly well suited to describe this Christian psychology, and not necessarily from an antagonistic position.

Chapter 6

Beowulf and the Origins of Civilization

The Role of Psychoanalysis

Now we can pursue the further relevance of psychoanalysis to the reading of *Beowulf*. Here I offer a model for understanding heroic literature, and epic in particular, as an idealization of a certain sort, inviting certain forms of psychological identifications in the audience—socially desirable identifications, to be sure, but necessarily effected in the individual. In the case of *Beowulf*, these identifications are facilitated by vast silences in the text—analogous to the silence of the psychoanalyst, another facilitator of such identifications. In this way, heroic literature produces an analyzable psychological effect in the audience, much as tragedy does with its catharsis.

Also, insofar as *Beowulf* is a Christian poem, I would like to restore the psychological dimension to our discussion of the Anglo-Saxon conversion. The conversion is central to our understanding of Anglo-Saxon culture and literature but is always treated as if it were a purely ideological phenomenon, a more or less simple matter of shifting alliances, reforming institutions, and substituting terms. But Christianity, by cultivating the superego in the individual and institutionalizing a cultural superego in the Church, imports its own psychology along with new social structures and doctrines.

This Christian psychology invites psychoanalytic interpretation, so its historical origins in the conversion should be analyzable as well. The notoriously difficult relations between Christian and pre-

Christian traditions and values in Anglo-Saxon culture, and in *Beowulf* in particular, can be understood historically and theologically, of course; but they can also—and perhaps even better—be understood psychologically, as an interesting case of ambivalence at the cultural level.

As I read *Beowulf* and other heroic literature, I am led to wonder about the relation of individual to social and cultural psychology. Like Freud, I am tempted to analyze culture as if it were an individual—to speak, for example, of its growth, its mourning, or its ambivalence, or of myths (and to some extent literature) as its dreams. But how can such analogies be defended—how can *psychoanalysis* be defended—among today's competing critical ideologies? Many have renounced both the concept of culture (a "facile totalization" as Jameson would say, at best only a dominant culture repressing myriad subcultures struggling for expression), and the concept of the individual (a bourgeois fabrication built on a humanistic conception of human nature, the myth of the autonomous ego). And even if those concepts could be retained, could we discover a clear train of linkages between them to account for all their tempting analogies?

I pragmatically dismiss these philosophical objections. Jameson's "political unconscious" might seem to offer a linkage between the insights of psychoanalysis and Marxism, one source of these criticisms; but that concept is as mystical in its Hegelian way as the Jungian collectivities from which it is derived via Northrup Frye, and it cannot be counted as psychoanalytic. Louis Montrose's "politics of the unconscious" is closer, perhaps, but dialogue between psychoanalysis and Marxism is still bound to be uncomfortable at best. At the very least, we will wish to clarify those areas of psychoanalytic theory where the linkages between the individual and the group must lie— the theories of identification and the superego.

Not to forget the text itself (so easy in theoretical discussions like this), I will point to certain passages in *Beowulf* characterized by silence and ambivalence, the psychological signatures of Anglo-Saxon heroic and elegiac poetry. But I am not so much interested in "psychoanalyzing the text" as in understanding how the text, with its deep, uninterpretable silences, might be said to sit in the analyst's place and psychoanalyze its audience—then and now—by acting as a screen for our projections.

This approach hardly replaces earlier approaches to the poem and in fact builds upon them; in the end, psychoanalysis being the omnivorous hermeneutic that it is, it interprets them, and itself, right along with the poem. Psychoanalysis is not inimical to other critical discourses, but it is not exactly complementary either. Psychoanalysis is concerned with all the mental states relevant to the poem and its understanding, and therefore our other critical responses to the poem are an important part of its subject. When I come to grapple with particular problems in the poem, it will be seen how psychoanalytic judgments tend to grow out of philological, textual, literary, and historical analysis, considered along with our more immediate psychological responses to the poem.

Nor can psychoanalysis, at least as I invoke it here, claim to interpret the poem better or more comprehensively than other contemporary approaches. I certainly do not consider psychoanalysis an "ultimate horizon" (Jameson's term again) or a programmatic hermeneutic. I can only claim to address the sorts of psychological questions that the poem prompts in a student of Freud. But these are important, if not ultimate, questions. Primarily they concern origins: not only the origins of civilization but the origins of the poem too, and also the origins of our critical attitudes toward it. All these questions turn out to be related psychologically. The individuality of the author and the reader, I will suggest, is one issue that binds them all into a single problem.

For the philologist, the folklorist, the new critic, the oralist, the postmodernist, and the new historicist—that is, for just about every scholarly reader—the author of *Beowulf* is decentered, erased, ignored, diffused into a web of preexisting traditions and historical forces, or evaporated into the ephemerality of oral culture. On the other hand, if I am right, the author was a highly original genius, a strong poet who helped shape those traditions in large part, at least as we perceive them now. Why is this position, which I find almost inevitable, so at odds with most traditions of *Beowulf* scholarship? What is it about the poem that invites such resistance to the idea of authorship, at least in those who have set about to conquer the poem intellectually?

It is partly because the roots of *Beowulf* scholarship lie in folklore and philology: the idea of an author never had a chance. Today it is orality and ideology. The poem does invite this response, I must admit, by passing itself off as traditional, even though it is demonstrably unique and original in many important respects, and even though there is scant proof of its traditionality outside its own claims and our uncommon willingness to believe them.

These two readings of the poem (the traditional *Beowulf* and the original *Beowulf*) imply not just ideologies but critical psychologies as well; for if the poem sits in place of the analyst, much of our response to questions of origin and authorship will be influenced by our dispositions toward the authority of the text and toward authority in general. The ideology served by our interpretations may be humanism, romanticism, nationalism, Marxism, or feminism; but weighed psychoanalytically, our interpretations will always be to some extent vicissitudes of the family romance, operations of the ego, expressions and sublimations of our own narcissism. We are social beings; but reading the poem here at the desk late at night remains an extremely private, individual act. That individuality is not insignificant, or imponderable, and it might be factored right into our interpretations.

Our attitudes toward authorship and the authority of the text will be the inverse of our attitudes toward the autonomous ego, the self. If these are indeed ideological commitments (Humanism! Marxism!), they still have psychological roots and can hardly be dissociated from our conceptions of ourselves as relatively free individuals, or as members and representatives of groups, or as expressions or victims of historical forces. Such self-representations are largely characterological, hammered out in childhood; as the poem sits in place of the analyst, the analyst ultimately sits in place of our parents. Epic especially may be said to serve with singular devotion that universal (though not ultimate) ideology that Lacan calls the Law of the Father and that Freud explored in his theory of the superego. Both theories are good descriptions of the Anglo-Saxon concept of fate, *wyrd*. Thus our own highly individualized relations to the superego are bound to inform our interpretations of a poem like *Beowulf*.

The role of psychoanalysis in critical thinking today is largely determined by the ideological drift of other schools: its role is to reassert the value and legitimacy of the individual (whether the author or the reader) as a focus of critical attention and the importance of the unconscious and the irrational in interpretation—and in mental life generally. Psychoanalytic readings of texts, psychobiographies of their authors, and psychohistories of their contexts notwithstanding, however, the greatest contributions of psychoanalysis to literary criticism are probably just the internalization of the simplest Freudian insights—unconscious intention, for example, or the overdetermination, condensation, and displacement of meaning, or art as sublimation. Another obvious example is Harold Bloom's realization that literary influence is not just one poet's having learned from another, like a student from a teacher, but more a matter of the deeply "agonistic" relations of parent and child.

The anxiety of influence is not a matter just for poets. Every reader's relation to a text is similarly complex, if we treat reader response responsibly in light of Freud. The common reader's response is also oedipal to a degree. That is the simple insight I would like to internalize here. Psychologically, the suspension of disbelief is not rational or entirely willing; it is a complicated, spontaneous act of projection and identification. That is where we must start; though in the end, projection and identification will lead us, like the Oedipus complex itself, back to the theory of the superego.

As a genre, epic is involved with the task of superego construction at both the individual and the cultural levels. Freud summarizes: "Strengthening of the superego is a most precious cultural asset in the psychological field. Those in whom it has taken place are turned from being opponents of civilization into being its vehicles" (*Future*, p. 11). That strengthening is one of the tasks of epic, the poetic accompaniment to the birth of civilization.

But the epic cannot discriminate among its audiences: it sets about constructing our superegos as well as its original audience's. So in the case of epic especially, interpretation is likely to express our own invaded psychologies as well as the author's. In this regard, *Beowulf* is an extreme, and therefore an extremely interesting, case.

Why *Beowulf*?

Beowulf has a bad reputation: Woody Allen advises English majors, "Just don't take any course where they make you read *Beowulf*." Despite its foreignness and its difficulty, however, and despite its

funereal obsession with death, *Beowulf* is now commonly taught to
ninth graders, along with the *Iliad* and the *Odyssey*, as if it were an
adventure or fantasy story. This trivialization accounts for some of
the poem's bad reputation, but not all of it.

Beowulf is a hard text. Its language, style, and values seem as distant and strange as those of Homer and the Greek tragedies. Like
them, *Beowulf* opens up a metrical world parallel to our own, different but strangely akin, throwing our ideas and attitudes, some of
them unconscious, into new light. But our kinship with the world of
Beowulf—our perspective in this new light—always remains haunt-
ingly out of focus. Today a good reader of *Beowulf* has to be an expert
time traveler and mystery unraveler—an expert scholar and interpreter; but even so, it remains uncertain what we can learn from the
poem that is not wholly contingent on our own attitudes and beliefs.
It is not at all clear that a "clean" interpretation is possible. This may
be true of all texts to a degree, but again, *Beowulf* is an extreme case.

The poet and his first readers already had something of the same
problem, however. The world of *Beowulf*, set in the heroic past, was
already distant from them, akin to but strangely different from their
Christian Anglo-Saxon world. Between the world of the poem and
the world of its poet lay not only the gulf of meter but the complex transformations, social and psychological, of the development
from tribe to state and of the conversion to Christianity. The relation of the Germanic tribal elements in the poem to Christianity has
always been its most notorious crux and the driving force of its criticism. *Beowulf* is an ethical poem of the Christian Anglo-Saxons, but
its ethics are not Christian, and its hero is not an Anglo-Saxon; so it
is not clear how the poem's ideals might actually have functioned in
the actual world of the audience.

Many scholars meditating on this problem have concluded that
an Anglo-Saxon audience could not have accepted the poem's non-
Christian ("pagan") ideals, so it is commonly argued that the poem's
heroic warrior virtues are actually metaphors for Christian ones.
Lately it is even commonly said that the poem's greatness may lie precisely in the way it subtly undermines those heroic ideals—in effect,
undermines itself. Robert Hanning, for example, argues that the poet
"completely reverses all tendencies toward harmony in heroic history, and offers instead a soured, ironic version of what has gone on

before, embodying a final assessment of a world without God as a world in which time and history are themselves negative concepts" (p. 88). T. A. Shippey claims "that the poet is demonstrating the inadequacy of heroic society; that he sees this the more forcibly for being a Christian; and that his rejection of overt finger-pointing first gives the pleasure of ironic perception, and second shows the glittering insidiousness of heroism, the way it perverts even the best of intentions" (pp. 37–38). The latest major statement of this position is Bernard Huppé's *Hero in the Earthly City*. These are modern readings of *Beowulf*. They are not entirely false, but they are unlikely simplifications, because they still leave many questions unasked.

A few questions I like to ask are these: (1) How do the psychologies of tribal and civilized societies differ? (2) What are the psychological dynamics of the transition from one to the other, and of religious conversion? (3) How and why do we idealize the past? and (4) How do we identify with and internalize a work of literature? In any case, we can assume from the start that *Beowulf* bore a complex, indirect, and nonmimetic relation to any historical reality, including the Anglo-Saxon *ethos* either before or after the conversion.

I have mentioned our kinship with the poem and also the Anglo-Saxons' kinship with it; but then there is a third kinship, ours to the Anglo-Saxons. We still live in a largely Anglo-Saxon world, and even over a millennium the child is father to the man. Different as we have become from the Anglo-Saxons and from each other, in our cultural origins we still sometimes see stark enlargements of our deepest traits, which otherwise now go unobserved—though they have hardly disappeared for all that. The hall may have become the office, its rituals a system of contracted salaries, duties, and taxes, the wars corporate (or even academic); but the relations of such traditionally male-dominated institutions to women, the family, and religion remain as teasingly unresolved as ever and are still the subject of much of our literature. So too the broken oath, the failed promise, the conflict of loyalties, the silent hero, the alienation of the individual from society, and the problematic roles of women and kinship in social life.

These are the great Germanic themes—Germanic, more than biblical or classical. Our modern English-speaking world is indebted to those three traditions equally, and the Germanic leg of this cultural triad is firmly rooted in *Beowulf*. It is perhaps the oldest, most ambitious, and most deeply resonant text in that tradition; it is the nearly inaudible, Germanic *basso profundo* of English and other Germanic literature. For all its Christian elements, it is still our most pregnant Germanic text. *Beowulf* is not just another poem. It seems to lay bare our Germanic, our Anglo-Saxon origins.

But the investigation of our own origins has to be fraught with all the usual perils of self-reflection—nearsightedness first of all, blindness to what is too close; also ambivalence, denial, avoidance, and vague fears of what might be discovered beneath the mask—in short, anxiety and guilt. As a result, *Beowulf* both reveals and disguises some surprisingly familiar structures of our cultured Germanic, Anglo-Saxon, English-speaking minds—our antifeminism, for example, our repression of affect, our materialism, and our denial of death.

This system of relations—of us to *Beowulf*, of *Beowulf* to the Anglo-Saxons, and of the Anglo-Saxons to us—constitutes the meaning of *Beowulf*. There is not much agreement about this meaning, though the poem's best students do like to claim that *Beowulf* is a poem for our day. But it has always been a poem for the day. That is because silence was a positive virtue to the Anglo-Saxons. Thus *Beowulf* (like the Old Testament, but unlike the classical epics) has its deep silences—so much is left unsaid!—in which we can hardly help but read our selves, and out of which we draw our interpretations. Like the sagas, the poem seldom speaks, for example, of its characters' motivations or feelings; so it is easy to assume they are like us, or like our stereotyped ideas of them. Not only speech but heroic behavior is also typically restrained. Behind this restraint, can we assume great passions are being repressed? Which ones? Fear perhaps, hiding behind all its predictably heroic reaction-formations?

Family and economic life are wholly invisible in the poem too; and the poem's attitudes toward women, and toward themes as fundamental as religion and heroism, are famously ambiguous. The poem might be said not to articulate its themes at all, leaving the reader a very wide range of interpretive freedom. Thus the heroic, or the overreaching, or the sinful, or the existential, or the Christian, or the Christlike Beowulf—the folk-Beowulf, the kingly Beowulf, the monastic Beowulf: like *Hamlet*, *Beowulf* supports with its silence whatever reading we most wish, and modern readers seem to wish many things of it.

Interpretation is not a science even in straightforward cases, and *Beowulf* is a rock on which interpretations are easily broken. The history of *Beowulf* scholarship (like Anglo-Saxon scholarship generally) has been a history of the projection of cherished beliefs upon the poem, both individually and collectively. They form the great tradition of Protestant, English, Gothic, pan-Germanic, Romantic, Victorian, and modern readings of Anglo-Saxon culture—a tradition of cherished beliefs that the Anglo-Saxons were really Protestant, or democratic, or noble savages, or Aryan folk, or anxiously self-contradictory existential Christian warriors.

The modern interpretation of *Beowulf* was born in Tolkien's analysis of its martial heroism in 1936, on the eve of World War II: "While the older southern imagination has faded for ever into literary ornament, the northern has power, as it were, to revive its spirit even in our own times. It can work, even as it did work with the *goðlauss* viking, without gods: martial heroism as its own end. But we may remember that the poet of *Beowulf* saw clearly: the wages of heroism is death" (p. 77). This is in fact a very wise—and very modern—interpretation, one that genuinely makes *Beowulf* a poem for Tolkien's day; only three years later the great ship-burial at Sutton Hoo was exhumed and immediately reburied to protect it from the Nazis. Tolkien was not in a position to romanticize Germanic heroism or to trivialize it. To him the poem's theme is obvious: the poet saw clearly that the wages of heroism is death. One could say just as easily, however, that the poet saw clearly that the wages of heroism is victory, or glory, or peace.

Unbelievably, only a half-century later, Tolkien's Christian existentialism, which has served so many interpretations well and which is so moving in itself, looks almost sentimental to postmodern eyes, like Churchill's posturing. Tolkien's own fiction is in some measure responsible for the reduction of *Beowulf* to adolescent literature. We await a postmodern *Beowulf*; for surely, poised between holocausts as we sometimes feel ourselves to be, our more complete disillusionment is bound to discover itself in those same poetic silences even more forcefully.

This book does not deliver a postmodern *Beowulf*. My theme, the origins of civilization, is Freudian in spirit and therefore distinctly old-fashioned in the postmodern climate. By the suspicious totalization "civilization" I mean a stage in social evolution characterized by cities as well as by literacy, statutory law, and civil government—as opposed to an earlier stage characterized by villages, orality, revenge, customary law, and kinship structures. These are well-worn anthropological concepts, still useful since Freud's day, though they will never be precise enough to resist philosophical attack, because the development from one stage to the other involves large and complex areas of overlap. But is it necessarily reductive or essentialist to define such structures contingently, within the numberless historical accidents we call a society, or the ceaseless flow we call history? Must it always be mean-spirited, patronizing, or romantic to explore the otherness of tribal societies still struggling on the margins of civilization, or explore, as in this case, the deepest roots of our own civilization?

For in our generation we have witnessed this other holocaust too: civilization's eradication of tribal societies everywhere. We are bound to mourn this loss forever. We share this mourning with the *Beowulf* poet, and it is one of our deepest ties to the poem. For now especially, in this generation, the relation of civilizations to the "primitive" societies that preceded them, and from which they developed, remains an urgent issue in the great tradition of Montaigne, Rousseau, and Freud. My focus is the transition in England. For the English-speaking world, and for much of the rest of the world too now, Anglo-Saxon England, along with early Greece and ancient Israel, was one of those formative stages determining the direction of future development. It remains one of our earliest cultural memories, traces of which can still be found deeply embedded in the present.

Interestingly, the Anglo-Saxons themselves, like the Greeks and the Jews before them, once they entered into the stream of civilization, were immediately obsessed with their own origins, with the transition they had just endured. *Beowulf* was not written in the heroic past but about it, and in particular about the trauma of its loss. In large part the poem creates that heroic past retroactively, thematizing cultural origins and the transition to civilization. Like the Pentateuch, and like Homer and the Greek tragedies, *Beowulf* and many of its companion poems in Old English dwell on the origins of civilization, mourning the loss of the prehistoric tribal past, now redefined as a heroic age. This mournful obsession defines the heroic, the epic, and the elegiac generally, and the Anglo-Saxon case with special clarity.

More than my theme is Freudian in spirit. I too am affected, as I think through this mournful obsession, attempt to re-create the audience's psychological relations to that imaginary heroic world, and experience their identification with those consoling idealizations of what has been lost. Criticism too has its psychological component: the greatest inhibitions to interpretation, in literature as well as life, seem to me to be psychological before they are philosophical, and they are barely open to "critical" discussion at all because they occur at the personal (and often unconscious) level, even if collectively. These are the inhibitions Freud called projection, resistance, and transference and countertransference.

I have already mentioned *projection* as a special problem in reading Old English poetry because of the ethical value the Anglo-Saxons placed on silence, as well as our unconscious *resistance* to perceptions that pose a threat to us. *Transference* and *countertransference* are more specifically psychoanalytic terms. The first refers to the projections of the analysand upon the silent analyst; the second refers to the limitations placed on analysis by the analyst's own neuroses, which necessarily cloud and distort interpretation unless he or she is aware of them. That is why the analyst must be analyzed. Countertransference is the specific mechanism of projection and resistance in the psychoanalyst, but the concept might easily be extended to interpretation in general.

In short, who we are means quite a lot to our interpretations, and the best we can do is account for ourselves every step of the way. In this regard, the neuroses I bring to *Beowulf* are neither religious or heroic; but scholarship has its own neuroses, so it might be pertinent here to report two recent dreams.

Falling asleep recently while thinking about *Beowulf*, I dreamt of a sphinx, not quite buried in the desert sand; in fact, no matter how hard I tried to bury it, one eye always remained uncovered. The sphinx is *Beowulf*, of course, but it is also my superego. I take this as a good sign.

I had the second dream the night before delivering a conference paper on the poem. I dreamt about a little girl who had a fascinating, unusual doll, every part of which—arms, legs, head, torso—seemed to be made from other dolls, all of different colors and proportions. I knew where it had come from: the little girl's brother had collected all the old, broken dolls he could find around the neighborhood, and he had loaded them into his red wagon and pulled them home behind his bicycle; then he had made a single doll out of all their parts, and had given it to his little sister. Far from thinking it was junk, she thought it was beautiful and loved it—first of all because it was unlike any other doll, yet like them all; also because it was so interesting, and because her brother had made it for her and made it so well.

The doll, of course, is *Beowulf*; I am the little girl, and the poet is her brother. In the construction and meaning of the doll may be seen something of my understanding of the poem's genesis, and the relation of its traditions to its originality. Perhaps because I first studied *Beowulf* while also reading Lévi-Strauss, in the dream I represent the poet as a *bricoleur*. When I sleep, it seems, I am still a structuralist.

So I am the little girl; but the dream is in the third person, because I am also the brother, piecing together (like the poet) my own *bricolage*, my effigy of *Beowulf* constructed from past scholarship; and you are the sister I am trying to please. In scholarship as in poetry, practice tells me, originality is still mostly *bricolage*, a new and loving reconstruction of the materials we have inherited from the past. Among other things, the dream tells me that as a scholar I do not identify so much with the hero of the poem as with the poet and with others who have made this identification. I take this as a good sign too.

My double identification in the dream, with both the girl and her brother, illustrates certain features of identification—its shifting ambivalence and overdetermination—which will be important in our interpretation of the poem. The most important of these features is that insofar as I am a reader of *Beowulf* I identify with the girl, but insofar as my reading is itself a creative act, I identify with her brother the artist. This is how overdetermination works.

Actually, the situation is much more complex than that, the images more overdetermined; for the characters in the dream are clearly modeled on my wife and her older brother (she was my *Beowulf* student, he is a craftsman), as well as my earliest memories of me and my own older brother (an inveterate scavenger with his red wagon). My scholarship is never entirely free of even the most intimate themes of my life. Enough said about that.

Like the poem, then, the dream is richly overdetermined and deeply ambivalent. In fact, the neatness of all this splitting makes me think that my ambivalence itself is probably the dream's latent thought, and that *Beowulf* has unconsciously become a symbol of it for me. Thus the ambivalent image of the poem itself: it is only a junk-doll, but a unique, beautiful, and meaningful one.

The dream also brings rather delicate problems of gender to consciousness. *Beowulf* is a markedly antifeminist poem, and making it a gift to the little girl is my attempt at compensation, though necessarily condescending: she is still being strongly marginalized, after all. I do not see any way around that, since the poem so strongly marginalizes the female reader already. My simultaneous identification with her, however, indicates my deep ambivalence about the patriarchal project of the poem and the patriarchal project of its criticism (not to mention the patriarchal structures of professional life, teaching, and marriage). Beyond that, moreover, the bond of love between her and her brother, both of whom I identify with strongly, though in different ways, indicates how far from such ideological criticism my personal responses to the poem really are.

The fulfilled wish of the dream is the harmony of opposites, *concordia discors*. Pursued long enough, the analysis would come to rest in the thought that although I am a child, I am also a parent—a form of the original oedipal paradox: What walks on four legs in the morning, two in the afternoon, and three at night? Much unresolvable conflict and ambivalence is harmonized in the manifest dream, and the junk-doll *Beowulf* is an overdetermined symbol of this harmony.

The ease with which the problem of understanding *Beowulf*, more than other poems, shades into the problem of understanding myself suggests to me (naturally) that the high indeterminacy of the poem provokes strong psychological responses which may well be a clue to its *raison d'être*. Just such an indeterminacy in the Greek tragedies seems intended to provoke catharsis. What does *Beowulf* intend for us in this way? If the overdetermined symbols and vast silences of the poem function like the silence of the analyst, the poem will function as a screen for our projections, which can be manipulated by the plot and predictably drawn toward resolution.

Identification of one sort or another is essential. Our relations to poetry are always highly personal. Even Keats's negative capability is only the heightened ability to make identifications without the interference of transference and countertransference. When statements about art claim to be impersonal, objective, and scientific, we are probably in the presence of resistance. The compulsion to objectivity is both a denial of affect and an exaggerated claim of importance—"my thought, my theory, my method is universal, ultimate, transcendental"—two sides of the same neurotic coin. There is still a lot of positivistic and rationalistic scholarship being produced about *Beowulf*, in a spirit of resistance to the more modest and self-effacing claims of both modernism and postmodernism.

I am finally coming to see the necessity and the value of what Bloom calls a "strong misreading." Thus objectivity is not exactly the goal of my interpretation; objectivity is not what is left when the psychological inhibitions to interpretation are finally overcome. *Disillusionment* strikes me as a more useful, less impersonal concept. This disillusionment is not necessarily negative or morbid; like the reality principle, it is an agent of the ego, something close to an active psychological force. Perhaps it is a version of Freud's death instinct, progressing naturally, though against resistance, from infant narcissism to the bier. Perhaps it would be more comforting to think of it in Socratic terms as the humility that naturally comes with self-knowledge.

Not surprisingly, the silences of *Beowulf* seem to me symptomatic, or proleptic, of even these latest developments in our cultural and personal histories. I see *Beowulf* as an artful, cagey, and defensive last stand against disillusionment with both heroism and religion; affirming and denying the comforts of both those illusions at the same time; post-heroic, Christian but secular. That is not the same as saying that the poem undermines its own ideals, though: ambivalence is not the same as ambiguity. Ambivalence is a psychological term pointing to the attitudes, conscious or unconscious, of the author and the audience, as well as to the poem. Ambiguity is a hermeneutic problem involving the critical faculties. Ambivalence, on the other hand, is a vicissitude of the passions, requiring a certain amount of disillusionment for its appreciation. This is one of the qualities ninth graders do not bring to *Beowulf*.

I suspect that behind the silence and restraint of Germanic heroism there are indeed great passions being repressed, and that there is therefore great ambivalence. The elegies, especially "The Wanderer" and "The Wife's Lament," tell me so.

> I know for a fact
> in an earl it is always a noble habit
> to seal fast the breast's locker,
> the heart's coffer, think what he may.
> The weary mind cannot withstand fate,
> or a troubled spirit be of assistance.
> Eager for glory then, often the dreary
> he binds fast in his breast's coffer.
>
> ("The Wanderer," ll. 11–18)

The Wanderer's psychology is neither Christian nor Roman, nor even consistent. It is easy enough to understand the masculine, stoic, "noble" impulse to lock sorrow away in the silence of the heart, to repress it; it is more difficult to understand that doing so might actually cure the troubled spirit. To the Wanderer, the mind is only weary if its weariness is spoken, but he is certainly a bad advertisement for this assumption. As in the other elegies, his hoarding of language in silence is overfilled and broken even as it is being described and affirmed. Readers cannot decide, therefore, whether the Wanderer is at peace or in despair, whether he awaits God's grace or has already achieved it, or gains it in the course of speaking—or whether the conflicting attitudes in the poem can even belong to a single voice. The poet could have made such issues plain, but rather he invites these questions, perhaps because he cannot answer them, perhaps because he cannot even ask them. We are thrust into his ambivalence regarding them as soon as we accept the irreducibility of the poem to a set of true or untrue statements. Strong arguments for any one of the interpretations I have listed are to some extent, then, projections of the reader's own attitudes, various rationalizations of the same provocative inkblot. And *Beowulf* presents us with an even greater screen than "The Wanderer" on which to project our fears, desires, and ambivalences.

Hero to Hero

A year after the essay that is now Chapter 4 first appeared in *Psychiatry*, Colin Chase reviewed it in the *Old English Newsletter*: "Despite his claim that psychoanalytic anthropology is both 'universal and particular,' Earl is quick to dismiss particular literary problems if they clash with his general theory. Having classified Beowulf as an 'ego ideal,' for example, Earl dismisses the question of whether Beowulf's behavior at the end of the poem is in fact ideal as being 'beside the point' " (p. 96). I would like to answer this criticism by considering the psychoanalytic relationship between the two heroes Beowulf and Byrhtnoth (hero of "The Battle of Maldon") in some detail. The conceit of this argument will be that Byrhtnoth represents the epic's intended audience, so we might explore his identification with Beowulf as a sort of thought-experiment.

I like to imagine Byrhtnoth as a reader of *Beowulf*. I even like to imagine *Beowulf* inspiring the English at the Battle of Maldon, as Henry Adams (in *Mont-St.-Michel and Chartres*, following William of Malmesbury and Wace) liked to imagine the *Chanson de Roland* inspiring the Normans at the Battle of Hastings. It makes a certain sense, even if it never happened. For all we know, *Beowulf* was written after the Battle of Maldon and was influenced by it. For all we know, *Beowulf* never had any readers at all. But even these possibilities do not detract from the interest of our thought-experiment: how might Byrhtnoth have read *Beowulf*? Not in the sense of W. F. Bolton's question, how Alcuin might have interpreted *Beowulf*; but in psychoanalytic terms, what would the structure of Byrhtnoth's identification with the epic hero have been?

Identification with the hero is not a simple matter, considered philosophically or psychologically. The hero is an idealization, and both idealization and identification are complex areas of psychoanalytic theory (see, for example, Loewald, Schafer, Smith, Wolheim, Chasseguet-Smirgel, and Borch-Jacobsen). What exactly is the hero an idealization of? Do I identify with him as a representation of my ego?—or what I would like to be, or what I should be, or even (the possibilities are endless) what I most fear or hate? What if the hero, like God, were an idealized parent figure, with all the conflicted feelings *that* could involve? These and other questions suggest themselves. Nor is there any reason the possibilities should not be mixed; as in my dream of the *Beowulf* doll, so with mental representations generally: overdetermination is the rule.

Earlier we defined identification roughly as a failure or refusal to distinguish the self from an object. But which part of the self is being extended in this way, the id, the ego, or the superego? And most important, what results are brought about by such identifications, especially with a literary character? My first thought is that whereas the tragedy aims at relieving, in its oddly negative way, certain feelings in the audience temporarily—like a laxative—the epic is more positively ambitious: it aims at structuring and reinforcing prevailing social relations by creating and maintaining certain shared attitudes in the audience. Identification is the means to this end, but it is indirect and complex; it is certainly not a matter of encouraging everyone in the audience to imitate the hero—for what kind of society would that be?

According to Aristotle, the epic hero (Achilles) is flawed like the tragic hero (Oedipus). The flawed hero—an idealization conspicuously short of ideal in some regard—presents special problems of identification. Our identification implicates us in the hero's flaw and the guilt that it symbolizes. Certainly in the case of the tragic hero, who is being conspicuously punished by the gods for his *hamartia*, identification with him either produces, or is produced by, feelings of guilt in ourselves, the audience. The death of the hero with whom we have identified then brings cathartic relief from these feelings in the form of self-punishment. To some extent at least, we go to the tragedy to punish ourselves and feel the better for it.

I have always resisted the common notion that Beowulf has such a tragic flaw, because I do not want to confuse epic with tragedy or encourage the elucidation of this flaw as the aim of criticism; but Beowulf and Byrhtnoth do raise questions of this sort. There is an especially puzzling contradiction encoded in the Anglo-Saxon version (perhaps the Germanic version generally) of the heroic ideal and in our responses to it. In both *Beowulf* and "The Battle of Maldon" this contradiction appears as a suicidal logic of unresolvable conflicts, complete with easy rationalizations of unarticulated ambivalence. These rationalizations ("the conflict of loyalties," or "Christian versus Germanic," for example) have been the traditional subject of literary criticism, so here we must take a non-psychoanalytic detour.

If we come to *Beowulf* primarily through its Germanic background, we tend to see Beowulf's fateful decision to face the dragon alone as exemplary of Germanic heroism; the dragon evokes the Midgarth-serpent, an apocalyptic symbol of fatality itself. On the other hand, if we come to the poem from a Christian angle, we tend to find Christian wisdom in it; the dragon is a symbol of *malitia*, evoking the Beast of the Apocalypse, and Beowulf's defeat is a flawed moral action: he is brought low in the end by his pride and avarice. Which is only to say, perhaps, that from a Christian point of view, Germanic heroism looks a lot like a combination of pride and avarice.

Whatever our perspective, the result of Beowulf's fateful decision is the same: his people, vigorously berated for abandoning him in the hour of his greatest need (though he did insist on going alone, didn't he?), are certain to be destroyed also, now that he is dead. The messenger predicts,

> So shall the spear be
> many a morning cold fast in fist,
> upheld in hand, no sound of harp
> to wake warriors, but the wan raven
> chattering eagerly over the doomed,
> telling the eagle how he and the wolf
> gulped their food as they stripped the dead.
>
> (ll. 3025–31)

After this grim prophecy, Wiglaf delivers his terse summary judgment:

> Often for the will of one, many an earl
> suffers punishment: so it happened to us.
>
> (ll. 3077–78)

But is this moral judgment, or simple wisdom? The first clause reads like an Old English maxim, almost as matter-of-fact as "frost shall freeze" or "a king shall be on the throne." It is difficult to believe that Wiglaf is actually criticizing the dead Beowulf here; but it is just as difficult to understand how this could not amount to criticism, especially of a king. Did Beowulf insist on going against the dragon alone, or did his men abandon him? Is his heroism exemplary or cautionary? Is the dragon evil, or is the hero cursed for opening the hoard? Is Beowulf wise, over the hill, kingly, proud, or foolish? As with "The Wanderer," the meaning is very much of our making.

"The Battle of Maldon" comes with a similar wrinkle. Byrhtnoth's *ofermod* is either "great courage" or "overweening pride," depending on your attitude (and your glossary) — much as the word "pride" today has two morally opposed meanings, as a secular virtue and a religious vice. *Ofermod* may be the sin of Satan in the poem "Genesis," but it is difficult to accuse Byrhtnoth of that. After all, "Maldon"'s famous climactic wisdom (again in maxim form), which no one has ever thought to criticize, is *mod sceall þe mare* — "*mod* must be the more." But then again, is Byrhtnoth not responsible for the lives of his men? Does he not condemn them by the heroic code's expectation that a warrior will fight to the death when his lord has fallen? This in spite of Rosemary Woolf's demonstration that there is no Germanic tradition of suicidal battle: the ethic of suicidal heroism is so powerful in "Maldon" precisely because it is freely chosen. Even in the eleventh century the Anglo-Saxon army was motivated by appealing to local ties of lordship rather than national loyalties (see Abels). Could not Byrhtnoth's men also have complained, "Often for the will of one, many an earl / suffers punishment: so it happened to us"?

The two cases are different, of course. Whereas Beowulf is an entirely fictional character, Byrhtnoth's action is historical and not just literary — though to what extent we will never know. Since Byrhtnoth is a literary hero as well, it is hard to know how to proceed with this thought. It is hard to know if the anachronisms in the poem belong to the hero or the poet. Both "The Battle of Maldon" and *Beowulf* are composed in an archaic style, including an archaic social structure and code of behavior. Did Byrhtnoth really have a *comitatus* like an ancient Germanic warlord? Did tenth-century soldiers really feel the force of the heroic code defined by Tacitus nine hundred years before?

Well, yes and no, in the postheroic, prefeudal tenth century; but to understand Germanic heroism in whatever form it takes, we must always start by going back to Tacitus for the ideal. His famous formula has not yet yielded all its secrets.

> It is shameful for the lord to be excelled in valor, shameful for his companions not to match the valor of the lord. Furthermore, it is shocking and disgraceful for all of one's life to have survived one's lord and left the battle: the prime obligation of the companions' allegiance is to protect and guard him and to credit their own brave deeds to his glory: the lord fights for victory, the companions for the lord. . . .

Banquets and provisions serve as pay. The wherewithal for generosity
is obtained through war and plunder. (p. 47)

This passage illuminates quite brightly the problem I am raising in
our poems, the contradiction in the Germanic heroic code. The heroism of Wiglaf and of Byrhtnoth's companions is self-evident, set as
it is in high relief against the flight of others. Their heroism is essentially their obedience—faithfulness to their oath, willingness to die
for their lord, no matter what the cause, no matter how hopeless.
Byrhtnoth's men die for him and for honor, not for the king, or for
England, or Christendom; and their more immediate loyalty (*treow*),
which seems to be the chief point of the narrative, is certainly offered
as exemplary.

But how do we judge the behavior and the heroism of Beowulf and
Byrhtnoth themselves? Their valor and generosity—the only lordly
virtues mentioned by Tacitus—are not in question. It is not their
fortitudo but their *sapientia* we doubt. On this subject Tacitus is curi-
ously silent, as are our poems. The "literary problem"—in Chase's
words, "whether Beowulf's behavior at the end of the poem is in
fact ideal"—reflects a problem in the heroic ideal itself and cannot be
solved.

The most Tacitus offers by way of a motive for lordly heroism
is victory, in the pregnant formula, "The lord fights for victory,
the companions for the lord." Perhaps if we could hold on to this
thought, we could still charge our heroes with entering battle with
something other than victory in mind (Pride! Avarice!). But in this
little formula, "The lord fights for victory, the companions for the
lord," we can see the deeper problem of Germanic heroism: there are
two heroic codes, one for the lord and one for his companions; and
whereas the ethical principles pertaining to the latter are perfectly
clear, even to Christians, no principle at all is educed to explain why
a lord fights—except to win, to prove his valor, and to acquire the
wealth needed to pay his men. No wonder it looked like pride and
avarice to Christians. Even Tacitus saw the self-perpetuating circu-
larity of violence in the structure of Germanic society, for which war
was an economic system requiring valor and obedience, but not necessarily nobility of purpose.

Nevertheless, the ideal of the obedient thegn prohibits criticism or contradiction of the lord, no matter what—with the result that lordly heroism, in poetry and life, could operate in relative freedom from ethical constraints. Though we would like to derive a consistent code of honor from the behavior of Beowulf and Byrhtnoth, Gunnar and Njal, Sigemund and Sigurth, the most important trait they all share is that like Greek tragic heroes they resist such criticism and analysis. In both our poems the result of this lordly freedom is suicidal annihilation—which pushy Christians like Alcuin might fairly interpret as a moral judgment, but which seems rather to operate more like a law of physics in the secular world of the poems. Heroic action is emphatically not practical action; nor is it necessarily imitable or even ethical, much less moral. Most important, no one tells the hero what to do; he *knows* what to do—and who is to gainsay it?

Now we may return to our psychoanalytic argument. The sort of idealization I have been describing, one that demands obedience and resists criticism—requiring, that is, the submission of the ego— is well known to psychoanalysis. In *Group Psychology and the Analysis of the Ego* Freud analyzed the military as a typical group and connected it to his "scientific myth" of the ur-group, the "primal horde." In the primitive family, according to this myth, the father tyrannizes his sons, who eventually join together to kill him. Thereafter, their shared guilt for this primal crime holds the group together; that is, the dead father is not really eliminated but is internalized in the members of the group as a tyrannical voice of authority, the ego ideal or superego.

The theory has its problems, to put it mildly; but interpreting it has become something of a glamour area for criticism (see, for example, Freeman; Girard; Badcock; Chasseguet-Smirgel, pp. 76–93; and Borch-Jacobsen). For Freud it was a way of illustrating the relations between the Oedipus complex and group psychology. His conclusion, that "the group appears to us as a revival of the primal horde" (p. 116), lets us take his account of the horde simply as a metaphoric description of strong groups: "A primary group . . . is a number of individuals who have put one and the same object in the place of their ego ideal and have consequently identified themselves with one another in their egos" (p. 125). This insight hardly depends upon the myth.

The myth goes on to suggest (pp. 88–89) that it is the epic poet who first forged the collective ego ideal, in the form of the hero—which is to say, apropos of our argument, that the hero is defined by the audience's shared guilt in relation to him. The heroic ideal, then, is not simply a model of excellence or virtue to be imitated but is also a forbidden and unattainable desire, highly defended against, sharply distinguished from the ego itself, and highly critical of it.

Mutually exclusive as these two descriptions sound, the superego is definitively both at the same time. "Its relation to the ego," Freud writes, "is not exhausted by the precept: 'You *ought to be* like this (like your father).' It also comprises the prohibition: 'You *may not be* like this (like your father)—that is, you may not do all that he does; some things are his prerogative'" (*The Ego and the Id*, p. 34). At the behavioral level, the result of this quite normal ambivalence is a guilt-ridden obedience to the ideal. In a warrior society, where obedience must be instilled as a cardinal virtue, this effect can be amplified by the construction of an artificial superego, to be shared by the group. This is the sort of ideal we are identifying with in the epic hero—or rather, we are identifying with each other in our egos, by means of our shared identification with him as our common superego. Two sorts of identification are involved. Regarding the latter especially, we must not forget that "identification, in fact, is ambivalent from the very first" (*Group Psychology*, p. 95); so the idealization of the hero, which frees him from criticism, is accompanied by self-criticism among his followers—and the audience.

Thus the faithful Wiglaf's speech excoriating the unfaithful companions is not anticlimactic after Beowulf's death, nor is the messenger's speech prophesying the nation's extinction. These speeches have the effect of chastising the audience, whose shared guilt in relation to the hero, it turns out, is one of the most important bonds holding the warrior society together, since it is the basis for the identification of the members of the group with each other. And thus also, Wiglaf's implicit criticism of the hero ("Often for the will of one . . .") remains only implicit. Its restraint, which to us seems an uninterpretable ambiguity, actually masks his (and our) ambivalence toward the hero.

Because the hero is an ideal of this sort, however, he is invulnerable to our criticism. He need not be exemplary to retain his authority. The endless debate over whether Beowulf behaves correctly at the end of the poem is thus beside the point—because consciously at least, we are expected to identify our ego with the thegnly, not the lordly, hero. Our identification with the lordly hero as superego will remain largely unconscious, like so much of the superego's activity, and to that extent be felt only as anxiety or guilt. Prufrock was right after all: "No! I am not Prince Hamlet, nor was meant to be; / Am an attendant lord."

The hero's invulnerability to criticism—including our criticism— has behavioral and psychological repercussions within the poem and critical repercussions for us. Just as we detected two sorts of hero- ism in Tacitus's account, Freud discovered two psychologies in his account of the group: "From the first there were two kinds of psy- chologies, that of the individual members of the group and that of the father, chief, or leader. The members of the group were subject to ties just as we see them today, but the father of the primal horde was free. His intellectual acts were strong and independent even in isolation, and his will needed no reinforcement from others" (*Group Psychology*, p. 125). For some reason, *Beowulf* criticism has chosen not to respond to this heroic freedom but to respond instead to the group ties, as if they applied to the hero as well. So critics are always passing judgment on Beowulf, good or bad, which the poet and his world would probably have found presumptuous and irrelevant.

It is easy to see the social function of such an ideal of heroic free- dom, for it corresponds not only to fatherhood but also lordship in the real world. In the late tenth century, warriors like Byrhtnoth were eldermen, officials of the king's government, responsible for the well-being of large areas of England. It was obviously in their inter- est to promote the principle that although the lord is responsible *for* those below him, he is not responsible *to* them. It was to an audience of warrior-aristocrats like Byrhtnoth and his men that heroic poetry was traditionally addressed. This audience certainly promoted this concept generally, in an effort to keep society tightly bound to them by vows of unquestioning obedience.

Most men in this audience, being of the thegnly class, would have identified with Beowulf in the first part of the poem, insofar as he is an utterly exemplary thegn. Beowulf serves both Hygelac and Hroth- gar faithfully, without any ambition to supplant or even succeed them, and totally without consideration of their conspicuous faults. But in the last part of the poem, this audience would probably have shifted their identification—at least in part—to Wiglaf, who comes to occupy the position of the faithful retainer. Beowulf himself, then, at the end of the poem, is a representation not of the ego but the superego—inspiring, but terrifying in his heroic freedom and superiority; revealing by his very existence our inadequacy, and punishing us for our inability to be like him. (Christianity has its own language for the same thought.)

When we consider Byrhtnoth in particular as the audience, the situation is complicated by the fact that he is at once both thegn to King Ethelred and lord to his own men. Thus insofar as he is the king's man, he too would shift his identification toward the faithful Wiglaf. The lesson that you defend your lord at all costs, without judging him, had some relevance in the reign of Ethelred the Unready; it has a special self-defeating urgency in the reign of any bad king, when criticism is most tempting. *But it is never your place to criticize your lord*: for by definition that would amount to challenging his lordship, and thus lordship generally, including your own. Unquestioning obedience is essential to the system.

It is not so simple, of course, not to criticize a bad king: "Be Kent unmannerly when Lear is mad!" Byrhtnoth has something of the same problem as Kent, perhaps, and his devotion to the *ideal* of the king could easily be interpreted as criticism of the reality. Accordingly, the focal question in "Maldon" scholarship seems recently to have become whether Byrhtnoth's action praises or criticizes Ethelred. Wiglaf too has something of the same problem: he can help his king only by disobeying him. "Wait on the hill, it's not your adventure," Beowulf had said (ll. 2529–31). Thus Byrhtnoth's identification with Wiglaf would have led him to the excruciating outer limits of the ideal of obedience, where it becomes heroic by becoming its opposite.

But insofar as Byrhtnoth himself is a lord, he would also maintain his identification directly with the hero, right through to the end of the poem. That is, his identification would become split—much as in my dream I was able to identify simultaneously with both the girl and her brother, though in different ways. In fact, it is this doubleness of vision in the poem that lay behind the doubleness of the dream; the repeated splitting of identification in the poem became associated in the dream with other nodes of ambivalence, like child-parent, male-female, passive-dominant, and self-other. These may not be neatly parallel, but they all reflect the theme of my individuality in relation to the determining structures of history and society—that is, the relation of the ego to the superego.

(Now suddenly I can see the most surprising, and therefore perhaps the most important meaning of the dream. Not only do I identify with the boy and the girl, but there is a third, more infantile, identification as well. Like the doll, I too am "unlike any other, and yet like them all"—a unique individual as well as a typical member of the group. Insofar as I identify with the doll, then the boy and girl naturally represent my parents. I watch my own children play out their family romances like this with their dolls every day.)

The problem of our individuality in relation to the group cannot be solved; the contradictory relation of our freedom to necessity is a problem that cannot be solved; the ego's relation to the superego is destined to be ambivalent. These are antinomies we learn to live with. Not fortuitously, this lesson is an epic as well as tragic theme, and thus a deep theme in *Beowulf*, which is a hymn to the individual hero as much as to the group he belongs to—and which he transcends, at least in desire. Insofar as I wish to be autonomous (and this wish is indestructible, being infantile)—that is, insofar as I actually wish to *be* the superego rather than be governed by it—I will identify (perhaps unconsciously) with the hero himself; but insofar as I must always remain an agent of history, I will retain my conscious identification with the loyal thegn. The end result is guilt, the fuel of obedience. Christianity could only have clarified and deepened this already amplified dynamic.

At the Battle of Maldon Byrhtnoth stumbled into one of those rare moments of lordship's terrible responsibility, when even in his highly codified world he was free actually to choose between desperate alternatives, to fight or not, to die or not, to commit his men to death or spare their lives, to dare to be more valorous and heroic even than the king. In his freedom, Byrhtnoth could identify with Beowulf himself. That secret infantile wish came true: in the most crucial moment of his life, he finally got to become the superego.

What kind of behavior would such a thrilling identification recommend? What could Byrhtnoth learn from Beowulf? Be generous, be valorous; not much beyond that. It is true that a code of honor, minimal, contradictory, and extremely subtle, can be deduced from heroic poetry. It is seldom articulated, though, because its first rules seem to be silence and restraint. It is a Hemingway heroism of power, generosity, valor, restraint, *treow*, revenge—and occasionally the nobility of spirit to forgo revenge. But this loose, unformulated code provides little guidance at the heroic moment, when unresolvable conflicts arise and a decision must be made, when responsibility and power fall to you. When you are the hero, there is no one to tell you what to do.

In epic, this heroism is usually tested against death, because the real issue of heroic behavior is how to engage necessity with freedom. Epics as diverse as *Beowulf*, *Njalssaga*, and *The Nibelungenlied*, as well as the ancient cycle of poems in the *Edda*, all offer us primarily models of heroic dying. It might fairly be said that in identifying with these heroes Byrhtnoth could have learned little else than how to die well—that is, how to embrace his fate freely and without fear. Students of Freud may wonder at this point how the hero, if he really represents the superego, could actually die. This harsh backlash of the idealization is symptomatically Anglo-Saxon: even the ideal submits to necessity and goes down in this world. Freud always assumed anyway that the id, ego, and superego have buried alliances in the unconscious.

What could Byrhtnoth have learned from *Beowulf*, then, except to plunge toward death against all odds, without the interference of complicating practical or moral considerations? As Beowulf had said to his companions, " 'It's not your adventure,/ nor any man's measure but mine alone' " (ll. 2531–32). As the French said of the Charge of the Light Brigade, "*C'est magnifique, mais ce n'est pas la guerre.*" But as readers—and as thegnly readers at that, most of us—ours is not to reason why. The forms of identification these poems invite from us do not invite us to question whether Beowulf and Byrhtnoth behaved correctly or not. Rather, they invite us—try to coerce us—into an identification with our fellows and an unquestioning obedience to the hero's authority.

In the current critical climate "The Battle of Maldon," even more than *Beowulf*, is a sitting duck for disquieted critics unwilling to obey or admire this authority; it is a preposterous, excessive illustration of the self-destructive contradictions built into the Anglo-Saxon male master discourse. The feminine is entirely absent from the poem. How I have wished for an image like the one in the medieval battle in Eisenstein's *Alexander Nevsky*, when the women appear in the night after the battle, walking with their lamps among their slain husbands, sons, and fathers in the icy landscape, a tender pathetic critique of male heroism—not so much valkyries as victims. I see the next generation of critics holding up their lamps to the carnage at Maldon, asking "Why?" and expecting no good answer. The poem's literary values will be irrelevant to such an ideological critique. The poem's coercive, patriarchal demands will fall on deaf ears. Byrhtnoth, we are bound to be told, richly deserved what he got. And those who are still inexplicably moved by the frightening psychodynamics of heroism, the masculine forces at work in heroic literature, will find there is no satisfactory reply to these charges. Nonetheless, on the anniversary of the battle's millennium I am moved to praise the hero one last time:

> O Byrhtnoth, better had you died in bed,
> Than your descendants in a thousand years
> Should scorn that white, heroic, severed head:
> For who among your judges are your peers?

The Riddle of *Beowulf*

I must admit, however, that my interpretation of *Beowulf* and its effects on the audience sits rather uneasily with my own individuality and my own resentful attitudes toward authority. The oedipal failure the poem tries to enforce is intended to socialize us into a radically authoritarian world. It is balanced, thank goodness, by the spectacle of the hero's awesome, if unobtainable, freedom. This freedom may choose to express itself traditionally, but it is still freedom, feeding our most infantile desires even as it punishes us for them. For the reader-as-critic, like us, caught in the poem's thoroughgoing ambivalence, this freedom is the hero's and the poem's freedom from all our reductive interpretations, and their freedom from our demands that they be simpler or other than they are.

One would think modern, if not postmodern, readers would be interested in this freedom from criticism, but no. Not content with stressing the hero's traditionality, his allegiance to established values,

or his role as an ethical or moral example, *Beowulf* criticism has pro-
ceeded to reduce even the poet to a cultural vector field as well. This
common attitude to the poem amounts to a two-pronged attack on
its most real authority, the autonomy and authenticity of its author,
who created the hero and (as Freud put it) "had in this way set himself free from the group in his imagination." "At bottom," Freud
concludes of the epic poet, "this hero is no one but himself" (*Group
Psychology*, p. 88). Recent advances in oral theory do not dissuade me
of this, at least in the case of *Beowulf*, this most original poem with
its invented hero.

The Oedipus complex tempts us to parricide, but that is not its
best resolution! Criticism, having too little interest in our unconscious response to the poem, has set out to kill off both the hero and
the poet in revenge for their power and superiority. In trying to fulfill
this wish, criticism only rebels against the poem's authoritarian intentions like an adolescent, declaring itself victor prematurely. But you
can't fool the superego. The poem will survive all our depredations.

And now I see the meaning of my dream of the sphinx whose eye
could not be covered. The sphinx is, as I knew immediately, the riddle
of *Beowulf*, and the eye is the ever-observant, omniscient superego.
They are identified in such a way that the poem looks down through
the ages to criticize me, even as I am in the act of criticizing it. My
criticism seems, at least when I am asleep, only like so much sand
heaved futilely against the truth.

But I am scholar enough to have a second, reflexive association
with the sphinx, whose riddle is of course the riddle of Oedipus, the
riddle whose answer is Man. I did not yet understand, when I had
the dream, that my reading of *Beowulf* could be largely determined by
oedipal themes—as I have come to discover. Not only is the reader's
relation to the author always oedipal to a degree, in the sense that
Bloom suggests; but in the case of *Beowulf* the poem invites a meditation on the unconscious themes of our own individual and cultural
origins—invites it with that same silence of the psychoanalyst, who
allows us to relive and reformulate our own oedipal dramas, but
consciously this time, by loudly plucking the deepest chords of ambivalence within us.

Reference Matter

References

Abels, Richard. *Lordship and Miltary Obligation in Anglo-Saxon England.* Berkeley: University of California Press, 1988.

Aristotle. *On Poetry and Style.* Trans. G. M. A. Grube. Indianapolis, Ind.: Bobbs-Merrill, 1958.

Arnold, C. J. *An Archeology of the Early Anglo-Saxon Kingdoms.* London: Routledge, 1988.

Augustine. *Confessions.* Trans. R. S. Pine-Coffin. New York: Penguin, 1961.

——— . *The Teacher.* Trans. Robert P. Russell. Washington, D.C.: Catholic University Press, 1968.

Bachelard, Gaston. *The Poetics of Space.* Trans. M. Jolas. Boston: Beacon Press, 1969.

Badcock, C. R. *The Problem of Altruism.* Oxford: Oxford University Press, 1986.

Bassett, Steven. "In Search of the Origins of Anglo-Saxon Kingdoms." In S. Bassett, ed., *The Origin of the Anglo-Saxon Kingdoms.* London: Leicester University Press, 1989.

✓ Bauschatz, Paul. *The Well and the Tree: World and Time in Early Germanic Culture.* Amherst: University of Massachusetts Press, 1982.

Bede. *Ecclesiastical History of the English People.* Ed. Bertram Colgrave and R. A. B. Mynors. Oxford: Clarendon Press, 1969.

Benson, Larry. "The Literary Character of Anglo-Saxon Formulaic Poetry." *PMLA* 81 (1966): 334–41.

——— . "The Originality of *Beowulf.*" *Harvard English Studies* 1 (1970): 1–43.

Beowulf. Ed. Fr. Klaeber. Lexington, Mass.: Heath, 1950.

Bieler, Ludwig. *Ireland: Harbinger of the Middle Ages.* London: Oxford University Press, 1966.

Bloom, Harold, and David Rosenberg. *The Book of J*. New York: Grove Weidenfeld, 1990.

Blumenberg, Hans. *The Legitimacy of the Modern Age*. Trans. Robert Wallace. Cambridge, Mass.: MIT Press, 1985.

Bolton, W. F. *Alcuin and Beowulf*. New Brunswick, N.J.: Rutgers University Press, 1978.

The Book of Kells: Reproductions from the Manuscript in Trinity College Dublin. New York: Alfred A. Knopf, 1974.

Borsch-Jacobsen, Mikkel. *The Freudian Subject*. Trans. Catherine Porter. Stanford, Calif.: Stanford University Press, 1988.

Bosworth, Joseph, and T. Northcote Toller. *An Anglo-Saxon Dictionary*. 2 vols. London: Oxford University Press, 1898–1920.

Brooks, Nicholas. "The Creation and Early Structure of the Kingdom of Kent." In Steven Bassett, ed., *The Origin of Anglo-Saxon Kingdoms*. London: Leicester University Press, 1989.

Bullough, D.A. "Early Medieval Social Groupings: The Terminology of Kinship," *Past and Present* 45 (1969): 3–18.

Campbell, J., ed. *The Anglo-Saxons*. Oxford: Phaidon, 1982.

Carver, Martin. "Ideology and Allegiance in East Anglia." In Robert Farrell and C. Neuman de Vegvar, eds., *Sutton Hoo: Fifty Years After*. Oxford, Ohio: American Early Medieval Studies, 1992.

Cassirer, Ernst. *The Philosophy of Symbolic Form*. Vol. 2: *Mythical Thought*. Trans. R. Manheim. New Haven, Conn.: Yale University Press, 1955.

Chadwick, Hector Munro. *The Heroic Age*. Cambridge, Eng.: Cambridge University Press, 1912.

Chambers, R. W. *Beowulf: An Introduction*. 3rd ed. with supplement by C. L. Wrenn. Cambridge, Eng.: Cambridge University Press, 1959.

Chance, Jane. "The Structural Unity of *Beowulf*: The Problem of Grendel's Mother." In Helen Damico and A. H. Olsen, eds., *New Readings on Women in Old English Literature*. Bloomington: Indiana University Press, 1990.

Chaney, William A. "Æthelberht's Code and the King's Number." *American Journal of Legal History* 6 (1962): 151–77.

Chase, Colin. "*Beowulf*." In Rowland L. Collins, ed., *The Year's Work in Old English Studies*, *Old English Newsletter* 18 (1984): 96.

——— , ed. *The Dating of 'Beowulf.'* Toronto: University of Toronto Press, 1981.

Chasseguet-Smirgel, Janine. *The Ego Ideal*. New York: Norton, 1984.

Chickering, Howell. *Beowulf: A Dual-Language Edition*. New York: Anchor Books, 1977.

Clover, Carol. "The Politics of Scarcity: Notes on the Sex Ratio in Early Scandinavia." In Helen Damico and A. H. Olsen, eds., *New Readings on Women in Old English Literature*. Bloomington: Indiana University Press, 1990.

Collingwood, R. G., and Myres, J. N. L. *Roman Britain and the English Settlements*. Oxford: Clarendon Press, 1937.

Cunningham, Clark. "Order in the Atoni House." In W. Lessa and E. Z. Vogt, eds., *Reader in Comparative Religion*. New York: Harper and Row, 1972.

Curtius, Ernst Robert. *European Literature and the Latin Middle Ages*. Trans. W. Trask. New York: Harper and Row, 1953.

Dalma, Juan. "La Catarsis en Aristoteles, Bernays y Freud." *Revista de Psiquiatria y Psicologia Medical* 4 (1963): 253–68.

Delasanta, Rodney. "Nominalism and Typology in Chaucer." In Hugh Keenan, ed., *Typology and English Medieval Literature*. New York: AMS Press, 1992.

Derrida, Jacques. *Of Grammatology*. Trans. Gayatri Spivak. Baltimore: Johns Hopkins University Press, 1974.

Dobbie, E. V. K., ed. *The Anglo-Saxon Minor Poems*. Anglo-Saxon Poetic Records 6. New York: Columbia University Press, 1942.

——— , ed. *Beowulf and Judith*. Anglo-Saxon Poetic Records 5. New York: Columbia University Press, 1953.

Donahue, Charles. "Potlatch and Charity: Notes on the Heroic in *Beowulf*." In L. E. Nicholson and D. W. Freese, eds., *Anglo-Saxon Poetry*. Notre Dame, Ind.: University of Notre Dame Press, 1975.

Donaldson, E. Talbot, trans. *Beowulf*. In M. H. Abrams, ed., *The Norton Anthology of English Literature*, 5th ed. Vol. 1. New York: Norton, 1986.

Donoghue, Daniel. "Word Order and Poetic Style: Auxiliary and Verbal in *The Meters of Boethius*." *Anglo-Saxon England* 15 (1986): 167–96.

Dumézil, Georges. *Gods of the Ancient Northmen*. Trans. E. Haugen. Berkeley: University of California Press, 1973.

Dumville, David N. "*Beowulf* and the Celtic World." *Traditio* 37 (1981): 109–60.

——— . "Sub-Roman Britain: History and Legend." *History*, n.s. 62 (1977): 173–92.

Earl, James W. "Apocalypticism and Mourning in *Beowulf*." *Thought* 57, 226 (Sept. 1982): 362–70.

——— . "Augustine, Freud, Lacan." *Thought* 61, 240 (Mar. 1986): 7–15 (special issue: J. W. Earl, ed., *Psychoanalysis and Religion: Postmodern Perspectives*).

——— . "*Beowulf* and the Origins of Civilization." In Allen J. Frantzen, ed., *Speaking Two Languages: Traditional Disciplines and Contemporary Theory in Medieval Studies*. Albany: State University of New York Press, 1991.

——— . "Beowulf's Rowing Match." *Neophilologus* 63 (1979): 285–90.

——— . "Hisperic Style in the Old English 'Rhyming Poem.'" *PMLA* 102 (1987): 187–96.

——— . "Identification and Catharsis." In Joseph Smith and William Kerrigan, eds., *Pragmatism's Freud: The Moral Disposition of Psychoanalysis*. Psychiatry and the Humanities, vol. 9. Baltimore: Johns Hopkins University Press, 1986.

———— . "King Alfred's Talking Poems." *Pacific Coast Philology* 24 (1989): 49–61.

———— . "The Necessity of Evil in *Beowulf.*" *South Atlantic Bulletin* 44 (1979): 81–98.

———— . "The Role of the Men's Hall in the Origin of the Anglo-Saxon Superego." *Psychiatry* 46 (1983): 139–60.

———— . "Transformations of Chaos: Immanence and Transcendence in *Beowulf* and Other Old English Poetry." *Ultimate Reality and Meaning: Interdisciplinary Studies in the Philosophy of Understanding* 10 (1987): 164–85.

Eco, Umberto. *The Limits of Interpretation*. Bloomington: Indiana University Press, 1990.

———— . *The Name of the Rose*. Trans. W. Weaver. New York: Harcourt, Brace, 1980.

Eissler, Kurt. *Discourse on Hamlet and "Hamlet": A Psychoanalytic Inquiry*. New York: International Universities Press, 1971.

Farrell, Robert. *Beowulf: Swedes and Geats*. London: Viking Society for Northern Research, 1972.

Finley, M. I. *Early Greece: The Bronze and Archaic Ages*. New York: Norton, 1970.

———— . *The World of Odysseus*. Rev. ed. New York: Viking, 1978.

Foley, John Miles. "*Beowulf* and the Psychohistory of Anglo-Saxon Culture." *American Imago* 34 (1977): 133–53.

———— . "Literary Art and Oral Tradition in Old English and Serbian Poetry." *Anglo-Saxon England* 12 (1983): 183–214.

———— . "Texts That Speak to Readers Who Hear." In Allen Frantzen, ed., *Speaking Two Languages*. Albany: State University of New York Press, 1991.

———— . "Textualization of Orality in Literary Criticism." In A. N. Doane and Carol Pasternack, eds., *Vox Intexta: Orality and Textuality in the Middle Ages*. Madison: University of Wisconsin Press, 1991.

Frank, Roberta. "Germanic Legend in Old English Literature." In Malcolm Godden and Michael Lapidge, eds., *Cambridge Companion to Old English Literature*. Cambridge, Eng.: Cambridge University Press, 1991.

———— . "'Mere' and 'Sund': Two Sea-Changes in *Beowulf.*" In P. R. Brown et al., eds., *Modes of Interpretation in Old English Literature*. Toronto: University of Toronto Press, 1986.

Frantzen, Allen J. *The Desire for Origins: New Language, Old English, and Teaching the Tradition*. New Brunswick, N.J.: Rutgers University Press, 1990.

———— . *King Alfred*. Boston: G. K. Hall, 1986.

Freeman, Derek. "*Totem and Taboo*: A Reappraisal." In Warner Muensterberger, ed., *Man and His Culture: Psychoanalytic Anthropology After "Totem and Taboo."* New York: Taplinger Publishing Co., 1970.

Freud, Sigmund. *The Complete Letters to Wilhelm Fliess.* Ed. and trans. Jeffrey M. Masson. Cambridge, Mass: Harvard University Press, 1985.

——— . *The Standard Edition of the Complete Psychological Works of Sigmund Freud,* 24 vols. Ed. and trans. James Strachey. 24 vols. London: Hogarth, 1953–74.

Vol. 2: *Studies in Hysteria* [1895; with Josef Breuer].

Vol. 4: *The Interpretation of Dreams* [1900].

Vol. 14: "Mourning and Melancholia" [1917].

Vol. 18: *Group Psychology and the Analysis of the Ego* [1921].

Vol. 19: *The Ego and the Id* [1923].

Vol. 20: *Inhibitions, Symptoms, and Anxiety* [1926].

Vol. 21: *The Future of an Illusion* [1927].

Vol. 21: *Civilization and Its Discontents* [1930].

Fustel de Coulanges, Numa-Denys. *The Ancient City.* Garden City, N.Y.: Anchor Books, 1963.

Gildas. *The Ruin of Britain and Other Works.* Ed. and trans. Michael Winterbottom. Totowa, N.J.: Rowman and Littlefield, 1978.

Gilson, Etienne. *The Christian Philosophy of Saint Augustine.* Trans. L. E. M. Lynch. New York: Random House, 1960.

Girard, René. *Violence and the Sacred.* Trans. P. Gregory. Baltimore: Johns Hopkins University Press, 1977.

Greenfield, Stanley B., and Daniel G. Calder. *A New Critical History of Old English Literature.* New York: New York University Press, 1986.

Gregory the Great. *King Alfred's West Saxon Version of Gregory's Pastoral Care.* Ed. Henry Sweet. London: Trübner, 1871.

Hanning, Robert W. "*Beowulf* as Heroic Poetry." *Medievalia et Humanistica,* n.s., 27 (1974): 77–102.

——— . *The Vision of History in Early Britain.* New York: Columbia University Press, 1966.

Harris, Joseph. "*Beowulf* in Literary History." *Pacific Coast Philology* 17 (1982): 16–23.

——— . "A Note on eorð scræf/eorð sele and Current Interpretations of *The Wife's Lament.*" *English Studies* 58 (1977): 204–8

Hermann, John P. *Allegories of War: Language and Violence in Old English Poetry.* Ann Arbor: University of Michigan Press, 1989.

Hill, John M. "The Good Fields of Grief: Remnants of Christian Conversion." *Psychological Review* 2 (1978): 27–43.

——— . "Revenge and Superego Mastery in *Beowulf.*" *Assays* 5 (1989): 3–36.

Hill, Thomas D. "Literary History and Old English Poetry." In Paul Szarmach, ed., *Sources of Anglo-Saxon Culture.* Studies in Medieval Culture, no. 20. Kalamazoo: Western Michigan University Press, 1986.

————. "Notes on the Imagery and Structure of the Old English 'Christ I.'"
Notes and Queries 19 (1972): 84–89.

Hodges, Richard. *Dark Age Economics*. London: St. Martin's Press, 1982.

Hodgkin, R. H. *A History of the Anglo-Saxons*, 2 vols. Oxford: Oxford University Press, 1952.

Howe, Nicholas. *The Anglo-Saxon Myth of Migration*. Bloomington: Indiana University Press, 1990.

Hume, Katherine. "The Concept of the Hall in Old English Poetry," *Anglo-Saxon England* 3 (1974): 63–74.

Huppé, Bernard. *The Hero in the Earthly City*. Binghamton: State University of New York Press, 1984.

Hurwit, Jeffrey. *The Art and Culture of Early Greece: 1100–800 B.C.* Ithaca, N.Y.: Cornell University Press, 1985.

Husserl, Edmund. *Cartesian Meditations*. Trans. D. Cairns. The Hague: Martinus Nijhoff, 1963.

Irvine, Martin. "Medieval Textuality and the Archeology of Textual Culture." In Allen Frantzen, ed., *Speaking Two Languages*. Albany: State University of New York Press, 1991.

Isaacs, Neil D. *Structural Principles in Old English Poetry*. Knoxville: University of Tennessee Press, 1968.

James, Edward. "The Origins of Barbarian Kingdoms: The Continental Evidence." In Steven Bassett, ed., *The Origins of Anglo-Saxon Kingdoms*. London: Leicester University Press, 1989.

Jameson, Fredric. *Postmodernism, or, The Cultural Logic of Late Capitalism*. Durham, N.C.: Duke University Press, 1991.

Jankuhn, H. "The Continental Home of the English." *Antiquity* 26 (1952): 14–24.

Jochens, Jenny. "Medieval Icelandic Heroines." *Viator* 17 (1986): 35–50.

Jolliffe, J. E. A. *The Constitutional History of England*. London: Adam and Charles Black, 1937.

Kaske, Robert E. "*Sapientia et Fortitudo* as the Controlling Theme of *Beowulf*." In Lewis Nicholson, ed., *An Anthology of 'Beowulf' Criticism*. Notre Dame, Ind.: Notre Dame University Press, 1963.

Ker, W. P. *Epic and Romance: Essays on Medieval Literature*. New York: Macmillan, 1908

Kerrigan, William. *The Sacred Complex: The Psychogenesis of Paradise Lost*. Cambridge, Mass.: Harvard University Press, 1984.

Keynes, Simon, and Michael Lapidge. *Alfred the Great*. New York: Penguin, 1983.

Kiernan, Kevin S. *'Beowulf' and the 'Beowulf' Manuscript*. New Brunswick, N.J.: Rutgers University Press, 1981.

————. "Reading Caedmon's 'Hymn' with Someone Else's Glosses." *Representations* 32 (1990): 157–74.

Kitto, H. T. F. *The Greeks*. New York: Penguin Books, 1951.

Krapp, George P., ed. *The Paris Psalter and the Meters of Boethius*. Vol. 5 of *Anglo-Saxon Poetic Records*. New York: Columbia University Press, 1932.

Krapp, George P., and E. V. K. Dobbie, eds. *The Exeter Book*. Vol. 3 of *Anglo-Saxon Poetic Records*. New York: Columbia University Press, 1936.

Kroeber, Karl. "The Evolution of Literary Study," *PMLA* 99 (1984): 326–39.

Küng, Hans. *Freud and the Problem of God*. Trans. E. Quinn. New Haven, Conn.: Yale University Press, 1979.

Lacan, Jacques. "Conference de Presse du Dr. Lacan." *Lettres de l'École Freudienne*. Bulletin intérieur de l'École Freudienne de Paris, 1974.

Laín Entralgo, Pedro. *The Therapy of the Word in Classical Antiquity*. Trans. L. Rather and J. Sharp. New Haven, Conn.: Yale University Press, 1970.

Langer, Ulrich. *Divine and Poetic Freedom in the Renaissance*. Princeton, N.J.: Princeton University Press, 1990.

Lapidge, Michael. "*Beowulf*, Aldhelm, the *Liber Monstrorum*, and Wessex." *Studii Medievali*, 3d ser., 23 (1982): 151–92.

Lees, Clare A., and Gillian Overing. "Birthing Bishops and Fathering Priests: Bede, Hild, and the Relations of Cultural Production." *Exemplaria* 6 (1994): 35–65.

LeMée, Jean, trans. *Hymns from the Rig-Veda*. New York: Knopf, 1975.

Lerer, Seth. *Literacy and Power in Anglo-Saxon England*. Lincoln: University of Nebraska Press, 1991.

Lesser, Simon. *Fiction and the Unconscious*. Chicago: University of Chicago Press, 1957.

Lévi-Strauss, Claude. "Do Dual Organizations Exist?" In *Structural Anthropology*. Garden City, N.Y.: Anchor Books, 1967.

Lewis, C. S. *A Preface to Paradise Lost*. Oxford: Oxford University Press, 1942.

Loewald, Hans. *Papers on Psychoanalysis*. New Haven, Conn.: Yale University Press, 1980.

Lord, Albert B. *The Singer of Tales*. Cambridge, Mass.: Harvard University Press, 1960.

Lowe, Walter. *Evil and the Unconscious*. Chico, Calif.: Scholars Press, 1983.

Magoun, Francis P. "Bede's Story of Caedmon: The Case History of an Anglo-Saxon Oral Singer." *Speculum* 30 (1955): 49–63.

———. "On Some Survivals of Pagan Belief in Anglo-Saxon England." *Harvard Theological Review* 40 (1947): 33–46.

Mandelbrot, Benoit B. *The Fractal Geometry of Nature*. New York: W. H. Freeman, 1977.

Meissner, W. W. *Psychoanalysis and Religious Experience*. New Haven, Conn.: Yale University Press, 1984.

Miller, David L. "'Attack on Christendom!' The Anti-Christianism of Depth Psychology." *Thought* 61 (1986): 56–67.

Milton, John. *The Complete Prose Works*. Ed. Don M. Wolfe. 18 vols. New Haven, Conn.: Yale University Press, 1953–82.

Mitchell, Bruce. "The Dangers of Disguise: Old English Texts in Modern Punctuation." *Review of English Studies*, n.s. 31 (1980): 385–413.

———. *Old English Syntax*. 2 vols. London: Oxford University Press, 1985.

Mitchell, Bruce, and Fred Robinson. *A Guide to Old English*. New York: Basil Blackwell, 1986.

Montrose, Louis. "*A Midsummer Night's Dream* and the Shaping Fantasies of Elizabethan Culture: Gender, Power, Form." In Margaret Ferguson et al., eds., *Rewriting the Renaissance*. Chicago: University of Chicago Press, 1986.

Myres, J. N. L. *Anglo-Saxon Pottery and the Settlement of England*. Oxford: Oxford University Press, 1969.

Neuman de Vegvar, Carol. "The Sutton Hoo Horns as Regalia." In R. Farrell and C. Neuman de Vegvar, eds., *Sutton Hoo: Fifty Years After*. Oxford, Ohio: American Early Medieval Studies, 1992.

Nichols, Michael, and Melvin Zax. *Catharsis in Psychotherapy*. New York: Gardner, 1977.

Niles, John D. *'Beowulf': The Poem and Its Tradition*. Cambridge, Mass.: Harvard University Press, 1983.

O'Brien O'Keeffe, Katherine. *Visible Song: Transitional Literacy in Old English Verse*. Cambridge, Eng.: Cambridge University Press, 1990.

Opland, Jeff. *Anglo-Saxon Oral Poetry: A Study of the Traditions*. New Haven, Conn.: Yale University Press, 1981.

Parry, Adam, ed. *The Making of Homeric Verse: The Collected Papers of Milman Parry*. Oxford: Clarendon Press, 1971.

Patterson, Lee. *Chaucer and the Subject of History*. Madison: University of Wisconsin Press, 1991.

Plato. *The Ion*. Trans. B. Jowett. In Charles Kaplan, ed., *Criticism: The Major Statements*. New York: St. Martin's Press, 1975.

Rahtz, P. "Buildings and Rural Settlement." In D. M. Wilson, ed., *The Archeology of Anglo-Saxon England*. London: Methuen, 1976.

Ricoeur, Paul. *Freud and Philosophy*. Trans. D. Savage. New Haven, Conn.: Yale University Press, 1970.

———. *Husserl*. Evanston, Ill.: Northwestern University Press, 1967.

———. *The Rule of Metaphor*. Toronto: University of Toronto Press, 1975.

———. *The Symbolism of Evil*. Trans. E. Buchanan. Boston: Beacon Press, 1967.

Robinson, Fred. *'Beowulf' and the Appositive Style*. Knoxville: University of Tennessee Press, 1985.

———. "Elements of the Marvelous in the Characterization of Beowulf: A Reconsideration of the Textual Evidence." In Edward Irving and Robert Burlin, eds., *Old English Studies in Honor of John C. Pope*. Toronto: University of Toronto Press, 1974.

———— . "Old English Literature in Its Most Immediate Context." In John D. Niles, ed., *Old English Literature in Context*. Cambridge, Eng.: D. S. Brewer, 1980.

Rorty, Richard. "Freud and Moral Reflection." In J. Smith and W. Kerrigan, eds., *Pragmatism's Freud: The Moral Disposition of Psychoanalysis*. Baltimore: Johns Hopkins University Press, 1986.

Schafer, Roy. *Aspects of Internalization*. New York: International Universities Press, 1968.

Scheff, Thomas. *Catharsis in Healing, Ritual, and Drama*. Berkeley: University of California Press, 1979.

Sedgefield, Walter. *King Alfred's Old English Version of Boethius*. London: Oxford University Press, 1899.

Shelley, Percy Bysshe. "A Defense of Poetry" (1821). In D. Reiman, ed., *Shelley's Poetry and Prose*. New York: W. W. Norton, 1977.

Shippey, T. A. *Beowulf*. London: Edward Arnold, 1978.

Sims-Williams, Patrick. *Religion and Literature in Western England, 600–800*. Cambridge, Eng.: Cambridge University Press, 1990.

Sisam, Kenneth. *Studies in the History of Old English Literature*. London: Oxford University Press, 1967.

Smith, Joseph H. "Identification Styles in Depression and Grief." *International Journal of Psycho-Analysis* 52 (1971): 259–66.

———— . "Samuel Johnson and Stories of Childhood." *Thought* 61 (1986): 105–17.

Snorri Sturluson. *The Prose Edda*. Trans. J. I. Young. Berkeley: University of California Press, 1966.

Stafford, Pauline. *The East Midlands in the Early Middle Ages*. London: Leicester University Press, 1985.

Stanley, E. G. "Old English Poetic Diction and the Interpretation of 'The Wanderer,' 'The Seafarer' and 'The Penitent's Prayer.'" *Anglia* 73 (1955): 413–66.

———— . *The Search for Anglo-Saxon Paganism*. Cambridge, Eng.: Cambridge University Press, 1975.

Sweet, Henry. *King Alfred's West-Saxon Version of Gregory's Pastoral Care*. Early English Text Society. London: N. Trubner, 1871.

Tacitus. *Agricola, Germany, Dialogue on Orators*. Trans. H. W. Bernario. Norman: University of Oklahoma Press, 1991.

Tolkien, J. R. R. "*Beowulf*: The Monsters and the Critics." *Proceedings of the British Acadamy* 22 (1936): 245–95.

Turner, Victor. "Encounter with Freud: The Making of a Comparative Symbologist." In C. D. Spindler, ed., *The Making of Psychological Anthropology*. Berkeley: University of California Press, 1978.

———— . "Process, System, and Symbol: A New Synthesis," *Dædalus* 106 (1977): 61–80.

Vance, Eugene. *Mervelous Signals*. Lincoln: University of Nebraska Press, 1986.

Vernant, Jean-Pierre. "Greek Tragedy: Problems of Interpretation." In R. Macksey and E. Donato, eds., *The Structuralist Controversy*. Baltimore: Johns Hopkins University Press, 1970.

———. *The Origins of Greek Thought*. Ithaca, N.Y.: Cornell University Press, 1982.

Virgil. *The Aeneid*. Trans. Robert Fitzgerald. New York: Random House, 1981.

Volkan, Vamik. "Re-Grief Therapy." In Bernard Schoenberg and Irwin Gerber, eds., *Bereavement: Its Psychosocial Aspects*. New York: Columbia University Press, 1975.

Wallace-Hadrill, J. M. *Early Germanic Kingship in England and on the Continent*. Oxford: Clarendon Press, 1971.

Wentersdorf, Karl P. "Beowulf's Adventure with Breca." *Studies in Philology* 72 (1975): 140–66.

West, S. E. "The Anglo-Saxon Village of West Stow." *Medieval Archeology* 13 (1969): 1–20.

Whitelock, Dorothy. *The Audience of 'Beowulf.'* Oxford: Clarendon Press, 1951.

———. *The Beginnings of English Society*. Baltimore: Penguin Books, 1952.

———. "The Interpretation of 'The Seafarer.'" In C. Fox and B. Dickens, eds., *Chadwick Memorial Studies*. Cambridge, Eng.: Cambridge University Press, 1950.

Wolheim, Richard. "Identification and Imagination." In R. Wolheim, ed., *Freud*. Garden City, N.Y.: Doubleday Anchor, 1974.

Woolf, Rosemary. "The Ideal of Men Dying with Their Lord in the *Germania* and 'The Battle of Maldon.'" *Anglo-Saxon England* 5 (1976): 65–81.

Wrenn, C. L., ed. *Beowulf with the Finnsburg Fragment*. 3rd ed. Rev. W. F. Bolton. London: Harrap, 1973.

Index

In this index "f" after a number indicates a separate reference on the next page, and "ff" indicates separate references on the next two pages. A continuous discussion over two or more pages is indicated by a span of numbers. *Passim* is used for a cluster of references in close but not consecutive sequence.

Abelard, Peter, 2, 5f, 10, 60
Aelfric, 7, 90
"Aldhelm," 98
Alfred, King, 64, 79, 87–99
Allen, Woody, 22, 165
Ambiguity, 3, 7, 12, 100, 168, 174
Ambivalence, 100, 132, 162, 168, 172–75, 177, 182, 187f
"Andreas," 17, 69
Anthropology, 16, 30f, 36, 100–105, 115, 117, 170
Apocalypticism, 29, 41–48, 76f, 133f
Archeology, 17, 31ff, 50f, 103
Aristotle, 138–52 *passim*, 177
Augustine, 6, 9ff, 43, 46, 58–67 *passim*, 87, 94–97, 152–60

Baker, Peter, 26
Bassett, Steven, 37
"Battle of Maldon," 39, 123, 133f, 176–87 *passim*
Bauschatz, Paul, 40
Bear's Son's Tale, 21f

Bede, 17f, 51–55, 61, 63, 68–73 *passim*, 77–87 *passim*, 92, 115, 117, 125f
"Bede's Death Song," 79, 87
Benson, Larry, 16, 21f, 90f, 98
Beowulf: interpretation of, 7–14, 18, 23–36, 71–78, 108, 123f, 166–77 *passim*, 183–88; authorship of, 11, 14f, 163f, 188; genre, 12, 18ff, 133f; originality of, 14f, 18–26, 163f; date of, 16–22 *passim*, 26; women in, 38f, 75f, 116, 123f, 168, 173; Christianity in, 46f, 73f, 77f, 166f
Bernays, Jacob, 141, 149
Bible, 39, 42f, 66, 69, 76, 84, 124, 130, 132, 178
Bloom, Harold, 14f, 165, 174, 188
Blumenberg, Hans, 2, 5
Boethius, 50, 73, 90
Bolton, W. F., 176
Book of Kells, 7, 92–93, 95
Bosworth, Joseph, 90
Bowra, C. M., 30
Breuer, Josef, 139, 141f, 149

Brooks, Nicholas, 32

Caedmon, 79, 81–87, 126
Canon formation, 12, 87f
Carver, Martin, 37
Cassirer, Ernst, 41
Catharsis, 137–44, 148–52, 173, 177
Chadwick, H. M., 19, 30
Chambers, R. W., 17, 21
Chase, Colin, 16, 175f, 180
Chaucer, Geoffrey, 1, 3f, 7, 22, 26
Chickering, Howell, 25f
"Christ I," 65–71
Clover, Carol, 35
Comitatus, 34, 57f, 60, 75, 108f, 117,
    179–84
Conversion of Anglo-Saxons, 17ff,
    31ff, 39, 44f, 49–55, 81, 101f, 110f,
    124–32, 160f, 166f
Curtius, Ernst Robert, 94, 96
Cynewulf, 79, 87

Dante, 60
Dark Age of Anglo-Saxon England,
    17, 31–40, 103
Deconstruction, 2f, 5, 95f
Delasanta, Rodney, 3
DeMan, Paul, 5
"Deor," 20, 84
Derrida, Jacques, 95f, 158
de Vries, Jan, 105
Dobbie, E. V. K., 20f
Donahue, Charles, 104
Donaldson, E. Talbot, 23, 82
Dreams, 11f, 70, 162, 171ff, 184f, 188
Dumézil, Georges, 33, 35, 105, 109, 119
Dumville, David, 16
Durkheim, Emile, 104–5

Eco, Umberto, 2, 10
Ego ideal, see Superego
Eissler, Kurt, 152
Elegies, 7, 56, 96, 162, 175
"Elene," 69
Epic, 18ff, 30, 38, 40, 133f, 137, 147,
    161, 164f, 170f, 177, 181f, 186

Essentialism, 5, 7, 12, 170
Exeter Book, 39, 65, 84
"Exodus," 17, 69

Fate, 40, 73, 138, 177, 186
Finley, M. I., 17, 31, 36, 38, 100
"Finnsburh," 19
Foley, John, 14, 30, 80, 91, 105
Fractal geometry, 6f, 10–15, 27
Frank, Roberta, 16, 21
Frantzen, Allen, 27, 82, 87f
Frazer, J. G., 30, 104–5
Freedom, 3, 15f, 26, 80, 122f, 168,
    181–88 passim
Freud, Sigmund, 5f, 11f, 36, 101–5,
    111f, 119–23, 128–63 passim, 169–71,
    174, 181–88 passim

Gildas, 19, 37, 46
Gilson, Etienne, 154, 158
Girard, René, 36, 104, 123
Gnomic poetry, 60f, 178f
Goethe, J. W. von, 141
Greenfield, Stanley, 82
Gregory I, Pope, 64, 66, 97, 121
Grettissaga, 21f
Guthlac, 126f

Hall, the, 29, 34, 46, 50, 53f, 67f, 100ff,
    114–29, 134ff, 167
Hamartia, 143, 150, 177f
Hanning, Robert, 19, 166
Harrisson, Jane, 30
Heidegger, Martin, 6, 10
Heorot, see Hall, the
Hermann, John P., 14
Heroic Age, 17ff, 29–40, 45, 170
Hesiod, 43f, 84
Hild, 81, 85f
Hill, John, 105
Homer, 17–21, 30–40, 134, 139, 143,
    166, 170, 177
Howe, Nicholas, 19
Hume, Katherine, 121
Huppé, Bernard, 167
Hurwit, Jeffrey, 35

Husserl, Edmund, 154–60
Hut, the, 34, 50, 114–21 *passim*

Idealization, 3, 34, 38, 40, 42, 59, 63, 100, 116, 133, 161, 167, 171, 176
Identification, 11, 101, 122, 131, 137–52, 161, 165, 172–77 *passim*, 183–86
Interlace, 7
Irvine, Martin, 14, 82

James, Edward, 34
Jameson, Fredric, 5, 162f
Jung, Carl, 12, 105, 123, 156, 162
Junius, Francis, 83ff

Kaske, Robert, 13, 35, 180
Keller, Helen, 6
Ker, W. P., 17, 30
Kerrigan, William, 152–55
Keynes, Simon, 88, 98
Kiernan, Kevin, 16, 18, 22, 24, 82
Kingship, 33–40, 52, 64f, 108–29
Kinship system, 34–40, 107–14, 123f, 170
Kitto, H. T. F., 30
Krapp, George, 89, 91
Kroeber, Karl, 20

Lacan, Jacques, 152, 158, 164
Laín Entralgo, Pedro, 140f
Lapidge, Michael, 16, 88, 98
Law, 36, 39, 64, 66, 107–13 *passim*, 170
Lees, Clare A., 86
Lerer, Seth, 82
Lesser, Simon, 148
Lévi-Strauss, Claude, 117, 172
Lewis, C. S., 30
Loewald, Hans, 130–32, 147–49
Lord, Albert B., 18, 30
Lordship, *see* Kingship

Magoun, Francis, 82, 104
Mandelbrot, Benoit, 6f, 10–14
Manilow, Barry, 84
Marxism, 5, 14, 162, 164
"Maxims I, Part 1," 39, 61–65, 73, 75

"Meters of Boethius," 6, 50, 88–98
"Metrical Preface to Wærferth's Translation of Gregory's *Dialogues*," 98f
Migration of Anglo-Saxons, 19, 31–35 *passim*, 52, 102, 129
Milton, John, 84ff, 152, 157
Mitchell, Bruce, 88, 98
Montrose, Louis, 162
Mourning, 47f, 129–34, 162
Myres, J. N. L., 32, 103
Myth, 16, 29f, 35–47 *passim*, 53, 76, 69, 105, 109, 115, 120–24 *passim*, 128, 162

Narcissism, 4, 6, 122, 146ff, 152
Neuman de Vegvar, Carol, 120f
Nibelungenlied, 109, 134, 186
Nichols, Michael, 142
Niles, John, 17
Nominalism, 1–7, 9f, 26

O'Brien O'Keeffe, Katherine, 79, 82
Ockham, *see* William of Ockham
Opland, Jeff, 18f, 30, 90, 104, 120, 134
Orality, 12–22 *passim*, 30, 49, 79f, 90–98, 121f, 134, 163f, 170, 188
Overdetermination, 9, 11, 100, 165, 172f, 176
Overing, Gillian, 86
Ovid, 94

Parry, Milman, 18f, 30
Pastoral Care, 64, 87–98 *passim*
Peirce, Charles S., 10
"Phoenix," 16
Plato, 69, 139f
Postmodernism, 2, 4f, 16, 27, 80, 87, 95f, 163, 169
Pound, Ezra, 61
Psychoanalysis, *see* Freud, Sigmund

Revenge, 36, 39, 75f, 113, 123f
"Rhyming Poem," vii
Ricoeur, Paul, viii, 10, 69, 138, 154, 160
"Riddle 26 (Book)," 91
Rig Veda, 43f

Robinson, Fred, 13, 21, 88, 98
Rorty, Richard, 138

Saussure, Ferdinand de, 6, 9, 157
Scheff, Thomas, 142
"Seafarer," 56–61, 65, 70f, 73, 106, 129
Semiotics, 2, 5ff, 10–16, 26f
Settlement of Anglo-Saxons, 32–40
Shafer, Roy, 145
Shakespeare: *King Lear*, 64; *Hamlet*, 143
Shelley, Percy Bysshe, 143f
Shippey, T. A., 167
Sisam, Kenneth, 87f, 91
Snorri Sturluson, 120
Soliloquies, 88, 98
Stafford, Pauline, 37
Stanley, E. G., 51
Structuralism, 13, 100, 172
Superego, 101, 114, 122, 127–37 *passim*, 144, 148–54 *passim*, 159–65 *passim*, 181–88 *passim*
Sutton Hoo, 150f, 169
Sweet, Henry, 87

Tacitus, 33, 50, 57, 64, 122, 179f, 183
"Thureth," 98
Tolkien, J. R. R., 13, 17, 74, 169
Toller, J. Northcott, 90
Tragedy, 20, 36, 39, 137–43, 147–52, 173, 177, 181

Turner, Victor, 104, 136
Tylor, Edward, 104

Unconscious, 1, 4f, 11f, 15, 138, 144f, 159, 165f, 171, 185, 188

Vengeance, *see* Revenge
Vercelli Book, 84
Vernant, Jean-Pierre, 17, 36, 38f
Virgil, 8, 38, 64, 84, 155f
Volkan, Vamik, 142
Volsungasaga, 109
"Vǫluspá," 43f, 46

"Waldere," 19
Wallace-Hadrill, J. M., 33
"Wanderer," 70, 96, 175
Wentersdorf, Karl, 21
Weston, Jesse, 30
West Stow, 32f, 117f
Whitelock, Dorothy, 17, 32, 59, 114
"Widsið," 20, 84
"Wife's Lament," 96, 117, 175
William of Ockham, 2f, 5, 16, 21, 23
Wittgenstein, Ludwig, 10, 157f
Wolheim, Richard, 138
Wrenn, C. L., 17
Wulfstan, 19, 46f, 133

Zax, Melvin, 142

Library of Congress Cataloging-in-Publication Data
Earl, James Whitby.
Thinking about Beowulf / by James W. Earl.
p.   cm.
Includes bibliographical references (p.   ) and index.
ISBN 0-8047-1700-1 (cloth : acid-free paper) :
1. Beowulf.   2. Epic poetry, English (Old)—History and criticism.
3. Free will and determinism in literature.   4. Literature and
anthropology—England.   5. Autonomy (Psychology) in literatre.
6. Freedom (Theology) in literature.   7. Literature and history—
England   8. Psychoanalysis and literature.   9. Liberty in
literature   I. Title
PR1585.E37   1994
829'.3—dc20   93-47132   CIP

⊗ This book is printed on acid-free paper.